BRITAIN and IRELAND

Country Inns and Back Roads

The Swan Hotel, Bibury, Gloucestershire

BRITAIN and IRELAND

Country Inns and Back Roads

**Fifth Edition
1988–89**

Country house hotels,
bed and breakfast, traditional inns,
farmhouses, guest houses,
and castles

**Norman T. Simpson
The Berkshire Traveller**

PERENNIAL LIBRARY

Harper & Row, Publishers, New York
Cambridge, Philadelphia, San Francisco, Washington
London, Mexico City, São Paulo, Singapore, Sydney

TRAVEL BOOKS BY NORMAN T. SIMPSON

Country Inns and Back Roads, North America
Country Inns and Back Roads, Britain and Ireland
Country Inns and Back Roads, Continental Europe
Bed and Breakfast, American Style

COVER PAINTING: The village of Evershot and "Tess's Cottage," Dorset,
by Lesliejohn Lucca
DRAWINGS: Janice Lindstrom

COUNTRY INNS AND BACK ROADS, BRITAIN AND IRELAND (*Fifth Edition, 1988–89*). Copyright
© 1988 by Harper & Row, Publishers, Inc. All rights reserved. Printed in the United States
of America. No part of this book may be used or reproduced in any manner whatsoever
without written permission except in the case of brief quotations embodied in critical articles
and reviews. For information address Harper & Row, Publishers, Inc., 10 East 53rd Street,
New York, N.Y. 10022. Published simultaneously in Canada by Fitzhenry & Whiteside
Limited, Toronto.

ISSN 0893-1186
ISBN 0-06-096273-9
88 89 90 91 92 FG 10 9 8 7 6 5 4 3 2 1

Contents

Preface

I love prefaces, introductions, or whatever they're called. They give an author a chance to say all the things he couldn't put in the book. He can explain the "mystique" of the book, acknowledge a few friends and teachers in his past, and generally spread an agreeable glow over everything connected with the work.

This preface is no exception.

My intense preoccupation with things British probably began when I was nine years old, reading Charles and Mary Lamb's *Tales from Shakespeare,* and it was given a glowing boost in high school by my teacher, Abraham Lass, who introduced us all to the entangling webs of the Thomas Hardy novels. Diggory Venn and Eustacia Vye, where are you now?

During my freshman year at Bucknell University, a splendid college in Lewisburg, Pennsylvania, I was cast as Feste, the jester, in Shakespeare's *Twelfth Night.* As the years moved swiftly onward, I was to take several other roles in the same play, including Orsino and Sir Toby Belch. While still attending an occasional class at Bucknell, I was further spurred by courses in Tennyson and Browning, taught by Professor C. Willard Smith; Shakespeare, by Professor Coleman; and British history, by Professor Johnson. (I'm sure *he'd* be very much surprised to learn the result!)

During World War II, I was stationed in India where I acquired an intense interest in the "Empire." I also saw Lawrence Olivier in the film *Henry V* at the Lighthouse Cinema in Calcutta. How that speech at Agincourt thrilled me!

That was one of my first British films. I didn't miss a single one of Dirk Bogarde's "Doctor" series, nor any of those early Hitchcocks, like *The Thirty-nine Steps* and *The Lady Vanishes.* Leslie Howard was my idol, a position he still shares with C. Aubrey Smith and David Niven. I spared no pains to see all of the Alec Guinness films, not to mention the six times I saw *Genevieve.*

In more recent years I've enjoyed some of the television imports like "Upstairs, Downstairs," "The Duchess of Duke Street," "Poldark," "The Jewel in the Crown," "Fawlty Towers," and all the other Master-

The Rising Sun Hotel, Lynmouth, North Devon

piece Theatre offerings hosted by that most urbane of Englishmen, Alistair Cooke.

My first trip to Britain was in 1973, a portion of which was described in *Country Inns and Back Roads, North America*. I knew eventually I would have to travel all over Britain and Ireland and write a book about my experiences.

In 1976, I included several British and Irish inns, country house hotels, and B&Bs in *Country Inns and Back Roads, Europe,* and a few years later, this entirely separate book was born.

The two books are revised alternately every other year. This revision is effective for 1988 and 1989, and I have made a provision for that in estimating the rates for a year in advance. I am sure the reader realizes that these are not firm quotations but merely estimates.

Everyone enjoys traveling in the British Isles: retired people, students, newlyweds, the first-time traveler, and the sophisticated, experienced traveler. This book has something for everyone, especially for the reader who may *never* get to Britain.

As far as cost of traveling in Britain and Ireland is concerned, I tend to look at the accommodations I have selected as a many-layered cake, a slice of which provides expensive frosting on the top and then continues through various gradations to include castle hotels, country house hotels, traditional inns, guest houses, and B&Bs. I try to provide a travel menu that allows the traveler to splurge on one night and perhaps be accommodated more modestly on the following night. While I have yet to find the perfect inn (hotel), the reader will notice very few, if any, negative comments.

The reader will find no ratings, stars, or rosettes displayed beside any entry. The length of my descriptions have nothing to do with the excellence of the accommodations. If I have used more space in writing about one place than I have for another, it simply means that as a writer I found an anecdote or story to share.

In Britain and Ireland I set out to find the same qualities that I look for among inns in North America: warm, friendly, personal lodgings that are the expression of the owner and his or her family. For the most part, these are proprietor-managed places and provide the opportunity for the traveler to get "the feel of the country."

As in North America, I looked for inns and country house hotels that I felt would continue to operate for many years to come. I searched for a feeling of stability.

If the reader finds as much about *people* as he does about half-timbered houses, hearty roast beef, Irish sunsets, Scottish castles, and English antiques, it is because I believe the heart and soul of these accommodations are the proprietor, his family, staff, and the guests themselves. The setting, food, lodgings, service, furnishings, diversions, and surroundings, of course, are of prime importance, but the main factor that makes this journey unique and enjoyable is personal involvement.

HOW THE BOOK IS PLANNED

I've divided this book into the principal touristic sections of Britain, plus London and Ireland. A large map of England shows these sections, and there are separate maps for Scotland and Ireland.

Each of these sections has its own keyed map showing the approximate location of every accommodation. Of further assistance is the Index, which lists the hotels alphabetically as well as showing rates and last times for dinner orders. There's also a map in this section showing the location of every county.

The italicized paragraphs following each narrative account of my visits contain essential information about the amenities offered and nearby recreational and cultural attractions. Reasonably explicit driving directions are also included.

To understand the italicized factual information, the following explanation may prove helpful:

NAME OF HOTEL, Village, (nearby larger town), County, Postal code.

TELEPHONE NUMBER: This is in two parts: The first number in parenthesis is the STD code. When outside of the immediate area of any of the accommodations, step into the nearest friendly red phone booth and dial all of the STD number plus all of the numbers that follow. In some cases, where an operator may be necessary, I have included the name of the individual exchange.

Many U.K. points can be dialed direct from overseas. The country code for England, Scotland, Wales, and Ireland is 011-44 plus the STD code and the individual number.

CREDIT CARDS: Except as noted, all places accept some major credit cards such as American Express, Barclaycard, MasterCard, or Visa. British traveler's checks are excellent.

RATES

Rates for a room for two people for one night with breakfast, except where noted, are included in the Index of this book. They are not to be considered firm quotations, but should be used as guidelines only. The traveler who is willing to travel British-style (booking a room with a shared bath) will appreciate the lower rates.

MAKING RESERVATIONS

A travel agent can frequently be the traveler's best friend. These people are professionals and know how to make the necessary contacts for reservations. Since a very high percentage of the hotels and inns pay travel agents' commissions, this should not be an additional expense for the traveler. However, in some cases, the smaller accommodations do not pay commissions, and the travel agent is entitled to charge the client a fee equal to the usual commission. It's also reasonable for the travel agent to charge the client for the cost of telephone calls or telex messages.

The best way to assure a firm reservation is to contact the inn or hotel by telephone and then send a deposit, which is held against the first night's stay.

Several of the accommodations listed belong to consortiums of hotels that provide a central reservation office.

Consortium	Telephone Number
Prestige Hotels	U.S.: 1-800-223-5581
Pride of Britain	U.S.: 1-800-323-3602
Relais et Chateaux	U.S.: 212-696-1323
Romantik Hotels	U.S.: 1-206-885-5804
Wolsey Lodges	England: 0449-740609

HOW TO TELEPHONE GREAT BRITAIN
TO MAKE A RESERVATION

If you are calling from North America, you may directly dial the numbers that are in this book. The first thing to do is to dial 011 if you want a station-to-station call, or 01 for calls requiring operator assistance (collect, person, etc.). Next, dial 44, the country code. Now refer to the telephone number given for each accommodation. One very important point: if calling from North America, omit the first zero; otherwise, dial the number as given. If direct international dialing is not available in your area, you will still get the dial rate on a simple station call; just dial 0 and give the details of your call.

If telephoning from point-to-point *within* Great Britain, read the instructions carefully that are posted in each telephone booth and be sure to dial the 0, which is omitted when dialing from North America to Great Britain.

The most economical way to telephone Great Britain is to call between 6:00 p.m. and 7:00 a.m., local North American time (British time is 5 hours later than Eastern Standard Time). This is for a call that does not require operator assistance. It costs about 25% more to dial direct between 1:00 p.m. and 6:00 a.m., and about 50% more to dial between 7:00 a.m. and 1:00 p.m. Operator-assisted calls are considerably more expensive. AT&T Information Service can fill you in on further details; dial toll-free 800-874-4000.

TELEPHONING THE UNITED STATES FROM BRITAIN

Before picking up a telephone to make an international call in a hotel or inn, it is wise to inquire as to the house policy on surcharges. International calls placed in a hotel or inn may be subject to stiff surcharges, unless the establishment is a participant in AT&T's TELEPLAN, which sets a uniform limit on such surcharges.

There are various ways to cut these extra telephone expenses if it is necessary to make out-of-country calls. Collect calls might have a small surcharge, as would be the case with credit card calls, if they are allowed. The person-to-person charge on a credit card call probably still would be less than the surcharge. Another method would be to place your call and ask your U.S. party to call you right back. To save time, you would want all the necessary numbers handy—access numbers, country and city codes, hotel and room numbers. Or, if possible, you could simply set up a schedule of places and times when you could be reached from the U.S.

The least expensive method, with no surcharge, is to call from main post offices, international airports, railway stations, or telephone buildings. Some public pay phones can handle international calls. Be sure to have a pocketful of change at the ready. (Be aware that, unlike American public telephone systems, British pay-telephones are on computers. When making any calls, you must keep an eagle eye on the display screen or listen for a warning signal so that you can quickly insert more change, otherwise you are in danger of being cut off in midsentence.)

AT&T has an International Information Service, from which all sorts of advice on international telephoning may be obtained. They publish two informative booklets and maintain a toll-free service at 800-874-4000.

LUGGAGE

For years I've been making two- or three-week extended trips to the U.K. and the Continent, using only carry-on luggage consisting of a garment bag and a soft travel bag. This eliminates any waiting for luggage or any other type of delay. The garment bag holds one jacket, which is necessary for the evening meal, and one pair of suitable dress trousers. I also include at least one sweater, an additional pair of trousers, and a raincoat, which serves many purposes. I usually carry three drip-dry shirts and three drip-dry shorts, and four pairs of wool socks. Of course, this means that I am doing a hand laundry every night, which, under the circumstances, will dry in just a few hours. The ladies will have a different list, but keeping your luggage to a minimum will simplify your travels all the way around.

CANCELLATIONS

In Britain, acceptance of a hotel booking by telephone or in writing is generally regarded as a legally binding contract. If it's necessary to cancel, advise the hotel immediately. If they are unable to re-let the room, the hotel may be entitled to claim compensation—usually two thirds of the agreed price—and any deposit would be included as part of this payment. Ask your travel agent about travel cancellation insurance.

AIR FARES TO BRITAIN AND IRELAND

Even in these days when escalating air fares keep pace with the rising cost of jet fuel, I find that it's possible to shop around and get bargains. All airlines have standby tickets that require an obvious flexibility of schedule. When this doesn't suit my convenience, I order my ticket in advance under one of several plans that effect a savings.

Although other airlines fly directly to Ireland, I've always found Aer Lingus extremely satisfactory.

ARRIVING IN BRITAIN

Visitors to England will, for the most part, arrive in London at one of two airports, although another gateway to the British Isles that is growing in popularity is Prestwick Airport, Glasgow, Scotland.

Heathrow

The large and somewhat complicated Heathrow Airport, just outside London, is most efficiently designed. Part of the hassle is reduced by luggage trolleys and moving walkways. Immigration and Customs are easily negotiated, and the traveler emerges into the International Arrivals Section, where currency can be exchanged and information about lodgings can be obtained if you haven't already done so. This is also where there are literally hundreds of people waiting for arriving friends and guests. Many of them have small signs with the name of the arriving person printed on them—that's how chauffeurs and other people meeting strangers get together.

Luggage is now handled very swiftly at Heathrow, and a tip of twenty pence per bag is usual, although the services are supposed to be free of charge.

It is possible to take a bus from Heathrow to Gatwick.

The most convenient way to the center of the city is the Airbus. Airbus 1 (A1) proceeds to Victoria Railway Station with stops along the way. The A2 goes to Paddington Station and the A3 to Euston Station. It takes about an hour and costs about five dollars.

A taxi will take a shorter time, but it is still at least an hour and fifteen minutes during the rush hour. The fare will be about twenty-five dollars plus tip.

One of the best ways to get into London is to use the Underground, which runs from Heathrow right to the center of the city. Follow the signs in the airport and use the moving walkways. This is another good argument for keeping the baggage to a carry-on weight.

If you have an overnight wait, I understand that the Sheraton-Heathrow provides very convenient accommodations, with free bus service to and from London and a coffee shop and pub that serve good, inexpensive food.

Gatwick

Charter flights deplane at Gatwick, but it now has many scheduled flights from North American cities.

Gatwick maintains that it has very fast baggage service, and there are little lounges with television sets that announce the arrival of the baggage for each flight.

Flightline 777 is a nonstop bus service between Victoria Coach Station at 164 Buckingham Palace Road in London and Gatwick. It stops just outside the terminal on the upper level. Victoria Coach Station, not to be confused with Victoria Bus Station, is about a half a mile from Victoria Railway and Underground Station. Coaches leave Gatwick every half hour all day long and then hourly in the evening. It takes about an hour and ten minutes and, of course, longer at the rush hour. The price is four dollars one way. A taxi costs forty dollars.

Often regarded as the most practical way to get to and from Gatwick is the train from Victoria Station. At Gatwick, the train stops inside the terminal on a lower floor. At Victoria, take the entrance next to the National Tourist Information Office to Platform 15. Trains leave every fifteen minutes all day long and every hour through the night. It is about a fifty-minute journey, although I understand that the express cuts it down to thirty minutes. The fare is six dollars.

There is an airport hotel at Gatwick in case you cannot get out or cannot get to town. The new ring road, M25, that encircles London eliminates the necessity of driving through the city to go north or northeast.

DEPARTING LONDON

As noted earlier, the Underground is a quick, reliable, direct method of getting to and from Heathrow Airport, and the train is the best way to and from Gatwick. For overseas flights, I find it's best to arrive at least ninety minutes ahead of time. You can always enjoy yourself watching the fascinating crowds after being ticketed or going through Passport Control. Major overseas airlines all have special reservation numbers for checking vital departure information.

RENTAL CARS

After much trial and error I found the most satisfactory car rental arrangements in both Britain and Europe, from the standpoints of convenience and cost, could be made through AutoEurope-Maine, whose offices in North America are at P.O. Box 1097, Camden, Maine 04843. The toll-free number for the U.S. is 800-223-5555 (Maine: 800-342-5202). For Canada it is 800-458-9503. Arrangements can also be made to pick up cars in principal cities and airports in Britain and drop them off in other countries.

I always advise travelers not to plan on driving their rented cars in the city of London. Take the Underground or the airport coach to center London and then a cab to your hotel. Pick up a rental car when leaving the city. The AutoEurope-Maine cars can be picked up and/or dropped off in London or at Heathrow, Gatwick, or Prestwick airports, or many other points.

Many experienced travelers visit London at the conclusion of their trip, engaging a rental car on arrival at the airport and spending the first night at one of several countryside accommodations listed in this book. At the end of their travels, the car can be dropped off at one of various locations, including Edinburgh, Glasgow, York, Oxford, Cambridge, Exeter, or even Heathrow or Gatwick. At some locations there is no charge for drop-off. The trick is to take the train back to London and avoid the traffic.

DRIVING TIPS

In Britain, automobiles are driven on the left-hand side of the road. This should not alarm anyone, since it's very easy to make the adjustment.

I'd suggest an automatic rather than a stick shift automobile. A U.K. operator's license is not necessary.

Enter the roundabouts (traffic circles) on the left and circle clockwise. The traffic already in the circle has the right of way.

MAPS

I find the British Tourist Authority's AA Motorists' maps particularly helpful and easy to handle. These can be purchased at most bookstores in England, or you can send for a catalogue and order them from:

> GHS Inc.
> British Travel Bookshop
> Box 1224
> Clifton, NJ 07012

USING BRITRAIL IN BRITAIN

Experiencing the English countryside by train can be a comparatively inexpensive and pleasant way to travel throughout Britain. In addition to its usual schedule, which covers a passenger network of 12,000 miles, Britrail has a number of special offers, among which is a plan for travel on the red buses and Underground in London.

A Britrail pass cannot be purchased in Britain, and must be obtained before you leave the United States. Britrail vouchers must be exchanged for tickets at Victoria Station in London. For complete information, write or call:

> Britrail Travel International
> 630 Third Ave.
> New York, NY 10017
>
> Telephone: 212-599-5400

COUNTRY INNS IN BRITAIN AND IRELAND

For the past twenty-three years I have defined the word "inn" in North America as a certain type of lodging that conveys something of the innkeeper's personality, along with friendly hospitality and service in unique surroundings.

However, I've discovered that in Britain the term "inn" has a more specific meaning. It's a type of pub (public house) that has a license clearly defining the hours when it must be open or closed. When overnight accommodations are available in a pub, they are frequently called inns. These are sometimes the old traditional inns, with colorful and imaginative names. The food and accommodations range from simple to sophisticated.

The popularity of traveling in Britain in recent years has seen the emergence of the "country house hotel." For the most part, these are sizable houses built a hundred or more years ago by affluent Britons for pleasure and residence away from the city. Today, they have been converted into very good, smallish hotels, usually set in several acres of grounds and woodlands, and located away from the towns and villages. They are not, by strict interpretation, inns. Proprietorship usually runs the gamut from retired naval and military types to younger couples who, like some North American innkeepers, are establishing new careers. If a British country house hotel were located in North America, it would be known as a country inn. If North American country inns were to be transferred to Britain, they would be called country house hotels.

The third category is the guest house. These are frequently in farms and private homes. Breakfast and dinner are usually served in the family dining room, and besides sharing the living room, there is usually that wonderful institution, only to be found in Britain, the residents' lounge, where there's usually a small "telly," a fireplace (or an electric fire), and many books and magazines.

The final type of establishment is the B&B, which is short for "bed and breakfast." Some B&Bs are splendid, others leave something to be desired. I have included as many of the former as possible.

DINING IN THE BRITISH ISLES

Basically, menus in Britain and Ireland fall into three categories. First, there's pub food, which is usually salads, sausages, cold cuts, meat pies, and pâtés. Pub food is most generally served at midday.

Some lunch and nearly all dinner menus include hearty British food such as roast beef and Yorkshire pudding; various cuts of lamb, veal, ham, and poultry, which might include pheasant, partridge, and other game birds.

At dinner, British dishes frequently share the spotlight with French cuisine, both traditional and *nouvelle*. I found a great many French chefs working in British kitchens.

There are local food specialties in various parts of Britain. Most of the time they are easily recognizable on the menu.

The latest times dinner may be ordered vary greatly from one place to another, and these times are listed in the Index in the back of the book.

ACKNOWLEDGMENTS

This book is really a team effort. Behind the scenes were literally dozens of individuals and organizations who gave generously of their time and advice in order to bring their experiences to this published fruition.

To start with, the British Tourist Authority in both New York and London was immensely cooperative in helping me plan my trips. Equally helpful was the Irish Tourist Board in New York and in Dublin.

The book was designed and the drawings created by my longtime associate, Jan Lindstrom.

Virginia Rowe, the editor, is responsible for the accuracy of all the facts and keeps a watchful eye on my literary style.

I am also grateful to the hundreds of readers of my earlier books who have been kind enough to share some of their favorite places in Britain and Ireland. This book will be revised again in 1990 and further suggestions are most welcome.

Maps in this book are reproduced with the kind permission of the British Tourist Authority.

England

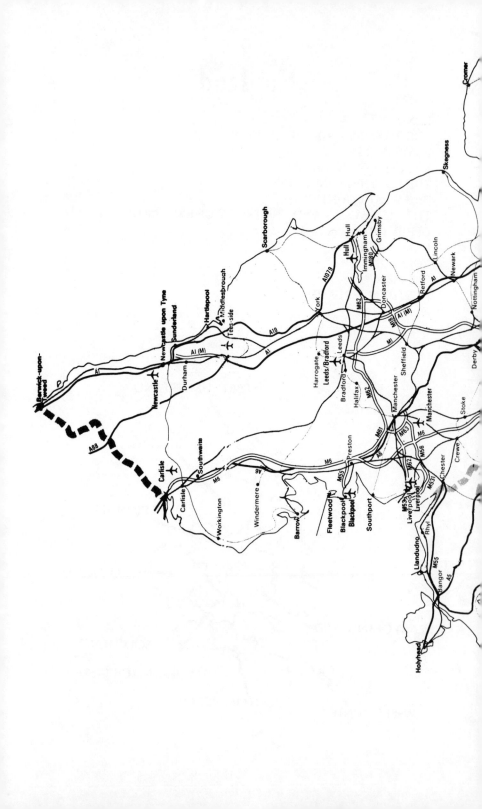

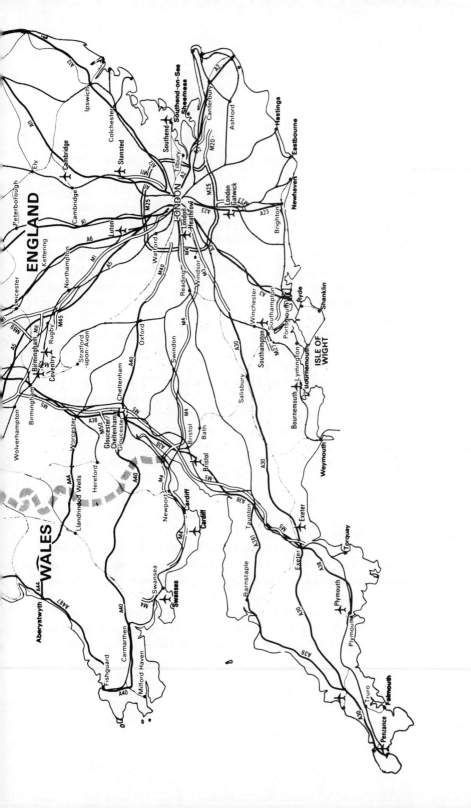

LONDON

Sooner or later, almost everyone visiting Britain goes to London, and well-a-day that they do because London is alive with interest, fun, and excitement. In this book I will not attempt an overview of this great city, but hope that the reader will be encouraged to visit London, walk as much as possible, and feel free to mingle, not only with the Londoners, but also the thousands of other visitors. I have walked the London streets very late at night in complete safety.

Now a word of caution and some advice for the first-time visitor to London. Do not attempt to drive an automobile within Greater London! The ground transportation from Heathrow or Gatwick is speedy and frequent. You will not need a car in the city of London. If you land at Heathrow, and your baggage can be handled conveniently, it is possible to take the Underground to center London, where a cab can then be taken directly to your hotel. (Please see "Arriving in Britain" in my introductory notes.)

Getting around London is easy. The London Underground is fast and efficient, goes everywhere, and is good for excursions that are some distance away. The double-decker buses, as well as the green buses, provide an opportunity to see London aboveground. The hotel concierge can supply a very essential map that gives all of the bus lines by number, and it's quite common to see tourists standing in front of a chart on a post, reading the numbers of the buses that are going to stop there. (See "Using Britrail in Britain" in my introductory notes.)

There are dozens of books about sightseeing in London; one of the best is London, Your Sightseeing Guide, published by the British Travel Authority.

London Hotels

Because almost everybody traveling to Britain will be planning to stop in London for a few days, I have included a group of moderate-sized London hotels in various price categories. (See rates in Index.)

Many of these hotels have representatives in the United States, but they can also be contacted directly for reservations. A telephone call at the low-rate time is well worth the effort. Once a reservation is made it should be followed up as soon as possible by an air-mail letter with a deposit.

THE BASIL STREET HOTEL
Knightsbridge, London

The Basil, as it is known in London, is the Americans' "home away from home." It is located right behind Harrods Department Store, near where Brompton Road, Knightsbridge, and Sloane Street all come together. It's just a few steps away from the Knightsbridge Station on the Piccadilly Line of the Underground.

All London hotels have an indispensable man, known as the Hall Porter. I'll use the Basil Hall Porter as a model for others. Guests soon discover that his desk is the nerve center to the smooth running of their holiday or business trip. Hall Porters provide information on everything from sightseeing and transport, to religious services, hotel reservations at the next destination, restaurants, theaters, mail, newspapers, messages, laundry, valet service, parcels, luggage, and taxis. He's on duty from 9 a.m. to 9 p.m., at which time his duties are taken over by the Night Porter.

Guest rooms at the Basil vary in size and decor. There are a few rooms without their own private bathroom that represent an exceptional value.

Besides several different dining rooms, the Basil also has the Parrot Club, a delightful meeting place for women, used mostly by daytime visitors to London, but also available to hotel guests.

The Basil lounge is a good place to meet friends in London, and also provides an opportunity to chat with other travelers. The afternoon teas are first-rate, and the dining room, with candlelit tables and a piano playing softly in the background, is most enjoyable for dinner.

I've stayed at the Basil several times, and I have American friends who prefer it above all other London hotels.

Reader Comment: "We followed your advice about not driving in London. We dropped the car in Bristol and took the train to London and the Basil. The staff was very accommodating, and it was a good place for our three-and-a-half-year-old. The Basil doesn't include a regular breakfast in the room rate, which is true of most London hotels."

BASIL STREET HOTEL, Knightsbridge, London SW3 1AH. Tel.: (01) 581-3311. Telegrams: Spotless London SW3. Telex: 28379. U.S. reservations: 800-223-9868. A 103-guestroom (mostly private baths) hotel located near Sloane Square, Hyde Park, and Harrods Department Store. Breakfast, lunch, tea, dinner, and snacks served every day of the year. Stephen Korany, Managing Director. (See Index for rates.)

Directions: From Heathrow Airport take the Piccadilly Line Underground (it's the only one available) to Knightsbridge Station, which is just a few steps away from the hotel. From London air terminals, take airline coach to central London, and then a taxicab.

DUKES HOTEL
35 St. James's Place, London

Dukes, like the Stafford, is located close to Piccadilly and the London theater district, although both of them are very quiet. Dukes was originally composed of "chambers" for the younger sons of the nobility; it has been a hotel since 1908. I've included it in *CIBR, Britain* since the first edition.

Dukes is probably the closest thing to a private London club—the essence of restrained elegance with a friendly and accommodating atmosphere. It's located on one of the few remaining streets in London enjoying romantic gas lighting.

The *London Times* is left at each door every morning. Although the dining room, which has been considerably enlarged, is open for breakfast, most of the guests prefer to enjoy breakfast in their rooms.

All of the rooms are furnished in a classic style with all the modern conveniences. They are on the medium-to-small size.

To find Dukes one has to have a sharp eye. You turn off St. James's Street, and about 200 yards on the left there is an entrance to Dukes between two buildings. There is a very small car park, used only for leaving your car while you check in. A valet parking service is provided.

I have a feeling that Beau Brummel, the arbiter of London fashion, who lived at 39 St. James's Place, would thoroughly approve of Dukes today.

DUKES HOTEL, 35 St. James's Place, London SW1A 1NY. Tel.: (01) 491-4840. Telex: 28283. U.S. reservations: 800-223-5581. A 36-guest-room and 20-suite luxury hotel in the heart of London's West End. Open every day. Breakfast, lunch, tea, and dinner served to non-residents. Adjacent to Green Park, Buckingham Palace. (See Index for rates.)

THE STAFFORD
16 St. James's Place, London

The Stafford is just about two blocks away from Dukes Hotel on St. James's Place, a quiet dead-end street, one of London's well-kept secrets. St. James's Place has its own history. Oscar Wilde lived here, and also Sir Francis Chichester. Some of the famous London clubs, such as Bootles, Whites, and Brooks were located here, and one of the principal walks was "Green Walk" between the mall and Park Wall, where Charles II met Nell Gwyn.

The Stafford housed various London clubs, then added buildings on each side, and then became the Stafford Hotel. During World War II, it was a club for Canadian and American overseas officers. I stayed there a few times and found the rooms very comfortable and the staff very amiable, although the Stafford has a reputation for being quite formal compared to similar hotels in America.

At the time of my most recent visit, there were window boxes filled with blooming tulips and daffodils and an air of springtime gaiety.

When I asked the general manager why Americans enjoy the Stafford, he replied, "As you know, we used to be a private house and we've been trying over the past four or five years to create as much of that private house or home atmosphere as possible.

"Changes have been made in the guest rooms and drawing rooms, and we've also built a garden suite with its own fountain. I think I've been dealing with Americans long enough to recognize the fact that what they frequently like is a 'home away from home' and the biggest compliment we can have from any of our guests is for them to say, 'It's nice to be back home again.'"

THE STAFFORD, 16 St. James's Place, London SW1A 1NJ. Tel.: (01) 493-0111. Telex: 28602. A 70-guestroom hotel located in the Mayfair district of London within walking distance of theaters, Oxford Street, and Buckingham Palace. Breakfast, lunch, tea, dinner served daily to non-residents. (See Index for rates.)

Directions: First-time visitors should take a bus to Victoria Station and a cab to the hotel.

For room rates and last time for dinner orders, see Index.

BRYANSTON COURT HOTEL
56 Great Cumberland Place, London

This is a very pleasant hotel located just a few blocks from Marble Arch. It is convenient for walking to Oxford Street and Piccadilly.

Great Cumberland Place is a quiet, dignified street, and the hotel has a demeanor to match.

BRYANSTON COURT HOTEL, 56 Great Cumberland Place, London W1. Tel.: (01) 262-3141. Telex: 262076. A 60-guestroom hotel on a quiet street a few blocks from Marble Arch. Open every day. Breakfast, lunch, tea, and dinner served to non-residents. E. Theodore, Resident Proprietor. (See Index for rates.)

DURRANTS HOTEL
George Street, London

Durrants Hotel is a former Georgian coaching inn, owned and run by the same family for over a half a century. It is in London's fashionable West End, opposite the Wallace Collection. It's within a short walk of Oxford Street, Piccadilly, and Marble Arch. It has a very pleasant lobby and entranceway, and a comfortable lounge area with deep leather chairs.

Durrants is a quiet, conservative hotel, generally preferred by travelers for whom London is a frequent stop.

DURRANTS HOTEL, George Street, London W1H 6BJ. Tel.: (01) 935-8131. A pleasant hotel just off Manchester Square and a few blocks from Oxford Street and Marble Arch. Open every day in the year. Breakfast, lunch, tea, and dinner served to non-residents. J. P. Leveque, Director. (See Index for rates.)

THE GORING HOTEL
Beeston Place, Grosvenor Gardens, London

The Goring is located within walking distance of the Thames Embankment, as well as the Royal Parks, Westminster Abbey, and the Houses of Parliament.

Departures and arrivals from Gatwick Airport are transported directly to or from nearby Victoria Station by train.

The Goring manages to be sedate and informal at the same time. One of its virtues is the fact that there is a beautiful lawn and garden in the rear, providing views of the posteriors of a group of small London townhouses.

THE GORING HOTEL, Beeston Place, Grosvenor Gardens, London SW1W OJW. Tel.: (01) 834-8211. Telex: 919166. A 100-guestroom family-owned hotel near Victoria Station and Pan Am Air Terminals. Breakfast, lunch, tea, dinner served daily to non-residents. William Cowpe, Manager. (See Index for rates.)

NUMBER SIXTEEN
16 Sumner Place, London

Number Sixteen is actually the name of a small, tidy hotel in a lovely residential area, close to the center of London.

It is located at 16 Sumner Place in the South Kensington area, which is also the name of the stop on the Underground.

It is actually four townhouses that were built in 1848 and have been preserved for their architectural charm. There is no hotel sign, but the street number is very plain. Inside, the reception area is most attractive and friendly. I saw many of the thirty-two guest rooms, which were furnished in a comfortable and appropriate manner.

There are two pleasant sitting rooms and also a private bar, which is open in the evening. A continental breakfast is served in your room.

Number Sixteen is one of the only two London hotels to have won an award for excellence from the *Good Hotel Guide*, and also has won the "London in Bloom" competition for its garden that stretches across the entire four-townhouse area in the rear.

Number Sixteen isn't for the traveler who ordinarily stays at one of the more palatial hotels near Marble Arch or Park Lane; however, you will not be the first London visitor to discover it. If form holds true, you will want to do what everyone does who visits it—tell the whole world about your new London hotel.

NUMBER SIXTEEN, 16 Sumner Place, London SW7 3EG. Tel.: 01-589-5232. Telex: 266638. A 32-guestroom (private baths) townhouse in a quiet section of London. Continental breakfast included in the room rate. Open year-round. A few moments from Harrods, Knightsbridge, Hyde Park Corner, and Piccadilly by cab, foot, bus, or Underground. Michael Watson and Tim Daniel, Hoteliers. (See Index for rates.)

Directions: After arriving at Heathrow Airport, take the Underground to South Kensington Station and ask directions to 16 Sumner Place; it is just around the corner. Otherwise, take the regular airport bus to central London and then take the short cab ride to the hotel.

THE RITZ
Piccadilly, London

When you walk into the high-domed lobby of this hotel and see that wonderful block-long corridor with the rich carpeting, the arches, the marble pillars, the mirrors, the palms, and the flowers, you know you have to be in the Ritz in London. The Ritz is located in Piccadilly, within walking distance of Bond Street, Oxford Street, and Knightsbridge.

Suites and guest rooms in the rear of the Ritz have a delightful view of Green Park. When I was there it was an April lunch-time, and the greensward was populated with Londoners anxious to catch a little of the high-noon sun.

There are several delightful suites on the various corners of the six floors, each of which has a different decorative theme. Most of the guest rooms are twin- or double-bedded, and they help the Ritz live up to its reputation as one of the world's most fashionable hotels.

Another point: Tea at the Ritz is almost a must. Make reservations for tea when you make your room reservations, even two or three months in advance. Tea is served in the Palm Court, a beautifully decorated room with a skylight, palms, flowers, and graceful Grecian statuary. It is the essence of elegance.

THE RITZ, Piccadilly, London W1V 9DG. Tel.: 01-493-8181. U.S. Reservations: 800-223-5581. Telex: 267200. A 128-guestroom (14 suites) luxury hotel in central London within a convenient distance of many of the London sightseeing spots. Open year-round. Breakfast, lunch, dinner, and afternoon tea served. Michael Duffell, Managing Director. Julian Payne, General Manager. (See Index for rates.)

HARRODS

I was browsing in the meat shop at Harrods, one of London's great department stores.

What a glorious fantasia of sights and enticing aromas greeted me! It was Elysian at the very least.

The first things I saw hanging from the domed ceiling, mind you, were hundreds of hams, sausages, pumpernickels, salamis, and dozens of their relatives in the "wurst" family. A great many of them were imported from different countries in Europe, and there were numerous items that were totally new to me.

Below them was a large center section of cases with such delights as pork pies, steak-and-kidney pies, ham pies, and chicken pies. There were twenty-seven varieties of salads, including oriental, Spanish, Russian. The displays themselves were beautiful. There were tins of caviar and small fish, and dozens of varieties of pâté. There were jellied eels, absolutely sumptuous-looking bacon, and beautiful quiches. I walked around the center at least three times planning picnics and cold buffets.

To further add to my delight, all around the outside of this square were counters with gorgeous displays of fowl, including turkey and pheasant. There were cuts of pork, lamb, veal, beef—just about everything. Particularly intriguing was the display of fish, including kippers, shellfish, halibut, sole, Scottish salmon, and many others. There was also a large fish sculpture in ice.

All of these great treats were beautifully displayed in a setting of intricately tiled pillars and ceiling. There were many colors of tiles forming a fascinating succession of patterns.

The next stop was the cheese department, equally exciting. There were all kinds of cheeses done in all forms—in crocks, jars, cans, sliced, in cases for slicing, and hanging from the ceilings. There were cheeses from all over the world—Beaumont, Brie, Port Salut, Jarlsburg, provolone, to name a few. There were cases of cheese of all colors—yellow, green, white, and speckled cheeses. I saw wheels of cheeses and cheese pâtés.

The aroma and sights are still in my mind.

In Britain, acceptance of a hotel booking by telephone or in writing is generally regarded as a legally binding contract. If it's necessary to cancel, advise the hotel immediately. If they are unable to re-let the room, the hotel may be entitled to claim compensation—usually two thirds of the agreed price—and any deposit would be included as part of this payment.

THE THAMES AND THE CHILTERNS
Counties of Oxfordshire,
Buckinghamshire, Bedfordshire
and Berkshire

The Thames Valley and the Chilterns extend from the London city limits to the western borders of Berkshire and include Oxford, the edge of the Cotswolds, and Bedford to the north.

The Thames meanders through towns and villages and eventually through London. It ripples down from its source in the Cotswold Hills, gathering momentum and becoming a full-fledged, navigable river. It passes through the peaceful countryside, historic towns, and lush meadows and by lovely old inns and waterside gardens; negotiates locks, rushing weirs, and leafy backwaters; slices between the wooded hills of Goring Gap; and slides lazily by Windsor, taking in memorable views of the town and castle.

The Chiltern Hills, many of which are crowned with ancient beech groves, are located roughly to the northwest of London, and the narrow country roads leading out of High Wycombe, Chalfont, and Wendover provide a very pleasant alternative route to Oxford.

The Thames and Chilterns are rich in history, architecture, and tradition. There are hundreds of years of family history to explore, and every one of its many great houses has its own unique story—of great men and wicked men, men who won battles, built empires, and gambled away fortunes.

THE THAMES AND THE CHILTERNS

THE ROYAL OAK HOTEL
Yattendon, Berkshire

It was Friday evening, and the pub of the Royal Oak was filled with people from Yattendon and the surrounding area who were having a good time and looking forward to the weekend. They were all partaking of that wonderfully English experience called "a pint at the local."

I remarked to Kate Smith, who shares in the pride of innkeeping with her husband, Richard, on all the signatures in the guest register of people from other parts of the world. She said, "I am constantly surprised at the number of people who find their way to our humble little inn. Actually, we try to keep a place that we would enjoy visiting ourselves.

"The Royal Oak started life as an inn during the 16th century and, despite the extensions and improvements carried out over the years, one feels that the founding landlord would still readily recognize the inn. There is no doubt that the strong oak beams and fascinating chimneys, together with the unusual brickwork, are unchanged in nearly five hundred years.

"With five bedrooms and five bathrooms, the hotel is small enough for a completely personal service, yet it's big enough to provide facilities demanded by the discriminating guest. A good English breakfast is served in the restaurant, and a continental breakfast may be served in the guests' rooms."

Only fifty miles west of London, the Royal Oak is in the center of the tiny village of Yattendon. Kate speaks of it as "the prettiest and quietest village in England." It is mentioned in the Domesday Record, dating to Norman times.

One of its earlier inhabitants, Sir John Norreys, was accused of having an adulterous affair with Anne Boleyn, one of Henry VIII's wives. He was executed at the Tower of London after refusing to compromise the Queen. The village includes a classic square surrounded by wisteria and vine-covered cottages and a blacksmith's shop, buildings that are virtually unchanged since Oliver Cromwell billeted his troops here before the second battle of Newbury. I understand that the cricket ground is one of the best in the area, and the village team will certainly welcome anyone who would like to play.

Winding lanes lead through the woods and farmlands to the Chilterns, the upper regions of the Thames, historic Oxford, and other beauty spots.

In addition to its multiple functions as a local pub and an internationally famous hotel, the Royal Oak is also a restaurant acclaimed by many of the food writers in Britain. I can certainly attest to the excellent roast duck I enjoyed at my evening meal. The dining room was very busy and Kate moved deftly among the tables, much concerned with her guests' comfort.

Because the village is only forty-five minutes from Heathrow Airport, many overseas guests arrange to spend either their first or last night in Britain at the Royal Oak. Either way, it would be a most enjoyable experience.

Reader Comment: "The innkeepers made us feel at home. It was our second visit, and we stayed an extra night. Great food."

THE ROYAL OAK HOTEL, Yattendon, Newbury, Berkshire RG16 OUF. Tel.: (0635) 201-325 or 201-244. A 5-guestroom village inn approx. 45 min. from London Heathrow Airport. Breakfast, lunch, and dinner served to non-residents. Open every day. Short distance from Thames and Chilterns recreational, scenic, and cultural attractions. Kate and Richard Smith, Innkeepers. (See Index for rates.)

Directions: Going west on M4 (from London or Heathrow) use Exit 12 and follow signs toward Pangbourne (A340). Take first turn left (200 yds.), signposted Yattendon. Go straight on to crossroads at Bradfield and follow signposts to Yattendon, 4 mi. [Don't miss Exit 12, because the next exit is miles to the west. I know.]

STUDLEY PRIORY HOTEL
Horton-cum-Studley, Oxfordshire

"Well, I trust you had a refreshing sleep!" A smiling Jeremy Parke greeted me in the dining room of the Studley Priory Hotel where the sun was streaming in through the stone mullioned windows. All around me the overnight guests were eating their breakfasts with what was obvious enthusiasm.

"I did, indeed," I responded. "However, I had a dream in the middle of the night that someone was galloping along the London Road, and that people were lighting bonfires and celebrating some portentous event!"

Jeremy smiled and said, "Oh, I think I can explain that. You fell asleep remembering our dinner conversation about Studley Priory, and I told you that the main part of the house was finished just one year before the defeat of the Spanish Armada. I'm sure it stirred your imagination."

Dinner the previous evening had been a gastronomic adventure; Jeremy explained that his *chef de cuisine* has introduced a radical new style of French cuisine. "It is Cuisine Légère. It includes a subtle new combination of tastes and imaginative uses of new ingredients." Starters were a quail consommé flavored with truffle and a velvety scallop soup with a dash of white wine. Main courses included baron of baby rabbit served with a delicate sherry vinegar sauce, calves' sweetbreads braised on a bed of vegetables, and an interesting group of three fillets of beef, pork, and lamb. The dining room is named for John Croke, who built this Elizabethan-style house and whose family owned it for over 300 years.

In 1966, Studley Priory was chosen as the home of Sir Thomas More for the film *A Man for All Seasons*. The hotel was used for exterior shots of the house and grounds.

A short walk through the grounds after breakfast gave me an interesting perspective on the lovely, mellowed Cotswold building, which stands in its own parkland with many magnolia, redwood, and oak trees. It was late April and as usual the daffodils were in glorious profusion. They would be

replaced throughout the summer by other colorful flowers. Nuthatches and goldfinches darted back and forth, busy at their springtime tasks.

There were pleasant views in all directions, including Blenheim Palace, the Cotswolds, and the Chiltern Hills. The grounds, while neat and tidy, had a good natural feeling and didn't seem overgroomed.

Walking out to the driveway to wish me a pleasant journey, Jeremy smiled and said, "You'd be surprised how many other guests have had that same dream!"

STUDLEY PRIORY HOTEL, Horton-cum-Studley, Oxford OX9 1AZ. Tel.: Stanton St. John 203 and 254. A 19-guestroom country house hotel in a handsome Elizabethan house, 7 mi. from Oxford. Breakfast, lunch, tea, and dinner served daily except the first 2 wks. in Jan. Just a few mi. from the Thames River, the Chiltern Hills, and the Cotswolds. All of the cultural attractions of Oxford are within a very short distance. Tennis and clay pigeon shooting on grounds. Squash, riding, and golf available nearby. Jeremy Parke, General Manager. (See Index for rates.)

Directions: Take the London–High Wycombe Road through Headington to A40 roundabout. Take the second left off the roundabout, signposted "Horton-cum-Studley 4 mi." Follow signs to Horton-cum-Studley. Hotel is situated at the top of the hill in the village. Turn right at an entrance to a drive.

THE GREY SPIRES OF OXFORD

Long before I had walked along the High or stood at the Carfax, the main crossroad of Oxford, or had seen for myself the Magdalen College deer park, or admired Wren's Sheldonian Theatre, or browsed in Black- well's Bookstore, I had dreamed of being in Oxford.

I expected to find a quiet town basking in the afternoon sun with groups of undergraduates casually strolling to appointments with their tutors, or trotting toward the cricket field, or dreaming on the river bank.

Instead, I found a vibrant, active city where town and gown alike enjoy the fruits of learning and pleasure. The quadrangles of the thirty-four colleges, each providing a superb example of almost every architectural period, are woven into the fabric of the commercial and residential life of the town.

Oxford has left its mark on some of the world's intellectual and literary giants. A list of scholars and graduates is a veritable "Who's Who" of English letters. Balliol College claims John Wycliffe, Adam Smith, Robert Southey, Matthew Arnold, and Algernon Swinburne. Thomas Moore,

Robert Burton, John Ruskin, and W. H. Auden were members of Christchurch.

Magdalen Hall looked down upon a youthful John Keats.

Perhaps of more contemporary interest is the fact that J.R.R. Tolkien was a Fellow and a Professor of English Language and Literature at Merton from 1945 to 1959.

Cardinal Wolsey, Roger Bacon, Geoffrey Chaucer, Shakespeare, Alexander Pope, Jane Austen, Wordsworth (a Cambridge man who wrote two sonnets about Oxford), Thomas Hardy, Henry James, and Dylan Thomas visited Oxford and came under its sway.

For an interesting satirical contrast between Oxford and Cambridge, first read Sir Max Beerbohm's novel, Zuleika Dobson, *and then read* Zuleika Goes to Cambridge. *The latter is attributed to "S. Roberts," which may be a Beerbohm pseudonym.*

THE BELL INN
Aston Clinton, Buckinghamshire

"Let me tell you the unusual story about that clock." Innkeeper Michael Harris and I were on a leisurely tour of the Bell Inn, and at the moment were standing in the main hallway.

"In 1797, William Pitt, who was responsible for the income tax, imposed a tax of five shillings a year on clocks. It applied equally to pocket watches, increasing to ten shillings a year for a gold watch. As a result, people refused to buy clocks and watches and many disposed of those that they owned. Thousands of craftsmen became unemployed. For the convenience of their patrons, and to attract those who no longer carried a watch or owned a clock, British innkeepers installed large clocks in their inns. The tax was repealed within a year, but the inn clocks remained popular, and many are in their original positions to this day. They are known as Act of Parliament clocks."

We strolled across the street to the old brewery, where there are fourteen additional guest rooms in the converted stables and malt houses that form an attractive group around the cobbled courtyard. "We tried to preserve the simplicity and charm of the old buildings as far as possible," he said.

"I think we take a justifiable pride in our food. The head chef has created a menu that has some traditional English dishes. However, fine French cooking predominates. Meals are à la carte and a *prix fixe* lunch is also offered every day except Sunday."

THE BELL INN, Aston Clinton, Buckinghamshire HP 225 HP. Tel.: (0296) 630252. A 21-guestroom luxuriously appointed village inn at the

foot of the Chiltern Hills, about 40 mi. from London. On Sun. and Mon.
eves. restaurant closed except to hotel residents. Open year-round. Con-
veniently situated for walking and sightseeing. Blenheim Palace, Wad-
desdon, Woburn, and other stately homes nearby. Golf, riding, tennis
available. Michael Harris, Managing Director. (See Index for rates.)

Directions: Take M1 out of London and use Exit 8 through Hemel
Hempstead and on to A41 through Berkhamsted. Take Tring Bypass
toward Aylesbury. The Bell Inn is 4 mi. from Tring.

MELBOURN BURY
Melbourn (near Royston), Hertfordshire

There is something about a house where several generations of one
family have lived and added their belongings and treasures over the years
that takes on a patina and feeling all of its own. It whispers of the lives that
were lived there, of the people and their interests. Melbourn Bury has
been in Sylvia Hopkinson's family since 1820.

When I stepped into the graceful entrance hall, with its beautiful
antique desk, oriental rug, and fireplace, I had an instant sense of culture
and refinement. That sense was further borne out when Sylvia led me into
her graciously proportioned, high-ceilinged drawing room. A baby grand
piano stood in one corner, and there were lovely antique pieces, a wide,
arched alcove framing the fireplace, pleasant groupings of comfortable
furniture, and everywhere paintings, books, and flowers.

French doors at one end looked out on a glassed-in porch, much like a
small conservatory, filled with fuchsias, miniature orange trees, lilies, and
many other plants. There were wicker chairs where one could sit and look
out over the lawn and gardens to a small lake ringed with weeping willow
trees, where Sylvia said ducks and geese often paddled about.

As we strolled around the rather extensive grounds, I admired the rose
garden, the little walkways, and an old brick wall covered with wisteria
while Sylvia, a delightful lady, told me a bit about the history of the house.
First, "bury" means a fortified house, and it was usually the largest house
in the village. There was a moat here at one time, parts of which still
remain, and a gable or two of the 16th-century house that stood here can
still be found.

Back in the house, she showed me the perfectly wonderful Victorian
billiards room, with an adjoining cozy library. I was really taken with the
little wooden leather-covered balustrade, or club fender, in front of the
fireplace for people to sit on.

Sylvia does the cooking, and I think she may get some help from her
husband, Anthony, and possibly her children, when they're home. "I try to

keep my meals balanced and not too rich," she told me. Breakfasts are the full English kind, with fresh fruit and juice, cereal, eggs, bacon, sausages, tomatoes, and toast and marmalade. Dinners are rather traditional, with roasts, pork chops with cider and apple sauce, and fresh lamb in season. "I check with my guests to find out their preference. I always have homemade soups and fresh vegetables. Americans particularly seem to like my 'Queen of Puddings,' a hot custard with apricot jam and meringue."

The very attractively furnished guest rooms have twin beds and their own bathrooms.

After a heavy day of sightseeing in nearby Cambridge, Melbourn Bury would be a most welcome and peaceful refuge.

MELBOURN BURY (Wolsey Lodges), Melbourn (near Royston), Hertfordshire SG8 6DE Tel.: Royston (0763) 61151. A 3-guestroom (private baths) gracious home 10 mi. south of Cambridge. Breakfast included in tariff. Dinner by prior arrangement. Closed Christmas and New Year's. Croquet lawn, billiards, lovely garden on grounds. Cambridge, Saffron Walden, Audley End, Wimpole, and other great houses, wool towns, and airplane museum at Duxford nearby. Children over 8 welcome. Sylvia and Anthony Hopkinson, Hosts. (See Index for rates.)

Directions: From London, take the A1 to Baldock and then the A505 or A10 to Royston and Cambridge. Approx. 1 mi. after Royston look for a black-and-white lodge and white gateposts on the left just after a fruit farm. The main house is 200 yards down the drive.

WOODLANDS MANOR
Clapham, Bedfordshire

This is a place where you are likely to meet American businessmen. Owner Richard Lee tells me that there are a number of American companies based in Bedford, including Texas Instruments, Prime Computers, and National Semiconductors.

I could see why they would like to stay in this gracious Victorian manor house. There is a pleasant and comfortable drawing room with many groupings of sofas and chairs, the dining room is inviting with its white linen and rose-and-white Limoges china and silver settings, and I understand the food is excellent.

The guest rooms that Mr. Lee showed me were quite attractively decorated. Some of the bathrooms boast rather unusual tortoise shell, marbleized walls, and fixtures in harmonizing colors.

All of the guest rooms have televisions, radios, and telephones, and such other amenities as hair dryers and trouser presses.

The dinner menu offers ten possible starters, including a fan of baked avocado, pear, and Stilton cheese with a spicy tomato sauce, curried mushrooms and pistachio nuts in a puff pastry, and a smoked mackerel mousse with a horseradish sauce. Among eight choices for the meat course were Dorset veal, pan fried with white wine and cream and Stilton cheese, roast breast of duckling with plum and port wine sauce, and calf's liver pan fried with sage, sliced onion, and bacon. A special menu is available for vegetarians.

The manor house is surrounded by a pleasant lawn with trees and gardens, and there are chairs and tables with umbrellas, where drinks are served when the weather permits.

WOODLANDS MANOR, Green Lane, Clapham, Bedfordshire MK41 6EP. Tel.: (0234) 63281; Telex: 825007. A 21-guestroom (private baths) Victorian manor house on the outskirts of the busy and historic town of Bedford, a few miles from Cambridge. Continental breakfast included in tariff. Restaurant serves breakfast, lunch, and dinner. Reservations necessary. Open year-round except Christmas week. Convenient to Woburn Abbey and the John Bunyan Museum in Bedford and the many cultural and historic attractions in Cambridge and Oxford. Trout fishing on the River Ouse and other recreational activities also available nearby. Richard Lee, Proprietor. (See Index for rates.)

Directions: From London, take the M1 to the A1. Turn off on the A603 to Bedford. In Bedford take the A6 toward Clapham. Continue 2 mi. to Green Lane on the right.

For room rates and last time for dinner orders, see Index.

FLITWICK MANOR
Flitwick, Bedfordshire

I think of Santa Claus when I think of Somerset Moore—he has that jovial, jolly quality that makes you feel happy to talk to him. I was trying not to eat *all* the delectable cookies on the tea tray Debbie, his manager, had placed before me, while he was telling me the story behind his remarkable collection of beautiful antique porcelain covered sardine dishes. You might want to ask him about them.

With his reputation as a fine chef, Somerset and his wife, Hélène, opened Flitwick Manor as a restaurant, and with its success they were soon able to move forward with their dream of creating a country house hotel.

They had chosen an impressive property for their endeavor. Standing on high ground above the town, this estate has a recorded history dating back to the 11th century, and the present manor house is of 17th- and 18th-century origins. The drive up to the house is lined with lime, or linden, trees, most of which are 250 years old. Somerset is justly proud of all the magnificent trees on the grounds, many of which have been listed by the Forest Commission. You should ask him about them—especially the juniper *recurva,* which I couldn't get over.

There are fifty acres of grounds, including woodland, a three-acre lake, an 18th-century grotto (called a "folly") with an ornamental pond, and gardens, both cultivated and wild. Somerset makes sure there are some wild areas for his bees. You'll want to ask him about those, too.

The reception area has an interesting, somewhat primitive feeling, with its simple brick fireplace, rather rough parquet floor, and medieval chairs. However, the sitting room is quite different. Paneled in lovely honey-colored pine, with a marble-faced fireplace and elegant furniture and fittings, it provides quite a luxurious feeling.

In fact, the entire house is most luxurious. I saw nearly every guest room, and was really impressed with the decoration—the furnishings, the choice of colors and fabrics—and, in short, the total aspect of every room. Even the bathrooms are outstanding. I don't think I've ever seen such an array of amenities, from every sort of toiletry, including razors, combs, and cosmetics, to baskets of fruit and an incredible assortment of both alcoholic and nonalcoholic drinks on the "honesty" drink tray. Every room also has a Scrabble game and a pack of cards in addition to television, a radio, and a telephone.

There isn't a view from a window that isn't enchanting, whether it's lawn, trees, and gardens, the cedar of Lebanon tree, a meadow, the pond, the lake, a village on a hill far away, or the kitchen garden with fruit trees, beehives, chickens, and a brick wall covered with wisteria.

Even the halls and landings display beautiful and unusual antique pieces and paintings. You should ask Hélène about those.

It goes without saying that the lounge and dining rooms are lovely. I was extremely disappointed that I couldn't stay for dinner. The cuisine is basically English with some French influence, and the menu lists a really mind-boggling selection of dishes for every course, with an emphasis on fish and other seafood. There are various mouth-watering treatments of lobster, crab, salmon, oysters, trout, eel, clams, shrimps, and sea bass. For instance, there is lobster cooked with brandy, cream, and truffles or a fillet of Scotch salmon in a puff pastry with asparagus tips and a sauce Maltaise. I noticed several starred items, which presented "a new concept in low-calorie eating." It's impossible for me to convey the full scope of the menu. You'll have to see it. Their brochure describes their sources for provisions, and I'm sure if you asked Somerset, he'd show you the kitchen.

Flitwick is in an excellent spot for seeing some of the interesting sights in Bedfordshire, particularly the Woburn Estate, with a stately house, a fabulous art collection, and a 2,000-acre park with rare deer. There is also the Fabergé collection at Luton Hoo, a house of descendants of Russian czars, and many other places of interest. You should definitely ask Somerset about them—I think you'll agree he's a lot of fun to talk to.

FLITWICK MANOR, Flitwick, Bedfordshire MK45 1AE. Tel.: Flitwick (0525) 712242. Telex: 825562. A 16-guestroom (private baths) luxurious country house hotel in the rolling countryside of Bedfordshire, halfway between Oxford and Cambridge. Breakfast included in the tariff. Lunch and dinner served to the public; reservations imperative on weekends. Open year-round. Croquet lawns, hard-surface tennis court, putting green, snooker, walks, Wellies, and bicycles on grounds. Woburn Estate, Luton Hoo, and other stately homes, golf, Silverstone motor racing, squash, swimming, horseback riding, surfing, and windsailing nearby. Mr. and Mrs. Somerset Moore, Proprietors; Janet Abbot and Debbie Bullock, Managers. (See Index for rates.)

Directions: From London, take the M1 north to the A5120 or 512. About 3 mi. from turnoff watch for entrance on the left.

SWALCLIFFE MANOR
Swalcliffe (near Banbury), Oxfordshire

Standing in the Great Hall and looking at the book Judith Hitching was showing me, *The English Mediaeval House,* in which the architectural history of Swalcliffe Manor is discussed, I felt a sense of awe. Here was a room where the lord of the manor, his family, the serfs, and the dogs had all gathered 700 years ago. I could just barely discern the medieval wall paintings over the mantel. Judith told me there are better-preserved paintings in the attic, where they were more protected from the smoke and light. In 1600 the house was sold to New College at Oxford, which owned and maintained it for over 350 years.

Judith, vivacious, friendly, and quite nattily turned out in a white turtleneck sweater and white duck pants, had some fascinating things to tell me about the house, which she and her husband, Francis, have owned for about five years. "It was built around 1200 by the lord of Broughton Castle, nearby, for his third son, and the same stonemasons who worked on the castle built this house. The castle is fabulous, with a moat and a drawbridge—a real fairy-tale castle. But I think our undercroft is better than theirs."

Now I have to tell you about the undercroft. This is a room with massive stone pillars and tripartite stone arches, something like flying buttresses (see Jan Lindstrom's sketch), which are usually found only in fortified castles or cathedrals, and are nearly always built to support a great tower. In the case of this undercroft, one expert declared that the only possible reason for it was for show—to impress people. And it certainly does its job.

When I entered the house and stepped into this undercroft, with its stone floor and walls and low, vaulted ceiling, I felt almost as if I were entering a time warp. However, Judith brought me back to the present as she graciously led me through 13th-century stone archways, into the Great Hall with its huge, walk-in fireplace, the Tudor dining room, a Georgian drawing room, and up narrow, twisting stone stairs to the three comfortably furnished guest rooms on the second floor. One 13th-century bedroom has a four-poster bed.

The Hitchings are a cosmopolitan pair—Francis writes and produces

documentaries and Judith continues, on a reduced scale, the catering service she had operated when they lived in London. "I'll still do a posh wedding or a special London party now and then," she says. Guests who make advance arrangements for one of her dinners are in for a treat, I am sure. Judith was named Gourmet of the Year in London a few years ago; "I've got a reputation to keep up," she says with a laugh.

Francis cooks the hearty English breakfasts of eggs, sausages, kedgeree, and the like, which are served *en famille,* as are the dinners, at the long dining table in the Tudor dining room.

In addition to being historically and architecturally fascinating, this seems to be a most comfortable and relaxed place to stay, with pretty gardens and lovely views, and certainly most hospitable hosts.

SWALCLIFFE MANOR (Wolsey Lodges), Swalcliffe (near Banbury), Oxfordshire OX15 5EH. Tel.: (029578) 348. A 3-guestroom (private baths) medieval stone manor house in a charming tiny village on the edge of the Cotswolds, midway between Stratford-upon-Avon and Oxford. Breakfast included in the tariff. Dinner by advance reservation only. Open from early March to late Nov. Croquet lawn, swimming pool, game room with ping-pong on premises. Country walks, antiquing, beautiful gardens, Blenheim Palace and many stately homes, Cotswolds nearby. No credit cards. Francis and Judith Hitching, Hosts. (See Index for rates.)

Directions: From London, take M40 to Oxford and then to Banbury. At Banbury Cross turn left on B4035 for about 5 mi. In the tiny village of Swalcliffe you will see the sign for Swalcliffe Manor on the right.

EAST ANGLIA
Counties of Sussex, Essex, Suffolk, Norfolk, and Cambridgeshire

East Anglia starts at the Thames estuary and runs north to King's Lynn and the Wash. It bulges into the North Sea to the east, and its coastline is opposite Europe. To the west it borders the Thames, the Chilterns, and the Heart of England.

Essex is the county closest to London. Its great attractions are the seaside towns and villages and the historic town of Colchester.

In the 13th century, Flemish weavers settled in Suffolk and established a cloth trade that was to make the county one of the great centers of medieval England. Some of the towns in midcounty like Long Melford and Lavenham still have great churches, houses, and colorful cottages. Suffolk is Constable country and the great English painter saw great beauty in the quiet pastoral scenes near Dedham. Newmarket is a famous racing center.

Norfolk has the famous inland waterways known as the Norfolk Broads. These reed-fringed lagoons are thought to be the remains of Saxon peat diggings that are now flooded and connected by a complex network of six rivers. Norwich is its ancient capital, and there are castles and many great houses in this section. Norfolk is also well known for its seaside resorts.

Cambridgeshire, besides being the site of the famous university, also has the cathedral town of Ely, where the King's School was founded by Alfred the Great. Other towns include Kimbolton, where Mary, Queen of Scots, was imprisoned for a time; Soham, one of the last areas of natural habitat for fenland wildlife; and St. Ives.

Many individuals from East Anglia have left their mark on England, if not the entire world. The great landscape painter John Constable was inspired by the tranquil countryside. Sir Isaac Newton was seated in the garden of this manor in nearby Lincolnshire when he formulated the law of gravity as he watched an apple fall from a tree. Oliver Cromwell, the Protector of England, attended the grammar school which is now the Cromwell Museum in Huntingdon.

EAST ANGLIA

MAISON TALBOOTH AND LE TALBOOTH RESTAURANT
Dedham, Essex

Seated in the pale sunshine of a promising April forenoon on the terrace of Le Talbooth on the banks of the River Stour, I was nearly overwhelmed by daffodils—daffodils growing in the flower beds, in wooden tubs on the terrace, on the dock—masses of them on the opposite banks.

Le Talbooth is a beautiful, old, white building with Tudor half-timbers interspersed with red brickwork. The wrought iron furniture and marble-topped tables on the terrace would shortly be accommodating other luncheon guests. Through the stone mullioned windows of leaded glass, I could look into the lounge area where some early arrivals were already enjoying good conversation in front of a small, bright fire.

Gerry Milsom joined me for a few moments before lunch. "We still have time to run over to Dedham Village," he said. "There's something over there that I think you might find rather extraordinary."

As we walked across the lawn, he told me that the house was built early in the 16th century. "The name 'Talbooth' probably derives from the fact that tolls were collected at the bridge. It may have been used to collect tolls also from the barges that worked their way from Harwich."

I remarked on how beautifully the building had been restored. "By the 1930s," he said, "the house was in a sad state of disrepair. Abandoned lime kilns occupied the site of the River Room, and the oak timber frame of the house, so characteristic of East Anglian domestic architecture, was concealed by the original lime plaster, crumbling and long past making good.

"We arrived on the scene in 1952 with everything in a near-shambles. It took a lot of time and a lot of work, but we finally opened. During the first week, the takings were 27½ pence!"

I might add, parenthetically, that now Le Talbooth is a rousing success and a founding member of the prestigious Pride of Britain Partnership.

As we sped over the country road towards the village of Dedham, Gerry explained that there are two establishments; one is the restaurant Le Talbooth, and the other is a country house hotel with the appropriate name of Maison Talbooth.

In the village I saw the old grammar school attended by the painter John Constable. Gerry pointed out a brick building with a sun dial on the front. "This building, Sherman Hall," he said, "has direct connections with the General Sherman who gained some notoriety during the American War Between the States."

Maison Talbooth is an elegant country house hotel with fine views of the Constable countryside. As Gerry says, "We work on the assumption that everybody who comes here really has a first-class home, and they don't want to experience anything less than they are accustomed to."

There was no reception desk; instead, we were met in the reception hall by a very attractive hostess who obligingly showed me through the individual rooms and suites, all with sumptuous furnishings. The bedrooms were beautiful, but words fail me on the subject of the bathrooms. Each of the ten was entirely different, and two of them had round sunken bathtubs large enough for two people. Very contemporary.

During the half-mile return trip to the restaurant, Gerry commented that the Vale of Dedham is known throughout the world because of the many Constable paintings. "There is a painting, hanging in the National Gallery of Scotland, of Le Talbooth itself in a view across the vale. We're fortunate enough to have a copy."

I still have fond memories of lunch, which included a delicious slice of pork brought to the table on a silver carving tray. The kitchen is staffed with enthusiastic men and women well versed in the art of French cuisine, who also turn out such regional specialties as Yarmouth herring with cream cheese, Colchester oysters, and Suffolk stew.

Gerry proved to be a walking fount of information about the virtues and attractions of East Anglia, and his last word before my departure was, "I hope all of your readers will visit East Anglia. It's the uncrowded, natural England for which so many people are searching."

MAISON TALBOOTH AND LE TALBOOTH RESTAURANT (Pride of Britain), Stratford Rd., Dedham, Colchester, Essex CO7 6HN. Tel.: (0206) Colchester 322-367. U.S. reservations: 800-323-7308. A 10-

guestroom luxury hotel and restaurant located about 8 mi. from the ancient city of Colchester. Lunch and dinner served every day. In the heart of Constable country, it is very convenient to many of the Essex and Suffolk cultural, scenic, and recreational attractions. Tennis, swimming, riding, golf, fishing, available nearby. Gerald Milsom, Proprietor. (See Index for rates.)

Directions: Follow A12 from London. Above Colchester, watch for exit at Stratford St. Mary and Dedham. Follow road down hill. Take right turn toward Dedham. Maison Talbooth is ½ mi. on right.

DEDHAM VALE HOTEL
Dedham (near Colchester), Essex

Gerry Milsom had prepared me to expect some changes at the Dedham Vale Hotel, although as I sat in the conservatorylike atmosphere of the Terrace Restaurant, I was certain that even in my most imaginative musings, I never dreamed of anything quite like this.

Actually, the entire redesigning of Dedham Vale came out of Gerry's vivid imagination. He is also the owner of Le Talbooth Restaurant and Maison Talbooth Hotel nearby. Dedham Vale was for many years the home of his father and mother, who operated this beautiful building as a hotel. "It was here that I got my first taste of the restaurant and accommodation business," he commented.

Basically, the entranceway was exactly as I had remembered it, through a very sedate front doorway into a quiet parlor. However, as Gerry led me through the doorway to the Terrace Restaurant, it opened on an entirely different world.

It was as if I had walked into a magical garden with glass walls and ceilings. There were large bushes and small trees adorned with gaily colored lights and a profusion of brightly hued flowers.

"We had an Edwardian-style glass conservatory in mind," Gerry said. "The glass panels provide an intimate view of the garden outside and we wanted a total alfresco feeling."

To add further to the fun and enjoyment, Gerry pointed out that the poultry and some of the main dishes served at the restaurant, such as chicken, duckling, and lamb, are barbecued on the largest rotisserie that I have ever seen. Other main courses, such as sirloin steak, fillet of pork, and halibut steak, are cooked on the grill. A heavily laden sweet trolley rounds out the evening meal.

However, the wonderful British features are still in glorious profusion, including the really outstanding garden, which is the habitat of wrens, wagtails, thrushes, and finches. The rustic bench is still snuggled up to the tremendous tree with a girth equal to some I've seen in northern California, and the miniature waterfall creates a counterpoint to the songs of the birds.

Ten of the original twelve guest rooms have now been converted into six handsome suites, all with their own bathrooms, television, radio, and telephone service.

"Between Le Talbooth and Dedham Vale Hotel we feel that our guests can now have a choice of two different types of atmosphere," Gerry remarked. "Things are a bit more informal here at Dedham Vale and the barbecued main courses provide an interesting contrast to the French menu at Le Talbooth."

Dedham Vale now operates the Terrace Luncheon Club with a smorgasbord buffet service.

DEDHAM VALE HOTEL, Dedham (near Colchester), Essex CO7 6HW. Tel.: (0206) Colchester 322273. A 6-guestroom (all private baths) hotel in Constable country, just a few miles from Colchester. Open every day. Continental breakfast included with room tariff. Dinner served nightly. Luncheon Club operates every day. Conveniently located to enjoy the meandering Stour River, Dedham Village, and other cultural, recreational, and scenic attractions in Suffolk and Essex. Gerald Milsom, Proprietor. (See Index for rates.)

Directions: From London on the A12, continue 6 mi. beyond Colchester and turn off at large sign on left marked, "Stratford St. Mary." After ½ mi., bear right over bridge crossing the A12. The hotel is 100 yds. away at the bottom of hill on left.

DEDHAM HALL
Dedham, Essex

"This entire area—the Vale of Dedham—is a walker's and painter's paradise." Bill Slingo and I were taking a stroll about the grounds at Dedham Hall as he explained some of the many interesting aspects of this splendid guest house.

"Actually," he continued, "the Vale of Dedham is a wide valley through which flows the River Stour, the boundary between the counties of Essex and Suffolk. John Constable discovered its wonderful, paintable qualities and it was made famous by his landscapes. Fortunately, the Ministry of the Environment has declared it an area of outstanding beauty and national importance, so it's changed very little since he painted it."

As we made the turn around Dedham Hall, he indicated a timber-framed, white plastered house with one side almost completely of glass. "Because so many of our guests are interested in painting, we made this old 14th-century building available for painting courses that are held

throughout most of the year. Visiting tutors are experienced in oils, water colors, and pastels. I do a bit of picture framing here if it's desired."

There are ten very comfortable guest rooms at Dedham Hall, and besides the full English breakfast, which includes homemade bread or croissants, Elizabeth Slingo provides a hearty dinner. Most of the eggs and meat come from the Hall grounds, and she's very proud of the home-grown vegetables. Dinner is served at 7:30 p.m., but reservations are necessary no later than 9:30 a.m., because everything is cooked to order.

"There are two sitting rooms and a small bar in the oldest part of the house, which dates back to 1380," Bill commented. "Relaxing there in the evening is sometimes one of the best times of the day."

Our turn around the grounds brought us back to the front entrance, and I could see the often-painted tower of Dedham Church rising above the trees. The village of Dedham and the surrounding countryside remain one of the most beautiful and unspoiled areas in England. Small wonder that John Constable was so inspired.

DEDHAM HALL, Dedham, Colchester, Essex CO7 6AD. Tel.: (0206) Colchester 323027. A 10-guestroom (4 rooms with private baths) guest house in the heart of Constable country. Rates include breakfast. Dinner served to houseguests and friends with 12-hr. advance notice. Closed Jan. and Feb. Inquire about painting courses held frequently with visiting tutors. Most conveniently located to enjoy Dedham Vale and wonderful walks in the country. Mr. and Mrs. William Slingo, Proprietors. (See Index for rates.)

Directions: Take Dedham exit from A12; follow through village and look for guest house sign on the left.

THE OLD VICARAGE
Higham (near Colchester), Suffolk

We American Anglophiles who watch "Masterpiece Theatre" regularly are certainly familiar with English countryside and with English country houses. That's why, when I stopped off at the Old Vicarage, I felt as if I had been there before. It's really a private house, because there is no sign indicating that there are accommodations available. The Parkers are country people who have "a few guests now and again." I think the great appeal is that it is indeed a private family; however, Meg Parker has a way of taking people up and making them feel as if they are very much part of everything that is going on.

I phoned from about a mile away in the center of the village and had no difficulty following her directions to reach the pink house. There were other personal guests visiting at the time, and for a few minutes we all gathered in the comfortable drawing room and talked travel, discovering that we had all visited several of the same places.

The guests went off to play tennis on the courts just outside the door, and Meg and I stayed long enough to have a late-morning cup of coffee and to get acquainted.

"That's the River Brett just behind us," she pointed out. "It joins Constable's favorite river, the Stour, just a little bit farther on. You know we are right on the Essex and Suffolk borders."

While we were talking we were joined briefly by a couple of friendly dogs, who rendered their approval of me and then went outside to enjoy the June sunshine. Meanwhile, we could hear the sounds of the tennis game going on, and another guest came through to take a plunge in the swimming pool.

The house itself, like other East Anglian structures, is Elizabethan in design. There are six guest rooms, three of them with private baths and the other three share two bathrooms. A full breakfast is included and Meg mentioned that there are times when she invites her guests to use the kitchen to prepare a light evening meal for themselves.

We continued our chat, strolling around the grounds and the most impressive garden. She pointed out that the sweet little church that adjoins the Vicarage dates back to the 14th century. "It is a typical small wool church," she explained, "so-called because the people who lived up here were all in the wool business. The church is still in use today, and on Sunday the church bells are rung by the village carpenter."

I think you'll have a lot of fun finding the Old Vicarage, but you'll have even more fun as a guest.

THE OLD VICARAGE (Wolsey Lodges), Higham (near Colchester), Suffolk. Tel.: (0206-37-248) Higham 248. A 6-guestroom (some shared baths) private home in the Constable country of Suffolk. Full breakfast is included in the room rate. Open all year. Tennis court and swimming pool on grounds. Conveniently located for excursions to the Suffolk coasts, as well as enjoying the footpaths and back roads. Meg Parker, Proprietress. (See Index for rates.)

Directions: Take the Stratford St. Mary exit from the A12 (halfway between Ipswich and Colchester), and follow the road toward Dedham and Langham to Stratford St. Mary. In Stratford St. Mary, there is a turning marked Higham; follow this 1 mi. and look on the right for a pinkish house with a black barn and 3 pink deer beside a sign marked "Church."

BELSTEAD BROOK HOTEL
Ipswich, Suffolk

I think it's fair to say that, with the exception of the GIs who served there during World War II, East Anglia remains relatively undiscovered by the North American traveler. During my visit to the four counties in this section, I made several happy discoveries and among them was the Colchester-Ipswich area, which can be enjoyed during a stay at the Belstead Brook Hotel.

Peacocks and Muscovy ducks strutting around the newly greening willow trees on the bank of the brook immediately caught my eye as I entered the hotel grounds. The many rosebushes already had buds; in a few weeks the garden would come completely to bloom—and just two miles away was the bustling center of Ipswich.

Belstead Brook is a family-owned hotel; the present manager is a young, handsome Englishman named Iain Hatfield. His father, George Hatfield, founded the establishment a number of years ago and is one of the most respected hoteliers in Britain. There's a pleasant air of comfortable sophistication about the hotel. The lounges, restaurant, and other public rooms have been decorated in harmonious colors and furniture. There are twenty-four guest rooms, all with contemporary furnishings, color TVs, radios, and intercom systems.

Several suites have been built that are entirely in keeping with the general atmosphere. Each has its own sitting room and bedroom with a king-sized bed, clock radio, a trouser press, and a whirlpool bath. These are known as the Garden Suites.

The dining room is particularly attractive with handsome candlesticks and bright red candles on each table. A bevy of very comely young ladies wearing long gowns serve the diners.

I enjoyed a steak and kidney pie accompanied by broccoli and parsnips. I'm particularly fond of buttered parsnips, and the English variety has a flavor that I've never found anywhere else. The dinner menu was à la carte and had an unusual number of selections, including fresh seafood from the nearby North Sea.

Iain Hatfield joined me for coffee and proved to be well versed in the history of both the hotel and this section of East Anglia.

"A favorite activity of our guests is to get maps of all of the footpaths nearby." He stopped when he saw I was smiling. "Oh, I see you've already learned how keen we Britons are on walking. We even have a little packet of eight different walks in southeast Suffolk with a map and a description of each."

Of no small importance to the international traveler is the fact that it is only a short drive to Felixstowe and Harwich, where there are ferries to Germany, Holland, and Scandinavia.

Incidentally, Iain Hatfield made a visit to America in the fall of 1985 to participate in the conference of *CIBR* inns at the Red Lion Inn in Stockbridge. We enjoyed having him and several other of the U.K. innkeepers who also made the trip.

BELSTEAD BROOK HOTEL, Belstead Rd., Ipswich, Suffolk IP2 9HB. Tel.: (0473) 684241. A 30-guestroom country house hotel on the pleasant outskirts of Ipswich. Breakfast, lunch, tea, and dinner served daily year-round. Ipswich is conveniently located for many attractive day trips in East Anglia, including Colchester, Yarmouth, Bury St. Edmonds, Lavenham, Harwich, and Felixstowe. Swimming, sailing, golf, riding, squash, tennis available nearby. Iain Hatfield, Manager. (See Index for rates.)

Directions: Take the A12 from London to the first significant roundabout in Ipswich and inquire at the nearest petrol station as to the location of Belstead Road, which is relatively close. Follow Belstead Road approx. 2 mi. through the residential area, keeping a sharp lookout for the hotel sign on the right.

In Britain, acceptance of a hotel booking by telephone or in writing is generally regarded as a legally binding contract. If it's necessary to cancel, advise the hotel immediately. If they are unable to re-let the room, the hotel may be entitled to claim compensation—usually two thirds of the agreed price—and any deposit would be included as part of this payment.

KING'S HEAD INN
Orford (near Woodbridge), Suffolk

Once a fortified port on the coast of Suffolk, Orford is a delightful fishing village bordering the North Sea. It has a high church tower that for centuries has served as a landmark for mariners. The town also boasts an equally high castle keep built by Henry II. The tower of this castle has a stunning view of the sea, harbor, and surrounding marshlands.

I saw all of this and more during my visit to Orford on a bank-holiday Saturday. I was originally interested in Orford because a New Hampshire village has the same name.

I dislike using the word "typical" in referring to inns or hotels anywhere, because the one thing of which inns can certainly boast is a remarkable individuality. However, the Englishman is able to feel at home in a pub wherever it may be located because of certain common denominators. For example, at the King's Head, patrons were picking up plates of food at the bar from hostess Phyl Shaw and her son, Alistair, and taking them out into the wonderful sunshine to sit against the wall of the inn or underneath the trees in a little adjoining park. I knew that just as the patrons of the King's Head were enjoying this holiday scene, it was also being reenacted in all parts of England.

The King's Head has a rather impressive evening menu that includes special dishes, such as fresh brill in a champagne sauce and fillets of sole, poached, rolled, and stuffed with lobster, scampi in a white wine sauce, fresh local lobster, and lots of other mouth-watering dishes.

Even though it was 2 p.m., at the height of the bar lunch rush, I stayed long enough to take a quick tour of the guest rooms, which, as with the

Silent Inn in West Yorkshire, were small but serviceable. Five double bedrooms share two bathrooms. There were basins with hot and cold water in each of the rooms.

In the rear of the inn is a crafts shop with a very good selection of baskets and several other locally made crafts. Next to that, in what was formerly a stable, is one of the most popular spots in the village—the ice cream shop.

KING'S HEAD INN, Orford (near Woodbridge), Suffolk 1P12 2LW. Tel.: (03945) Orford 271. A 5-guestroom (sharing 2 baths) traditional inn located in one of Suffolk's most natural villages. Breakfast, lunch, and dinner every day. Closed Jan. Closed from 3 p.m. to 5 p.m. every day, but arrangements can be made to check in in advance. Orford is a sailing center. The entire area has a great deal of historical interest. Conveniently located for all of the recreational, cultural, and natural attractions in this part of East Anglia. Phyl Shaw, Innkeeper; Alistair Shaw, Chef. (See Index for rates.)

Directions: Take A12 north from Ipswich. After passing Woodbridge, look for signs to Orford and follow them to the village. Inn is on the left.

FELMINGHAM HALL
North Walsham, Norfolk

An Elizabethan manor house! With few additions and permutations, it has been standing on this spot for four hundred years. Its architecture and design are quite different from the Georgian and Victorian so predominant in Britain. Built of red brick with plaster trim, the two main sections are separated by a smaller center section. At a distance, it looks like a small, willowy child standing between two sturdy adults.

The entrance is through a formidable front door into a large reception area and living room with a tremendous sunken fireplace, which would prove to be, I discovered that evening, a splendid gathering place for guests.

My bedroom was reached by well-worn stone steps leading to the second floor, and through its deep windows, it looked out in two directions over the fields and parkland. I could see the vegetable gardens on one side and many grazing sheep on the other. The date carved in the stone mantelpiece said 1569.

The Elizabethans apparently had large rooms, but they didn't have the central heating or the generous bathtubs or conveniences provided for today's guests. However, the remnants of their lives were around me, including many old trees and ancient brick walls adding to the atmosphere of this beautiful house.

After a few moments of rest and a quiet walk, during which I raised several pheasants and woodcocks in the fields, we were all summoned to an attractive dining room to enjoy the evening meal. Along with several other guests, I was served by a very pleasant young woman with whom I had a lively conversation about the nearby Norfolk Broads. Following a choice of starters, I enjoyed some Norfolk turkey, fresh vegetables, and a trifle for dessert.

Although Felmingham Hall was an Elizabethan country house originally owned by a wealthy family, today's owner, Mrs. Joyce, is working hard to provide contemporary comforts for her guests.

Before turning in, I took another short walk underneath the starry East Anglia skies and reflected that as glamorous as Felmingham Hall's past may have been, its present certainly bodes well for the future!

FELMINGHAM HALL, North Walsham, Norfolk NR28 OLP. Tel.: (069269) Swanton Abbott 228. A 12-guestroom (private baths) country house hotel, approx. 10 mi. north of Norwich. Dinner, bed, and breakfast year-round. Dinner served to non-residents. Many natural scenic attractions nearby, including the sea and the Norfolk Broads, museums, churches, art galleries, theaters in Norwich and Buxton. Available recreation includes color TV, bicycles, covered swimming pool on grounds; golf, tennis, riding, sailing, swimming, fishing, etc., nearby. No facilities for amusing small children. Mrs. J. Joyce, Proprietor. (See Index for rates.)

Directions: From Norwich, follow A140 to Aylsham. Take B1145 toward North Walsham. Turn right in Felmingham Village, continuing past Felmingham Church. Take 2nd right. Felmingham Hall is the 2nd left on this road.

THE NORFOLK BROADS

It's hard for anyone to suppress a smile when the term "Norfolk Broads" is introduced into the conversation. Double entendre *aside, the Norfolk Broads are among the greatest attractions of this section of East Anglia. These reed-fringed lagoons are thought to be the remains of Saxon peat diggings now flooded and connected by a complex network of rivers. Hidden canals link vast acreages of water drained from the local countryside, offering ideal waterways by which to explore the broadlands. There are more than thirty large water areas contained in the triangular area between Norwich, Lowestoft, and Sea Palling. Along with the canals, lakes, and rivers, they provide some two hundred miles of water for cruising and sailing.*

The essential character of the Broads can only be properly appreciated from a boat and there are boat liveries and tour operators in such centers as Roxham, Horning, and Potter Heigham.

One of the best ways to view the Broads by car is to take the main road between Ormesbey St. Margaret and Rollesby.

From Norwich to Great Yarmouth, the country is as flat as Holland, and like Holland, boasts windmills—five, if not more, can be seen along this stretch. In this part of the world, flat means beautiful.

CONGHAM HALL
King's Lynn, Norfolk

I had no trouble knowing which direction was west. From the great window in my bedroom overlooking the rear lawns of Congham Hall I could see the wonderful, lowering Norfolk sky moving in, leaving an ever-diminishing streak of red across the horizon. In some places this might bode a fair day on the morrow; however, in England the weather can be capricious, and the television in my room had informed me only a few minutes before that a string of showers from the southwest would soon be coming across the heart of England and into East Anglia.

However, in the spring one travels in England on a day-to-day basis, and this had been a beautiful day, starting with cheery good-byes to Gerald Milsom at Maison Talbooth in Dedham, and continuing on up to Bury St. Edmunds for a visit at the Angel, and then north through the wonderful Thetford Forest, past the gates of Sandringham, the Queen of England's estate.

Now I was at Congham Hall, a Georgian manor house built in the mid-18th century and set in forty-four acres of beautiful parkland. Strolling its paddocks, orchards, and country gardens, travelers can unwind and enjoy their holiday.

The conversion from a country house into a luxury hotel in 1982 has been accomplished by Mr. and Mrs. Trevor Forecast, with careful regard to its original classic interior. They brought with them considerable experience as hoteliers in other parts of Britain.

The entrance hall spans the depth of the house, with a view of the park at the far end. All of the guest rooms have a view of the surrounding parkland or the adjacent fields. There is a pleasant mix of conventional rooms and suites. The furnishings are both modern and traditional.

Dinnertime beckoned me below and I could hear the sound of merry tunes being played on a piano in the drawing room. I took one of the comfortable chairs, and the headwaiter immediately presented me with the evening menu. He explained that everything is cooked to order and so guests are able to make their choices in comfort in the drawing room. When their dinner has been prepared, they are then seated in the dining room.

The starters presented problems right away, they were so enticing. The first course was poached salmon, and the main courses included lightly grilled lamb livers, fillet of sole, roast fillet of pork, roast breast of duck for two, and roast saddle of venison. An eight-course meal is served here, including coffee and petit fours.

As the pianist drifted from Victor Herbert to Noel Coward, I was called in to dinner, and I found an attractively decorated dining room in rose-pink and lily. Dinner was most rewarding, and the sweets menu was quite in character with everything else. I chose hot spiced pears served in red wine and fresh homemade vanilla ice cream. I took coffee in the drawing room, lost in a reverie enhanced by the gentle sounds of the piano.

Congham Hall is a wonderful example of what is fortunately happening in many former country houses as they are being converted into excellent small hotels.

CONGHAM HALL (Pride of Britain), King's Lynn, Norfolk PE32 1AH. Tel.: Hillington (0485) 600250. U.S. reservations: 800-323-7308. An 11-guestroom (private baths) country house hotel at Grimston, just 6 mi. from King's Lynn. Breakfast, lunch, and dinner served. Open year-round. Centrally located to enjoy a visit to Sandringham, uncrowded beaches, tiny fishing villages, horseback riding, golf, bird sanctuaries, and the Norfolk Broads. Swimming pool, tennis court, and cricket on the grounds. Not suitable for children under 12. Pet kennels and stabling available. Mr. and Mrs. Trevor Forecast, Hoteliers. (See Index for rates.)

Directions: From King's Lynn follow A149 to the roundabout and pick up A148. Grimston is the nearest local village for Congham Hall—not Congham Village.

BURY ST. EDMUNDS

Shall I risk saying it at least once more? The traveler to Britain who goes from London to Stratford-on-Avon and on to the Lake Country and then to Edinburgh has really experienced about five percent of this enchanted isle. Witness East Anglia in general and Bury St. Edmunds in particular.

Bury St. Edmunds is the crown of East Anglia. Here in the vast Norman Abbey were buried the remains of King Edmund, martyred in A.D. 869 by heathen Danish invaders.

For centuries the town was a premiere center for pilgrimages, and it may come as a surprise to learn that at the Abbey high altar, twenty-five barons of England swore on the 20th of November, 1214, that they would enforce the observance by King John of the Magna Carta.

The main attraction of the town is the Abbey of St. Edmund, whose history is much too complicated for me to even attempt here. Suffice it to say that it is one of the great ancient monuments of England, and even though its architecture, reflecting over a thousand years of renovations and changes, is confusing, nonetheless it continues to attract travelers from all parts of the world.

THE ANGEL HOTEL
Bury St. Edmunds, Suffolk

"The Angel at Bury." The place to stay in Bury St. Edmunds is the Angel Hotel. It is on the old market square directly across from the Great Abbey gatehouse. It so delighted Charles Dickens that he resided there twice when giving readings of *David Copperfield*. His room, Number 15, is preserved today exactly as if he had just left it.

If first impressions are the most memorable, then the lasting impression of the Angel would be its Georgian facade, covered from top to bottom with vines that turn deliciously crimson in the autumn. This is but the first of many lasting impressions, not the least of which is a dining room, in the basement of the Angel, that has vaulted ceilings dating from the 11th century. There has been an inn or some kind of accommodation on this site almost from the time that the original abbey became an object for pilgrimages.

Since my first visit some years ago, I have been an enthusiastic supporter of travel in East Anglia, but I must confess that innkeeper Mary Gough really added considerably to my knowledge and appreciation of the area. Mary pointed out to me that East Anglia has strong links with the early settlers in America. "Two-thirds of the Mayflower Pilgrims came from Suffolk and Norfolk, and Thomas Paine was born in nearby Thetford."

She also told me that the Angel has been at the center of Bury's life for over seven hundred years. It's been used as a polling place and also as the Council House.

"We think we have a lot to offer the American visitor who has most probably visited Britain before. This is the real historic and living England, and we do not promise to make an American feel at home. At Bury, he will find none of the popular American hamburger stands or fast food restaurants. What he will find is a beautiful town, one of the undiscovered gems of this sceptered isle, amongst some of the loveliest, most gentle, quiet countryside and villages Britain has to offer. One might say that Bury is the hub of East Anglia and we're within a convenient drive of the racing at Newmarket, the great houses of Blickling, Sandringham, and Ickworth, and of course Cambridge is just a short distance away. It's not just the past, but the present and the future that makes the area so fascinating."

The Angel Hotel is very comfortable, and all of the guest rooms have private bathrooms and are all individually decorated. There are quite a few four-poster beds and private suites. Many of the guest rooms and the dining room look out across the square to the Abbey gatehouse.

THE ANGEL HOTEL, Bury St. Edmunds, Suffolk IP33 1LT. Tel.: (0284) 3926. Telex: 81630 Angel G. U.S. reservations: 800-323-5463. Telex: 286778 Barr Ur. A 45-guestroom in-town hotel in East Anglia, just a few paces from the site of the famous Norman abbey. Breakfast, lunch, and dinner served daily. Open year-round. Conveniently located for access to East Coast ports and ferries in less than two hours. Almost all of the recreational, cultural, and historic attractions of East Anglia within easy driving distance. The Gough Family, Proprietors. (See Index for rates.)

Directions: Once in Bury St. Edmunds, make inquiries for the Angel Hotel. It is on Angel Hill.

CAMBRIDGE AND THE FENS

Cambridge is a city of colleges and bridges. Clare Bridge, Trinity College Bridge, and the Bridge of Sighs span the river on the Backs, those picturesque banks of the Cam, with their peaceful green lawns running down to the river, shaded by willows, and carpeted with daffodils in the spring.

Cambridge University was founded in the 13th century and now consists of several different colleges, some of which are well known, including Emmanuel, Jesus College, Magdalene College, and Trinity College. Much to my surprise, I discovered that I was not the first writer to visit Cambridge, and that several of my predecessors, including Michael Drayton, wrote about it in 1622; Daniel Defoe had some comment about scandalous assemblies at unseasonable hours; Charles and Mary Lamb visited the town and the university, and Mary wrote about the excessive amount of walking that was necessary. Henry James spoke of the "loveliest confusion of Gothic windows and ancient trees, grassy banks, and mossy balustrades, of sun-chequered avenues and groves, of lawns and gardens and terraces, of single-arched bridges spanning the little stream."

North of the elegant landscaping of Cambridge's gardens and parks lie the Fens, an expanse of flatland now farmed and yielding cabbages, potatoes, carrots, sugar beets, and every other green and root crop. They proliferate in the rich black peat soil. There have been attempts to drain this land as far back as the Roman occupation, but it remained for a rather improbable figure in history, Charles II, to institute a scheme to drain large areas with the aid of Dutch experts. Now the water is confined to innumerable drains and rivers, many of which are higher than the shrunken peat land around them.

Cambridge and the Fens have many historic buildings, museums, Cromwell memorabilia, cathedrals, archeological sites, wildlife, nature trails, windmills, and sports. As far as I know, it is also possible to hire a punt, a romantic way to see Cambridge from the river.

Fitzwilliam Museum

SOUTHEAST ENGLAND
Counties of Sussex, Kent, and Surrey

All roads in Southeast England originate from (or lead to) London, consequently, almost every weekend, the motorways and main roads from London's Marble Arch are abuzz with small English cars being driven on the left-hand side of the road, at slightly-less-than-breakneck speed, through the pleasant countryside to the three southeast counties and the towns and villages of Chichester, Brighton, Eastbourne, Hastings, Rye, Folkstone, Dover, and Canterbury.

Surrey, the county closest to London, has beautiful hills, woods, and heathland, including Lythe Hill, the highest point in the south of England. There are many "great houses" in Surrey, and it has been the scene of some of the stirring events of England's past, including Runnymede where King John signed the Magna Carta in 1215 on the bank of the River Thames.

The county of Sussex, divided into East and West Sussex, extends from the southern borders of Surrey south to the coast, and eastward to Kent. Sussex has delightful combinations of peaceful forest, undulating downland, and attractive seaside towns and villages.

The South Downs (high rolling hills) sweep across Sussex from the border of Hampshire to Eastbourne, and there are several of the famous hill figures carved on the sides of the hills. Some of these are rather ancient, but a surprising number have been created since 1900. The Glyndebourne Opera is also in Sussex, as is the city of Chichester and its harbor.

The Kentish coast bends around Southeast England for 126 miles and is replete with many resort towns. This is the land of Anne Boleyn, Henry VIII's second wife, who was beheaded (and whose ghost still walks); Winston Churchill, whose home, Chartwell, is now maintained by the National Trust; Charles Darwin; and General Wolfe, who figured prominently in the history of the New World. It is a place of many cathedrals, abbeys, churches, castles, and ruins. One of the principal attractions is the old city of Canterbury with its famous cathedral.

Oddly enough, this section of England is not the prime objective for North American visitors who are far more apt to go from London north to Stratford-on-Avon, the Lake Country, and on to Edinburgh.

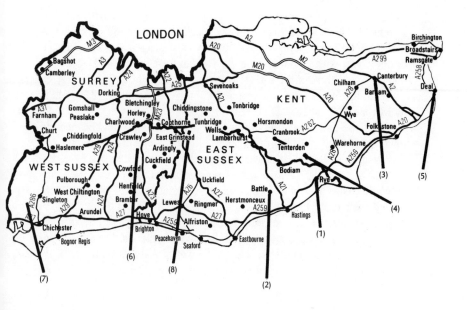

SOUTHEAST ENGLAND

MERMAID INN
Rye, Sussex

"Good night, Norman, I will see you at breakfast. Will 8:30 be suitable?" That was Michael Gregory speaking, owner and innkeeper of the Mermaid Inn in Rye. We had spent a most congenial evening in the dining room with a dinner of good England roast beef and Yorkshire pudding, and then in the lounge over second cups of coffee.

Naturally, most of the talk centered around the Mermaid. "How old is it, Michael?" I asked. "Do you really know?"

"Well, we think it was rebuilt in 1420 after the French had burned the town in 1377 on one of their frequent raids. Local legend says that the inn was visited by Queen Elizabeth I when she came to Rye in 1573.

"The inn has seen and made its own episodes in history," he commented. "During the Reformation many priests were sheltered here during their flight to France."

He took me upstairs to point out the initials "JHS" in one of their bedrooms. "This was the symbol of the escaping clerics," he said. Then he showed me the secret staircase, which was probably used many times as members of the clergy slipped away from their oppressors. In the huge

Back Lounge of the inn I saw the "Priest's Hole." "Just take a look up the chimney," he said. "That's another hiding place. A bit warmish, but quite safe.

"The history of the inn has always reflected the history of the town. Perhaps the most exciting period was during the times when smugglers' gangs were the bully boys of Rye. One group called the Hawkhurst Gang didn't do our reputation any good at all. They sat about in the windows of the inn cursing and carousing with their loaded pistols on the tables, and no magistrate would interfere with them.

"In February, 1735, a smuggler named Thomas More, who was out on bail, went to the Mermaid and dragged the bailiff by his heels from his room and into the street, taking the bail bondsman's warrants with him. The bailiff was taken to a ship in the harbor but was eventually rescued by the captain of another ship. I could go on at great length about famous people who visited here," Michael said, "and, of course, the ghosts."

Jan Lindstrom's drawing of the inn shows the Elizabethan half-timbers and entrance arch. The entrance hall reflects the motif of the entire building. The walls are faced with oak paneling and the timbered ceiling is supported by a kingpost. In a way, four centuries just fall away.

Michael and I said good night and I walked up the staircase past "Dr. Syn's Lounge," which is another whole piece of Mermaid tradition.

I fell asleep quickly, but in the middle of the night I awakened, hearing whispers in the hall and a clicking sound like the cocking of an ancient pistol. Footsteps went down the passageway and stairs and then it was quiet. When I asked Michael about it the next morning, he just smiled.

MERMAID INN, Rye, Sussex. Tel.: (0797) 22-3065. Telex: 957141. A 30-guestroom traditional inn located in one of England's most historic ports, 65 mi. from London. Open all year. Breakfast, lunch, dinner served to non-residents. Reservations may also be made for the Royal Hotel in Deal. M. Gregory, Resident Owner. (See Index for rates.)

Directions: From London, take A21 through Tunbridge Wells, and then A268 from Flinwell directly to Rye. There are dozens of alternate routes.

In Britain, acceptance of a hotel booking by telephone or in writing is generally regarded as a legally binding contract. If it's necessary to cancel, advise the hotel immediately. If they are unable to re-let the room, the hotel may be entitled to claim compensation—usually two thirds of the agreed price—and any deposit would be included as part of this payment.

RYE AT DAWN

Michael Gregory told me that Rye was fascinating at sunrise, and an early morning walk over hill and dale and into the town, with all its fascinating little shops, proved him to be altogether correct. The old houses and the flowers lining the cobbled streets; the church at the top of the hill with its ancient churchyard graves; Battings Tower, built in 1250, and redolent of English history; and that place on the hill where stood (until a bombing in 1940) the garden house of Henry James, who had lived there from 1898 to 1916, were all part of a magical sunrise walk through Rye.

POWDERMILL HOUSE
Battle, East Sussex

Douglas Cowpland was straightening me out about the Battle of Hastings. "First of all, it really is not the Battle of Hastings," he said, as we walked out toward the small pond in the front of this spacious Georgian country house. "The fact is that it should simply be called 'The Battle.' We are in a part of Battle Abbey Estate, originally six thousand acres; we have about fifty acres here. The Abbey itself was built in honor of the dead, and the original ruin is still there. You can walk from our grounds to the battlegrounds, and if you look to your left over the hedge, you'll see what is actually *the* 'Battleground.' We're in sort of a valley here, and for many years there were stories that the whole area flowed with blood. Of course, it really was the water washing through the ironstone in the area, creating a reddish tinge."

I could have listened to Douglas for hours, because I've always been intrigued by the events of 1066. In fact, this entire area is now called "1066 Country," and there's much to see and do relative to those portentous days, which certainly changed the life of all of us on both sides of the Atlantic.

However, Powdermill House occupied my immediate interest, particularly for the fact that it is a pure Georgian house and is filled, as far as my relatively unpracticed eye could see, with authentic Georgian antiques. This is because Douglas and his wife, Julie, are also well-known antique dealers with a shop in the village of Little Common, a few miles from Battle.

There are six guest rooms in the main house and others are in some buildings that are being reconstructed. To add to the fun of the stay, there are tennis courts and a lake with many Canada geese, resident Muscovy ducks, swans, white geese, and other birds and wildlife. There is also a small herd of rare Hebridean sheep.

"We're trying to encourage a wildlife park in that area over there beyond the lake," he said. "There are times when the visiting and resident wildlife are quite numerous."

At the time of my visit, Powdermill House was in the process of complete rehabilitation. However, I saw all of the guest rooms in the main house and also the drawing room, the dining room, and a room set aside as a new dining room that would be in use when this book goes to press. All will have Georgian furniture.

Julie Cowpland explained to me that dinner consists of a choice of starters and one main course, which, of course, is different every night, plus desserts and coffee.

Back to our little stroll at the pond. Douglas reached inside a bag and threw something that looked like food pellets on the surface of the water. Immediately, at least a dozen trout leaped out of the water, and the placid surface churned with activity for about thirty seconds before our finny friends disappeared into the deep.

POWDERMILL HOUSE (Wolsey Lodges), Powdermill Lane, Battle, East Sussex. Tel.: Battle (04246) 2035 or Cooden (04243) 5214. A 9-guest-room Georgian house converted into a picturesque guest house. Dinner served by appointment. Open all year. Located near Rye and Hastings. Adjacent to the grounds of Battle Abbey and the scene of the famous Battle of 1066. Swimming pool and lakes located on the grounds. Douglas and Julie Cowpland, Proprietors. (See Index for rates.)

Directions: From London take A21 toward Hastings. At Battle turn right on Powdermill Lane. From Brighton take A259. Turn off at Little Common and follow the road signs to Battle.

CANTERBURY

Canterbury dates back to Roman times and was used by the Romans as the seat of government for the tribes of Kent. In A.D. 597 St. Augustine traveled from Rome and converted the King of Kent and restored some of the town's earlier Christianity. The present cathedral dates from 1070 and was the scene of the brutal murder of Archbishop Thomas à Becket for his denial of the king's authority over the Church. It remains to this day one of the great and inspiring attractions in the United Kingdom.

In addition to the abbey and cathedral, it is possible to view the city wall bastions: the West Gate; Grey Friars, the first Franciscan settlement in England; the Weavers, a house for Flemish weavers in use in the 16th century; and the Poor Priests' Hospital, now used as the regimental museum.

Canterbury is a compact, inspiring city. Perhaps nowhere else is it possible to see so much history within a few hundred yards. It is a real center of English religion and learning.

Although not a native of Kent, Geoffrey Chaucer (1340?–1400) has proved to be the best press agent for Canterbury. The celebrated Canterbury Tales is made up of the stories of a group of pilgrims, representing all types of English life, as they journeyed through the April sunshine and showers from the Tabard Inn in Southwark (near London) to Canterbury and back. Chaucer apparently finished twenty-one of these humorous, earthy tales that reveal his love of nature and his fellow man.

It is said of Chaucer that he found English a dialect and left it a language.

HOWFIELD MANOR
Chartham Hatch, Canterbury, Kent

I was enjoying a second cup of coffee with Clark and Janet Lawrence in the wonderful, spacious kitchen of Howfield Manor, in the heart of the countryside and only ten minutes away from the cathedral city of Canterbury.

Breakfast had been outstanding—the orange juice freshly squeezed, the eggs from a local farm, and all the jams and marmalades made by Janet.

Clark is an American and Janet is English. They had kindly toured us through the house and we admired all of the five guest rooms, each with its own bath and other amenities such as a trouser press, hair dryer, and alarm clock.

We were now talking about the fun they have as hosts. "We would like to have a place for people to stay that is as nice as their own homes. People traveling today expect much more than just the bare essentials of the room. They want comfort, service, good bathrooms and towels, decent food, and most of all, the opportunity to talk to somebody knowledgeable about all of the things to do in the area."

As far as the latter is concerned, Clark pointed out to me that it is well to keep in mind that you can't do Kent in a day or even two, and it is preferable to find a central point from which to enjoy all of the many beauties and attractions of the area, including visits to Dover, Folkestone, and Deal.

Dinner at Howfield Manor is a set menu and by reservation only. Guests are seated family-style in the beamed dining room. Janet explained that she does a number of things, including salmon that comes from Scotland and cheese soufflés.

"I use lots of cream because the cream is so fantastic down here. What we aim for is good home cooking."

"Janet also does braised lamb with an egg-and-lemon sauce that's marvelous," said Clark.

The oldest part of the house, which is now the kitchen, dates back to 1181, when it was a chapel. The well used by the monks is in the dairy, which is now the Lawrences' private sitting room.

HOWFIELD MANOR, Chartham Hatch, Canterbury, Kent CT4 7HQ. Tel.: Canterbury (0227) 738294 or 738495. A 5-guestroom restored country house, just a few moments from Canterbury Cathedral. Dinner, bed, and breakfast. Open year-round. Conveniently located to enjoy all of the cultural and recreational attractions in the area, including a great many castles; Chartwell, once the home of Winston Churchill; Great Dixter, Mount Ephraim, and other famous gardens. An ideal stop-off point going to and from the Continent. Not well-suited for children under 14. Clark and Janet Lawrence, Proprietors. (See Index for rates.)

Directions: Take the M2/A2 from London to a point just outside of Canterbury. Look for a Little Chef/Esso service station and watch for Chartham Hatch U-turn. Do not take U-turn, simply take the side road that goes off to the right. Howfield Manor is just a few minutes away.

For room rates and last time for dinner orders, see Index.

KENNEL HOLT HOTEL
Cranbrook, Kent

Kennel Holt was one of the first places I visited in England. It was an Elizabethan, beamed, manor house, and today it is a country house hotel set in five acres of landscaped grounds with a natural pond, rosebeds, croquet lawn, and cobnut walks. It still sits at the end of a secluded lane, 300 yards from the main road, overlooking a wooded valley in the heart of the rolling orchard country of Kent.

These days it is amiably presided over by Patrick Cliff, a former RAF fighter and helicopter pilot, and his wife, Ruth, who, among other things, is totally in charge of the kitchen. She is a Cordon Bleu–trained cook.

There are eight guest rooms, all with color TV and private bathrooms.

There are over fifty historic houses, gardens, and castles within easy driving distance of Kennel Holt. I'm afraid I can't list them all, but I will mention Chartwell, Sir Winston Churchill's family home. The Cliffs have a very comprehensive book and maps of all of the fascinating places nearby.

Wing Commander Cliff points out that Kennel Holt would make an excellent first and last stop for guests using Gatwick and Heathrow airports. I should imagine that the peace and quiet, and the comfort of the log fires in the residents' sitting rooms would be most reassuring to all guests.

Kennel Holt is also just an hour away from London by train (Charing Cross Station).

If you'd like to have the pleasure of staying at a country house hotel and don't want to drive down into the country, you can be collected at Staplehurst Station and enjoy a few days in the Kent countryside.

KENNEL HOLT HOTEL, Cranbrook, Kent TN17 2PT. Tel.: (0580) Cranbrook 712032. An 8-guestroom country house hotel (all private baths) 50 mi. from London. Rates include dinner, bed and breakfast, and early morning tea. Minimum 2-night stay required with advance reservation. Open Apr. to Nov. Central location for touring Kent. No credit cards. Mr. and Mrs. Patrick Cliff, Resident Owners. (See Index for rates.)

Directions: Cranbrook is 1 mi. southeast at the A262-A229 crossroads, which is 10 mi. south of Maidstone. The hotel is on the A262 between Cranbrook and Goudhurst.

THE ROYAL HOTEL
Deal, Kent

Deal is a modest-sized town on England's southeast coast, barely sixty minutes by ferry from the European continent. I arrived on a very sunny morning in late April and was immediately delighted by one of the main streets, which has the English Channel on one side and the wonderful old business buildings of various sizes and shapes on the other. Compared to Brighton, Rye, and Dover, Deal is smaller, more conservative and quiet.

The Royal belongs in Deal. It's an unobtrusive structure whose front entrance is on the long street next to the water, and because it is the only building on the water side, the back of the hotel looks directly out over the Channel.

Visited by the great and near-great for over three hundred years, the most notable guests may have been Lord Nelson and Lady Hamilton. There are two adjoining sea-view rooms with their names on the doors. Another of the impressive rooms facing France is called the Wellington, named after the famous duke who was the victor over Napoleon at the Battle of Waterloo. There are several Wellington prints on the walls of the dining rooms and parlors in the hotel.

Besides these large and impressive rooms, there are smaller accommodations that are clean and quite comfortable, most of which have their own baths and all have direct-dial telephones. (When traveling in Britain, it is well to bring a bathrobe for journeys to "hall" bathrooms.)

The Royal is like visiting the home of a favorite aunt, because there are many delightful surprises. It is really very comfortable and natural. The British and French have known about it for years. I think it would be particularly enjoyable in June, September, and October.

THE ROYAL HOTEL, Beach Street, Deal, Kent. Tel.: (03045) 5555. Telex: 957141. A 28-guestroom seaside hotel (20 private baths/showers), 8 mi. from Dover. Open every day. Breakfast, lunch, dinner served to non-residents. The Royal is located on the beach overlooking the English Channel. Many golf courses nearby. Limited facilities for children. (See Index for rates.).

Directions: There are several roads from London to the Kentish coast. Consult the map for one of your choice.

LITTLE THAKEHAM (COUNTRY HOUSE HOTEL)
Storrington, West Sussex

I was walking through the pergola with the warm April sun on my back. The pergola, as hotelier Tim Ractliff explained, was the name given to the rose arbor, which leads through the orchard and provides a view into the woods in the south. "It sort of links up the house with the surrounding lawns and gardens," he said.

Speaking of gardens, this might well be called the Little Thakeham Country House Hotel and Gardens, because the gardens are indeed a most important part of the entire experience. They include paved walks, numerous varieties of flowering shrubs, and specimen trees. The long approach to the house is lined with walnut trees. Gertrude Jekyll, a leading landscape designer of the last century, created the Little Thakeham gardens.

I walked up toward the house, which appears ageless but was actually built around 1902. Tim remarked that the South Downs, visible in the distance, actually protect this section of Sussex from the rigors of the coast. The climate here is really quite mild.

Dominating the first floor of the house is a great hall with a marvelous fireplace and a minstrel gallery. Everything is done in beautiful beige stonework. There's another huge fireplace in the dining room. The antiques are most impressive, and mullioned windows create a wonderful manor-house feeling.

I've visited many British country house hotels and each of them has a unique identity and personality of its own. Although there are some similarities, it is impossible to become confused, and one never loses the sense of the particular place of each and its most favorable and special conditions.

The situation at Little Thakeham is exceptional because if the guests want to do nothing there is ample opportunity to enjoy reading, walking, motoring, a dip in the swimming pool, and the peace and quiet that the British look for continually. On the other hand, the Americans literally may want to do something, and there are visits to the nearby Glyndebourne Music Festival and the seacoast town of Brighton, as well as a game of tennis or croquet on the grounds. At the end of the day, it is wonderful to come back and sit in the lounge, meet and talk with other people, and feel completely as if for a moment you are home.

Dinner is a four-course set meal with a starter, a fish dish, and one main course that changes every evening. There are frequent evening concerts of chamber music, with wonderful sounds reverberating in the great hall. Little Thakeham is less than an hour from Gatwick and probably a little bit farther from Heathrow Airport.

LITTLE THAKEHAM (COUNTRY HOUSE HOTEL) (Pride of Britain), Merrywood Lane, Storrington, West Sussex. Tel.: Storrington (09066) 4416. U.S. reservations: 800-323-7308. A 9-guestroom country house hotel located south of London on the edge of the South Downs and not far from Brighton. Breakfast to houseguests, luncheon by appt., dinner served to the public. Open year-round. Minimum stay of 2 nights required. Conveniently located to visit Goodwood, Petworth, Parham Park, and Arundel Castle. The nearby Chichester Theatre is open during the summer, as well as Glyndebourne. Swimming pool, grass tennis court, and croquet lawns on grounds. Other outdoor recreation nearby. Timothy and Pauline Ractliff, Proprietors. (See Rates for index.)

Directions: From London take the A24 Worthing Rd., and about 1½ mi. after the village of Ashington bear right, off the dual carriageway. Follow the lane for 1 mi., and then turn right to Merrywood Lane. Little Thakeham is 300 yds. on the right. It's easy to get lost in this section of Sussex, so be prepared to make inquiries.

Rates for a room for two people for one night with breakfast, except where noted, are included in the Index of this book. They are not to be considered firm quotations, but should be used as guidelines only.

WHITE HORSE INN (COUNTRY PUB)
Chilgrove, Sussex

I happened to stumble willy-nilly into the White Horse Inn while making a wandering back road trip between Midhurst and Chichester. The whitewashed building with its red chimney sits back from the highway in the meadows, where there were some sheep and new lambs placidly grazing. The front entrance had many tubs of daffodils and other spring flowers heralding a welcome. I couldn't resist a visit.

The White Horse is a traditional English country pub. If it had rooms I would typify it as an inn or a residential pub. It can boast a marvelous countryside setting, an interior that would be quite at home in an English movie, and a very extensive menu of some considerable reputation in the south of Sussex.

"We serve lobster, grouse, pheasant, partridge, woodcock, mallard, teal, widgeon, hare, salmon, venison, calf's liver, and Aylesbury duck," owner Barry Phillips declared. "Our menu is à la carte. We offer lunch and dinner. And many people who are staying in Midhurst, Chichester, and other surrounding towns eventually find their way to us. They are surprised that in our rather small place we have such a wide variety of choices."

The most recent news from Barry Phillips is that he had the honor of a visit for luncheon from H.R.H. Prince Philip. I'm delighted to know that things are humming at the White Horse Inn.

WHITE HORSE INN, Chilgrove (Near Chichester), Sussex PO18 9HX. Tel.: (024-359) East Marden 219. A traditional country pub (no lodgings) 7 mi. north of Chichester near Goodwood House, Chichester Festival Theatre and the South Downs. Lunch and dinner served Tues. through Sat. except bank holidays. Closed a few weeks in fall and spring. B.C. Phillips, Owner. (See Index for rates.)

Directions: Proceed north from Chichester on A286 toward Midhurst. Through Lavant take B2141, signposted "Petersfield," and proceed 5 mi. to village of Chilgrove.

THE WOODED LANES OF SUSSEX

Surrey and West Sussex have some extremely attractive back roads that wander through forests, border meadows, and follow the course of the many brooks and rivers. It is easy to get lost on them, but not "perilously" so. It is beautiful in springtime, especially during the daffodil season, and I found myself stopping to look at gnarled old trees with ivy growing up the trunks, and lingering by the meadows with centuries-old stone and thicket walls. In the spring the rock gardens appear with all the lovely spring colors.

In this part of England what are called speed bumps in North America are known as "sleeping Bobbies."

GRAVETYE MANOR
(Near East Grinstead) West Sussex

The memories of my first visit to Gravetye (as it is known) were immediately revived as I followed the winding drive through the parklike grounds and saw the weathered stone and oaken door of the front entrance. The Sussex countryside was bathed in the light of an autumn sun, heightening the muted tints of beige, brown, and russet. The flowers of autumn in the famed Gravetye gardens, encouraged by the warmth, turned their faces toward the sun.

Gravetye is an Elizabethan manor house, built about ten years after the defeat of the Spanish Armada. According to the records, Roger Infield built it for his bride, Katherine Compton. Their initials, "R" and "K," are carved over the entrance to the formal gardens. To add to the romantic note, the likenesses of Roger and Katherine are carved in oak over the fireplace in the master bedroom.

The manor's most notable owner, William Robinson, had a worldwide reputation as one of the greatest gardeners of all time. He bought Gravetye and the one thousand acres on which it stands in 1884, and lived there until he died, well into his nineties, in 1935. It was here that he realized many of his ideas for the creation of the English natural "garden style," now admired and copied all over the world. His book, *The English Flower*

Garden, is still in demand. His simple good taste is much in evidence both inside and outside of the manor house. He paneled the interior with wood from the estate and enriched the rooms with chimney pieces and fireplace furnishings kept entirely in the Elizabethan mode.

Today, the proprietors are Susan and Peter Herbert, who have devoted time, effort, and considerable investment in carrying on Mr. Robinson's ideals, while at the same time preserving much of the tradition and antiquity. The Herberts' five children range in age from 4½ to 33 years old, so a future line of assistant innkeepers seems assured. In fact, the eldest has already begun his career at Gravetye.

The menu for lunch and dinner is basically French, but a note points out that if the guest's preference is for *simply* cooked food, this can be accommodated. Even now while writing this paragraph, my mouth begins to water at the thought of their parfait of chicken livers, with a delicate hint of port and the contrasting sharpness of green peppercorns. The "sweet" menu is a Mozart sonata.

There are basically two types of guest rooms. One group is done in the grand manner with canopied beds and walls that are intricately paneled. The master bedroom is a classic—the furniture is "manorial" to say the least.

The other type of room is a bit smaller and has a more modest demeanor. However, all of Gravetye's rooms enjoy the most fabulous views over the gardens and surrounding forest.

"Garden" is a key word at Gravetye. In a country where gardening is a national sport, the gardens here, covering many acres, are some of the most impressive I've ever seen. For example, the kitchen garden has over a full acre of leeks, parsley, endive, chicory, spinach, dill, thyme, mint, hyssop, broccoli, french beans, radishes, lettuce, and several different types of berries and fruits. Naturally, these all appear on the table. The Herberts have also developed their own smokehouse, producing smoked salmon, duck's breast, and venison. Fresh herbs are grown all year round under artificial climate conditions in the spacious glasshouses.

Thanks to Roger Infield, William Robinson, and Susan and Peter Herbert, Gravetye Manor has been preserved and is entering into its most useful and exciting period, because it is available for all of us to enjoy.

GRAVETYE MANOR (near East Grinstead), West Sussex RH19 4LJ. Tel.: (0342) Sharpthorne 810567. Telex: 957239. A luxuriously appointed 14-guestroom country manor hotel, 30 mi. from London. Open all year. Lunch, dinner served to non-residents. Beautiful gardens on grounds as well as trout fishing, croquet, and clock golf. Golf and horseback riding nearby. This area has many famous houses and gardens for touring.

Suitable for children over 7 years old. No credit cards. Peter Herbert, Managing Director. (See Index for rates.)

Directions: From London, leave M23 at Exit 10, taking the A264 towards East Grinstead. At roundabout take 3rd exit marked Haywards Heath and Brighton (B2028). Continue through Turner's Hill, and 1 mi. south of village, take left fork towards West Hoathly. Proceed for about 150 yds and turn left up Vowels Lane. Hotel on right after 1 mi. (Hotel drive 1 mi. long.)

It's not that the distances are very long in the British Isles, it's the many diversions along the way that sometimes make it impossible to estimate traveling and arrival times. Last order times for dinner are included in the Index so that you can see what time you must arrive in order not to find the kitchen door locked. If you are going to arrive later, call ahead—there isn't a hotel/inn listed here that will not make some provision to feed you if they know you can't make it before the kitchen closes.

THE SOUTH OF ENGLAND
Counties of Hampshire and Dorset

These counties, about two-and-a-half-hours' drive southwest of London, include the woods and heaths of the New Forest, the megaliths of Stonehenge, the great cathedrals of Winchester and Salisbury, Thomas Hardy and Jane Austen country, and among other great houses, Broadlands, the treasure-filled residence of the late Lord Louis Mountbatten.

Broadlands is located in Hampshire and contains an impressive collection of art, as well as numerous mementos of Mountbatten's naval and Asian campaigns. The River Test, one of Britain's trout streams, runs through the grounds of Broadlands, south of the town of Romsey and near Southampton.

Dorset has uplands rising to 900 feet and a splendid coastline. This is the country embodied in many of Thomas Hardy's novels, and where examples of the thatcher's art can be seen in countless villages.

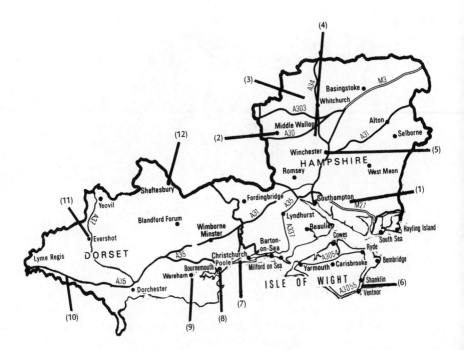

THE SOUTH OF ENGLAND

THE OLD HOUSE HOTEL
Wickham, Hampshire

"This is a duck's nest coal-burning hearth." Annie Skipwith was showing me the guest rooms at the Old House in Wickham. We were in a most attractive second-floor guest room, where the stately windows overlook the other Georgian town houses on the hollow square in the center of town.

Everything about this inn was delightful. The young innkeepers, Richard and Annie, were full of *joie de vivre*. They are a most handsome couple. Richard is a debonair Englishman, and Annie is a delightful French girl.

Each of the ten guest rooms is totally different. The furniture was refinished by Richard. The upstairs hall has some engaging prints, originally done by a man named Gould, and curtains have been found whose patterns match the prints. There are several small things that make it seem very much like a private house. For example, there is a little cabinet in one corner of the hallway downstairs, filled with carved pieces and china.

In the back of the house, formerly part of an old barn, the guest rooms have exposed beams, beautiful flowered wallpaper in tones of blue and green, and curtains to match. There was one double bedroom with dozens of books. In fact, there are books in every guest room on the nightstands.

There are porcelain doorknobs on the paneled doorways and all of the floors in this house of many levels are shining clean and well varnished.

On the first floor, a series of small lounges all show Richard's and Annie's interest in prints. One room has some excellent sailing prints and also a mounted collection of different-sized keg taps.

The restaurant is part of the old converted barn and has exposed beams with a big window that overlooks the garden in the rear. This is an excellent breakfast room.

The menu is made up of French provincial dishes. For lunch that day I had a dish with green peppers, tomatoes, onions, and garlic cooked in spices and herbs and then topped with a whisked egg white that, when put in the oven, turns into a four-inch meringue. It was just right. Other main courses were pot-roasted chicken and escalloped veal and sirloin served with tomatoes and garlic sauce and topped with olives.

In discussing the inn clientele, Richard said that for the most part people stayed for one night, although many businessmen stay here while traveling during the week. "They like our little garden in the rear and our countryside is appealing." Please note that the hotel guest rooms are not available on Saturdays and Sundays.

THE OLD HOUSE HOTEL, The Square, Wickham, Hampshire PO17 5JG. Tel.: (0329) 833049. A 10-guestroom in-town hotel, 9 mi. west of Portsmouth. Closed Sat. and Sun., 2 wks. in July and Aug., 2 wks at Christmas, and 1 wk. at Easter. Lunch and dinner served to non-residents. Restaurant closed all day Sun. and also for lunch on Mon. and Sat. Pleasant rose garden on grounds. Sailing and golf nearby. Mr. and Mrs. Richard Skipwith, Proprietors. (See Index for rates.)

Directions: From London take M3 southwest to Exit 5 and follow A32 to Wickham, 45 min. from Motorway exit.

FIFEHEAD MANOR
Middle Wallop, Hampshire

I felt a very strong kinship with this section of England, because Middle Wallop is just a few miles from the village of Stockbridge; however, it is not in Berkshire (pronounced "Barkshire" in Britain), but in Hampshire, frequently referred to on local signposts as "Hants." Another coincidence is the fact that Salisbury, Connecticut, is about the same distance away from Stockbridge, Massachusetts, as is Salisbury, Hampshire, from Stockbridge, England.

The proprietress of Fifehead Manor, Margaret van Veelen, recently wrote me of her discovery that George Washington was a direct descendant of a 15th-century Lord of the Manor of Wallop Fifehead.

I liked the feel of Fifehead Manor almost as soon as I arrived, because it seemed to be a family place. Being a Sunday, there were several families from the local area, who had driven over for a Sunday dinner. Some well-dressed children were playing outdoors in the October sunshine, and several others had taken some games and puzzles from the shelves in the living room and were stretched out on the carpet enjoying themselves. I soon discovered that Mrs. van Veelen is capable of carrying on an animated conversation not only in English, but also in French, German, and Dutch, and this rather modest manor had a decidedly international air, with several visitors from the Continent.

She was able to spare me a few moments from her supervisory duties to point out that during the bizarre history of this old manor house it has been a nunnery and, later, the home of the Earl of Godwin, whose wife at the time was Lady Godiva, the famous horsewoman of Coventry.

There have been so many additions to the oldest part of the house, dating from the 11th century, that it is a sort of architectural "Pictures at an Exhibition." For example, the center section has typically medieval stone mullioned windows, and the Victorian newer portion has gingerbread ornamentation. There were two fireplaces in the dining room, one Jacobean and the other Elizabethan.

Middle Wallop (wonderful name, isn't it?) is just a few miles from one of the most famous trout streams in all the world, the River Test. In fact, one of the specialties on the menu is fresh trout from the Test, prepared in several different ways. The menu also lists Dover sole, roast lamb, veal, and beef in various forms.

The rather large guest rooms in the main house have been augmented recently by the addition of attractive, modernized bedrooms in an old barn.

Because it is such a relatively short distance from Heathrow Airport, Fifehead Manor would make a most sensible place to stay for the first night or two after arriving in the U.K. It is very quiet and relaxed and only a short distance from Salisbury, Stonehenge, and Winchester.

"Our guests from North America often stay here to recover from their jet lag and then go west to Devon and Cornwall, or north to the Cotswolds," commented Mrs. van Veelen.

I can think of many an enthusiastic fisherman who would love to start a holiday wetting a line in the River Test!

FIFEHEAD MANOR, *Middle Wallop, Stockbridge, Hampshire SO20 8EG. Tel.: (0264) Andover 781565. A 16-guestroom rural inn (all with private baths), 10 mi. east of Salisbury, convenient to the famous trout-fishing Test River, and Stonehenge. Open every day except 2 wks. at Christmas. Breakfast, lunch, tea, and dinner served to non-residents. Mrs. M. van Veelen, Resident Owner. (See Index for rates.)*

Directions: Fifehead Manor is located on A343 at Middle Wallop. There are several different routes. It is best to locate Middle Wallop and work backwards to where you are (east of Salisbury).

A LAZY SUNDAY AFTERNOON

Stockbridge, England, and Stockbridge, Massachusetts, have one common denominator. They are villages with a long main street, although the Hampshire village's street is much longer than the one in New England. A dissimilarity is the fact that the English Stockbridge has fewer trees. This is a very important fishing area, and there are two streams that literally run through the town. These were frequented, on a sunny Sunday afternoon, by resident ducks. There were a few guest houses, a number of B&Bs, and one rather large hotel. Several small restaurants served teas and light lunches.

From Stockbridge, I took the country road that runs beside the Test River through the village of Houghton, which, I understand, is one of the great fishing centers. I turned left over the river on a humpbacked bridge into another world. It was, to say the least, the most idyllic of all English scenes, worthy of a Constable.

A series of these small bridges spanned the river as it wound its way through the woodland copse. Overhead, the leaves were turning yellow and brown against the wonderful blue English sky. A flock of crows added their own particular chorus to the chirping of other small birds.

The water on one side of my bridge was so placid and clear that the vegetation on the bottom looked like cabbages and cauliflowers. I could easily see the trout. However, on the other side of the bridge, the surface changed as the water rushed out into a broad channel where the sun danced and sparkled. The eddies spun around and around before proceeding on their short journey to the sea. A few ducks fished for their Sunday dinner. Along the banks there were blackberries, plump and ready for the picking.

I drove on and came to a small village with a fascinating triangular village green. A group of people were sitting in the sun at the Crown Inn enjoying a bar lunch. Some of the village lads were leaning up against their cars. A sign announced that it was "Hampshire Weekend," and there were small stalls nearby where people returning from church stopped off and purchased various crafts and other country things on sale. A very British girl prevailed upon me to "have a go" at one of them.

I saw a poster announcing that a "country and western dance" would be held with music by the Rustlers. Admission would be one pound and twenty-five pence, including supper, but an additional note said "no leather jackets."

ESSEBORNE MANOR
Hurstbourne Tarrant, Andover, Hampshire

There were many tiny, picturesque old villages along the winding course I took through the lush lowlands of the Bourne Valley, but my very favorite one was Saint Mary Bourne. I've never seen so many beautiful thatched cottages in one village. I had wandered off the main road from Basingstoke onto B3048, on my way to Hurstbourne Tarrant. This is not a well-known tourist area, and it is blessedly peaceful and pastoral. One of the principal industries in Saint Mary Bourne is raising watercress.

I think Esseborne Manor is a real find. From the moment I stepped into the bright, pretty foyer, and was greeted by Peter Birnie, a most affable chap, I could feel (I hate to say this) the good vibes.

Peter Birnie is one of four young and enterprising people who work together to make this country house hotel a delightful place to stay. Belinda Watson holds sway in the kitchen, and when I met her she was a little preoccupied because her fish was almost ready to be turned, and she was in the midst of hectic preparations for a special party. I understand she presents a traditional English cuisine with some regional French influences.

The menu, which changes seasonally, includes such items as saddle of venison, monkfish with stem ginger in a pastry case, partridge roasted with kumquats, port, and red currants, and calf's liver with plums and Madeira. I might as well tempt you with a recitation of some of her desserts, too: coconut ice cream with raspberry sauce, chocolate and brandy roulade with a coffee sauce, lemon and rosewater custard cups served with a compote of poached apple and lemon macaroons.

Another member of the team is the very personable Diane Brown, and there is also Philip Harris, whom I did not meet. I was really impressed with this congenial group, who are obviously dedicated to pleasing their guests.

This white, rather austere-looking mid-Victorian house is encircled by a lawn with lovely beech and lime, or linden, trees, and gardens in the middle of farmlands where cattle graze. There is a tennis court on one side and a croquet lawn on the other. Strolling around outside, Peter showed me their herb garden. "These are not just kitchen herbs, like sage, thyme, and tarragon," he explained, "but other kinds, too, like those used for colorings and scents—roses count as herbs, also narcissus. It's not a formal Elizabethan-style place, because we're not that sort of hotel."

Peter said they serve tea and snacks, when weather permits, in the kind of courtyard, where there is a fountain and a pond with fish in it.

The residents' lounge is light and cheerful, with many windows looking out across the lawn to the tennis court and beyond to a pasture with cattle. Creamy yellow walls, a comfortable sofa and chairs, bookshelves with lots of books, and a large Queen Anne table in the center, decorated with a huge poinsettia and covered with magazines of all sorts, create a wonderful, relaxed atmosphere. A backgammon table sits in a little bay window area.

The dining room is most pleasant and serene, done in soft grays, blues, and rose, with a pastoral wallpaper, mauve upholstered chairs, and white tablecloths. A little bar-lounge has a cozy feeling with a fireplace and casement windows looking out on the croquet lawn.

As we walked through the rest of the house and outside to the new courtyard rooms, Peter told me that they had guests from Germany and France, who were on a shooting holiday. Arrangements must be made in advance for pheasant and grouse shooting and deer stalking. There is also trout fishing on the famous River Test nearby. I was amused to learn we weren't far from Watership Down, which really *is* stuffed with rabbits. For sightseeing, there are all sorts of historic landmarks and pretty little villages, not to mention the ancient and historic towns of Winchester and Salisbury.

Peter showed me all of the guest rooms, which are named for small towns and villages they particularly like, such as Lymington, Maddingly, Chichester, and Westholme. The Ferndown Room is their honeymoon suite, and it is a pretty thing, indeed. Decorated in shades of white, lavender, and lime green, it has a curtained four-poster bed, a lavender settee, french doors opening out onto an enclosed garden patio, and a bathroom with a whirlpool bathtub and a stall shower.

All of the guest rooms are different, and they are all most attractive and pleasant. They all have telephones, radios, color television, and many other amenities.

Oh, in case you were wondering, "bourne" means small stream, and there is one that meanders through this lovely valley.

ESSEBORNE MANOR, Hurstbourne Tarrant, Andover, Hampshire SP11 OER. Tel.: (026 476) 444. A 12-guestroom (private baths) delightful country house hotel in a pastoral setting in the Bourne Valley, midway between Andover and Newbury. Full English breakfast included in tariff. Restaurant open for lunch Mon.–Fri.; dinner Mon.–Sat. Reservations necessary. Closed for 2 wks. at Christmas. Tennis court and croquet lawn on grounds. Fishing, golf, country walks, horse racing at Newbury, Hawk Conservancy and Wildlife Park, and many historic and cultural attractions nearby. No children under 10. No pets. (See Index for rates.)

Directions: From London, take the M3 to the A303 toward Andover, and the A343 toward Hurstbourne Tarrant. Continue 1½ mi. north to Esseborne Manor.

CHURCH FARM
Barton Stacey, Winchester, Hampshire

"This is listed as a Class II building with a star, being of architectural or historic interest." James Talbot's family has lived in this farmhouse for over fifty years, so he knows whereof he speaks. There is a lot of history in his home, part of which was a 15th-century tithe barn, built in 1450 and now classified as a historic building.

Original heavy beams run across the entrance hall and part of the living room. Original great wooden posts stand in the entry, and the floor is still laid with the original huge flagstones. Mr. Talbot can show you the glassed-in cutaway section of wall that displays the wattle and daub (hazel twigs with chalk slurry) method of construction used 500 years ago— which seems to continue to work pretty well.

James and Jean Talbot are a most friendly and informative couple. They have raised their family here, and now they welcome guests to stay in their two guest rooms in the main house or in the Coach House, which sleeps up to five people and has its own kitchen facilities. Mrs. Talbot's breakfasts are usually fresh orange juice, cereals, bacon and eggs, toast or croissants, marmalade, and coffee or tea. She will also prepare dinner, with prior arrangement, and some of her dishes include homemade soups, a special watercress mousse, smoked salmon, escalope of veal with mushrooms and pepper in a wine sauce, roast rack of lamb, fresh vegetables, and zabaglione.

Breakfast and dinner are served in the dining room, where there are some fascinating antique pieces. The dining table is a particularly beautiful round rosewood pedestal table.

This is a farmhouse and the guest rooms are simply furnished, but they are clean and comfortable. The atmosphere is relaxed and informal, if in a somewhat reserved English way.

There are many books in the attractive living room, which looks out on a croquet lawn. There are beautiful trees and peaceful meadows and, believe it or not, this farmhouse has a swimming pool and the use of a hard tennis court. Besides which, there is Mr. Talbot, who is an extremely knowledgeable man and can tell you many interesting things about this ancient house and the area.

CHURCH FARM (Wolsey Lodges), Barton Stacey, Winchester, Hampshire SO21 3RR. Tel.: (0962) 760268. A 3-guestroom (private and shared baths) medieval farmhouse set in the Test Valley, equidistant from Andover, Winchester, and Stockbridge. Breakfast included in tariff. Dinner by prior arrangement. Open year-round. Swimming pool, tennis court, and croquet lawn on grounds. Country walks, charming old villages, arrangements for fishing, stately homes, Stonehenge, and Winchester and Salis-

bury cathedrals nearby. No credit cards. James and Jean Talbot, Proprietors. (See Index for rates.)

Directions: From London, take the M3 toward Southampton. At Junction 8 take the A303 toward Exeter and the West. After passing the turnoff for A34, watch for Barton Stacey signpost (approx. 1½ mi.). Turn left and after crossing the River Dever, continue into the village. Turn right at the church and right again at signpost to Bramsbury. Church Farm is 300 yds. on your right, behind a thatched wall. (There is no sign.)

LAINSTON HOUSE
Sparsholt, Winchester, Hampshire

Winchester—the ancient capital of England and home of the famous cathedral begun in the 11th century and holding the bones of Saxon kings. Structures still stand there that date back to the 13th century—stretches of the city walls and Winchester College, founded in 1382. You have to look for these relics—time has not stood still in Winchester. It is a modern, vigorous city today.

I was headed beyond Winchester, toward the sleepy village of Sparsholt, just two miles west. I was looking for Lainston House, another relic of the past that refuses to remain so. As I drove up the sweeping drive, lined with trees that must have seen the passing of at least a century or two, I thought I could imagine what it must have felt like to be in a coach and four, approaching the great 17th-century manor house at the top of the rise.

I made a circle past a large brick tower, which I later learned was the

largest dovecote in England, and swept around with a flourish through two great round brick pillars into a courtyard with a circular drive, where, alas, there were only cars—no carriages with stamping horses.

A charming miss greeted me as I walked through the tall french doors into the spacious foyer. Her name, it turned out, was Diane McLeavy, and she was the deputy manager. I noted the parquet floor and oriental rug, and the walk-in, bronze-hooded fireplace, faced with 18th-century Delft tiles, while Diane went off to order tea.

While we waited for the tea things to arrive, Diane showed me the library-bar, which is clearly the pride of the house. This room is lined with golden cedar paneling, elaborately carved, which was once a magnificent old cedar tree on the grounds. When it was struck down by a storm in 1930, the wood was used to line this quite spectacular room, with its curved walls, elaborate carvings, and carved wood chandelier. The tree is memorialized in a lovely and touching small bas-relief carving in a panel by the windows, which explains that the room was "fashioned from him." The view from the tall windows is also quite spectacular, looking far down a grassy promenade lined with lime, or linden, trees, and off to an undulating line of hills on the eastern horizon.

Diane told me that Lainston House had been owned privately since the 1300s. As early as 1087 there is a record in the Domesday Book of the land being set aside for the monks of the priory of Winchester Cathedral. In the 17th century it was owned by Oliver Cromwell's secretary. The area was probably a hotbed of Royalists and Roundheads. The property still embraces 63 acres of the 127 acres that were advertised "to let" in the *London Times* of 1853. The house has had its share of colorful owners of questionable repute. During a short period in the mid-17th century, it even served as a lunatic asylum.

None of this frenetic past was evident, however, in the grandly proportioned drawing room where Diane led me for tea. The lovely room, with its very high ceiling, tall windows draped elegantly, flowers and plantings, books and magazines, created a most graceful and serene atmosphere, and the conversations of other guests, who were also enjoying tea, seemed to form a low, musical background that was most pleasant. There were chintz-covered sofas flanking two fireplaces, and several conversational groupings of chairs and tables. I sank down into one of the very comfortable sofas while Diane poured. It was a magnificent tea, served on fine china, with wonderful Devonshire cream on delicious scones and lots of jams in tiny jars.

I was curious about a small notice posted near one of the many paintings and drawings that lined the walls, and this is what it said: "As a special service to guests of Lainston who fish the hallowed waters of these rivers, Judy Strafford has offered to accompany you and paint your favorite beat of the river whilst you fish." (Judy is the Countess of Strafford.) Certainly an unusual memento of a fishing trip in England. I was unable to stay for dinner, but based on the superb tea and the manner in which it was served, my guess was that dinner would be excellent. Diane told me it is a traditional *haute cuisine,* with such specialties as medallions of beef, breast of duck with apple and celeriac, lamb with a tomato and tarragon sauce, and mousse Lady Chudleigh. The menu changes three times a year. There are two dining rooms, both with tall windows looking out on the lawn.

The guest rooms, in different shapes and sizes, are done in a variety of styles, and they are all attractively decorated with antique furnishings and matching curtains and bedspreads. The beds looked comfortable, the bathrooms were modern and immaculate, and all the rooms were outfitted with telephones, radios and television sets, and other amenities.

Outside, beyond the courtyard and a little enclosed topiary garden are the ruins of a tiny 12th-century Norman chapel, with the original font still standing and three walls with arched doorways somewhat intact—a place to dream about the seductive, naughty Elizabeth Chudleigh and her 17th-century peccadilloes; her portrait hangs in the hall.

LAINSTON HOUSE (Prestige Hotels), Sparsholt, Winchester, Hampshire SO21 2LT. Tel.: Winchester (0962) 63588. Telex: 477375. A 32-guest-room (private baths) luxurious manor house hotel on 63 acres of parkland, 60 mi. west of London, just outside Winchester. European plan. Breakfast, lunch, and dinner by reservation daily. Open all year. Croquet lawn, 2 tennis courts on grounds. Clay pigeon shooting, game shooting, fishing, horseback riding may be arranged; golf courses nearby. Winchester, the ancient capital of England, has many points of interest and cultural activities. Richard Fannon, General Manager; Diane McLeavy, Deputy Manager. (See Index for rates.)

Directions: On A272 Stockbridge Rd., 2 mi. northwest of Winchester in the village of Sparsholt.

LUCCOMBE CHINE HOUSE
Shanklin, Isle of Wight

Ah, the Isle of Wight! I have always heard much about it—the connection with Queen Victoria, its strategic position as an offshore naval base, and its present popularity for holiday excursions.

The day was marvelous; I had driven across Sussex and Hampshire, and at Portsmouth I found the foot ferry to Ryde. I left my luggage at the ferry entrance and drove about two blocks away to the multistoried car park.

I had decided to try the ferry that did not take autos (there are others that do). After a very pleasant voyage, along with many dozens of other holiday-seekers, I arrived at Ryde, where a train was waiting on the pier. My journey continued along the famous Sunshine Coast through several little towns, finally ending at Shanklin, where my hostess, Stella Silver, awaited my arrival with a car.

Stella proved to be as enthusiastic as she was informative and I got a running history of the island, as well as interesting information about the flora and fauna as we drove through the village of Shanklin. The road went out into the country with occasional glimpses of the sea.

She turned down into a sheltered and secluded valley (chine) and entered a long private drive with lovely ferns, trees, lawns, and a profusion of hydrangeas. I had arrived.

The house itself has an interesting history and is definitely Victorian in feeling, although there are Tudor half-timbers and casements on the upper stories. The Silvers have made it very attractive and homelike rather than grand. It looks like what it is—a comfortable, upper-middle-class home.

The bedrooms are sensibly decorated with period pieces, but there is an emphasis on comfort, with wool blankets and even clock radios.

The first thing I did after getting settled was to take a walk on the grounds, with a visit to the Watch Tower overlooking the coast. The Tower was built in the days when smugglers were active.

I was tempted to continue on the footpaths that lead in all directions, many with magnificent views of the sea.

All of this vigorous outdoor activity, on top of the ferry trip, made for a very healthy appetite, and after a consultation with Mr. Silver I placed an order for pork cutlets. Everything is cooked to order and the sauce for the cutlets was simply marvelous.

I awakened in the morning to the wonderful sound of one of the fourteen cascades that musically assist a small brook as it twists, tunnels, and tumbles through the chine down to the sea below.

By all means take the time (at least two nights) to visit Luccombe Chine House on the Isle of Wight. There are dozens of things to amuse a visitor, including riding, swimming, tennis, saunas, and so forth, but there's also the wonderful sense of tranquility in just looking out over the sea.

LUCCOMBE CHINE HOUSE, Shanklin, Isle of Wight, PO37 6RH. Tel.: (098 386) Shanklin 2037. A 6-guestroom (private baths) country house hotel located in a quiet corner of the Isle of Wight, overlooking the sea. Breakfast and dinner served daily. Open all year. Conveniently located to enjoy all of the myriad diversions and recreations of the Isle of Wight. Great walking country. No facilities for children. Paul and Stella Silver, Hoteliers. (See Index for rates.)

Directions: If you are not planning to stay for more than two nights, don't bring a car to Luccombe Chine House. There are several different ways to get to Shanklin, including the train from Waterloo Station in London to Portsmouth, then the ferry to the Isle of Wight, and then another little train to the end of the line. For full information about car ferries, foot ferries, etc., call Mr. and Mrs. Silver for schedules.

CHEWTON GLEN HOTEL
New Milton, Hampshire

Chewton Glen has real style. I don't mean this in a fashion sense— although the hotel certainly could be called stylish. It's more than having beautiful rooms, lovely grounds, excellent cuisine, and an attentive staff. It's probably an inherent attitude. I think the key may lie in something Joe Simonini, Martin Skan's right-hand man, said to me over dinner. "I came here from Tuscany twenty years ago when Martin first bought Chewton Glen, and I fell in love with the place. We have worked hard to make it the best hotel in the country, and I believe it *is* the best." I saw that sense of dedication and pride in other staff members, some of whom have worked there almost as long as Joe. I have to congratulate Martin Skan, the owner, for inspiring such loyalty and a desire for excellence in his very able, friendly, and cheerful staff. Everything is done with such *style!*

Martin, who looks a bit like a mature Roddy McDowall, had been telling me about the changes he had made since my last visit, and I was really impressed with all the differences. From the moment I drove into

the new courtyard, paved with York stone, encircled with plantings of tulips and pansies and other pretty flowers, with an antique bronze fountain in the center, I could see that Chewton Glen Hotel had a very new look.

Inside, I really had to gasp. The two lounges, called the Elphinstone Suite after some early owners, are simply delightful. Martin told me that the well-known designer Diane Prestwich was responsible for the blending of colors and textures of fabrics in draperies, swags, upholstery, cushions, and wall coverings, along with the wonderful comfortable, cozy feeling of these actually very spacious and elegant rooms. Nina Campbell did a smashing job in the Marryat Bar.

Since Martin had been called away, I enjoyed an excellent dinner with Joe. Fishermen bring their daily catch and, with the English Channel so close, there is a wide selection of fresh fish and other seafood on the menu. I chose salmon, broiled to perfection, with a sorrel sauce and a side dish of fat, tender, fresh asparagus. The chef sent us a tasty avocado pâté with his compliments. I just have to say that the meal, the wines, and the service couldn't have been more elegant. Joe is very proud of their wine cellar, which has received many accolades. A time-honored British tradition is the standing rib roast on a handsome silver trolley, wheeled deftly from table to table, and carved with great flair to the preference of each guest.

After dinner, Joe showed me a very fat loose-leaf binder, kept for their guests, that is packed with literally endless suggestions for diversion and recreation. Just about anything you could think of is in this book, including such information as time schedules for a sports center, nearby churches, and trains to and from London. There are maps for walks through the gardens and glen out to the sea, information on making arrangements for fishing, shooting, bicycling, horseback riding, boat cruises in the Channel, and helicopter rides. There are lists of antiques shops, jewelers, Laura Ashley, Benetton, home furnishings, and on and on.

Some of the more important sightseeing possibilities are Stonehenge, Salisbury Cathedral, Winchester Cathedral, and the famous Exbury Gardens of the Rothschild estate, boasting the most beautiful and extensive collection of azaleas, rhododendrons, camellias, and magnolias in the country. There are many stately homes in the area, including Broadlands, home of the Mountbattens; Wilton House, home of the Earl of Pembroke; Kingston Lacey House and gardens; Longleat House, which also offers a lion safari; and many more. Chewton Glen is just on the edge of the famous New Forest, and has an interesting history of its own, dating back to the early 1700s.

Actually, the hotel itself is on thirty acres of parks and grounds, with lovely old trees, beautiful flowering shrubs, terraces, a gorgeous swimming pool, tennis court, croquet lawn, and a 9-hole golf course, along with a pitch-and-putt course. There is a billiards room that has a wonderful clubby atmosphere, and the walls are covered with framed clippings of the many, many articles written about Chewton Glen and photographs, sketches, and cartoons, many by former guests.

Well, I could go on at great length about this superlative place. Needless to say, the guest rooms are all beautifully and individually decorated, with every sort of amenity. There are some two-story suites with their own private enclosed patios.

It would be a perfect overnight stay for voyagers arriving or departing on the *QE2*, being just a half-hour from Southampton, although a longer stay would enable you to enjoy more of the lovely surrounding countryside.

With all of this, what I liked best was the note that a pair of "Wellies" (Wellington boots) were available for guests, if needed. Now that's *style!*

CHEWTON GLEN HOTEL (Relais et Chateaux), New Milton, Hampshire BH25 6QS. Tel.: Highcliffe (04252) 5341. Telex: 41456. U.S. reservations: 800-223-5581. A 44-guestroom luxury resort-hotel 10 mi. from Bournemouth. Open all year. Breakfast, lunch, and dinner served to travelers. Reservations necessary. Tennis, 9-hole golf, putting, outdoor heated swimming pool, croquet lawn on grounds. Golf, riding, fishing, nature walks in the New Forest, and all manner of recreation and sightseeing nearby. Martin Skan, Proprietor. (See Index for rates.)

Directions: Chewton Glen is situated on the A337 between New Milton and Highcliffe. From London take the M3 to A33 to Southampton and turn left on M27. Leave M27 at A337, marked Lyndhurst, and then follow A35 to a sign marked New Milton on the left side of the road. IGNORE THIS SIGN. Proceed toward Bournemouth and turn left on the road marked Walkford and Highcliffe (opposite the Cat and Fiddle Public House). From this turning, drive 1.3 mi. through Walkford to second left turn, marked Chewton Farm Rd. Hotel entrance is on your right. (Ignore all signs to New Milton.)

THE NEW FOREST

The New Forest stretches over heath and woodland in a 145-mile-square area west of Southampton. It is one of England's most attractive and popular natural areas. There are free-roaming animals of all kinds, including pigs, cattle, and ponies, and motorists are required to drive with great caution.

Being British, the forest, naturally, has great walking areas and public footpaths, as well as some narrow gravel roads for automobiles. The flowers, trees, and bushes, beautiful in themselves, are inhabited by hundreds of species of birds.

It's been called the "New Forest" ever since William of Normandy chose this part of Hampshire for his royal hunting grounds, as it was convenient to his palace and castle at Winchester. However, the area has prehistoric burial mounds and earthworks showing earlier occupation.

King William II later imposed such outrageous laws on the New Forest that it is said his death during a hunting expedition might have been an assassination. Both King John, of Magna Carta fame, and Charles I have a close association with this wooded area.

Many of the ancient laws of the forest still exist, but I don't believe that poachers are beheaded any longer.

THE MANSION HOUSE
Poole, Dorset

Poole is a place where Americans can see the English at play. It is a rather curious combination of old and new. The Olde Towne, right off the waterfront, with its warren of narrow, twisty streets and ancient buildings, harks back to the 18th and early 19th centuries, when Poole merchantmen made their fortunes plying the Mediterranean and Atlantic loaded with codfish from Newfoundland. Today, it is a fascinating jumble of antiques shops, curio shops, pubs, and restaurants, alongside a maritime museum, where Poole's seafaring history is depicted. There are exhibits in the Guild Hall and a restoration of Scaplen's Court, a medieval merchant's house with a central courtyard and walled garden.

Modern Poole provides endless diversions for tourists, with ferries to Brownsea Island, a 500-acre National Trust nature reserve, where peacocks strut and Sika deer can be glimpsed in the woodlands and glades. There are secluded beaches as well as a tourist center with a cafeteria and guided tours. Other ferries and sightseeing buses are available for tours to a variety of places, including the many beautiful parks and stately homes in Dorset.

There are sandy beaches for swimming and surfing, boats for hire for fishing, all sorts of water sports, and two sports centers in Poole. Pottery has been made in Poole since Roman times, and demonstrations of the art are given year-around. Some good buys are available in the showroom of the famous Poole Pottery. There are parks and lakes and bird sanctuaries. It is very much an English vacation spot.

The Mansion House, tucked between St. James Church and the King Charles Pub, in Olde Towne, provides a pleasant headquarters and respite from the rigors of sightseeing. Built in the 1770s by one of the most prominent merchants in Poole, it has an imposing facade with a semicircular porch and Greek columns. Guest rooms are on the second, third, and fourth floors, while a well-known and popular restaurant serves lunch and dinner downstairs.

When I popped in unexpectedly at noontime, I could see that this was the place where businessmen of the town gather for lunch. Mr. and Mrs. Leonard were terribly busy, and I was unable to chat with them, but Cindy, the head receptionist, was good enough to show me through the house.

I found the guest rooms to be quite attractive, clean, and comfortable. They were all differently decorated and furnished, with pretty wallpapers and harmonizing curtains and bedspreads. There were nice little touches like apothecary jars filled with candies, little pots of plants, and paintings and books. The rooms were completely equipped with private baths, radios, television, telephones, trouser presses, and the like. The residents' lounge on the second floor had a handsome fireplace, a high ceiling, and tall arched windows, and was very attractively furnished.

The restaurant downstairs is quite handsome, with paneled walls and a very clubby atmosphere. I understand the food has received a number of accolades, and that the menu offers a wide range of dishes.

THE MANSION HOUSE, Thames Street, Poole, Dorset BH15 1JN. Tel.: Poole (0202) 685666. A 19-guestroom (private baths) small hotel in the Olde Towne section of a popular tourist area on Poole Bay in the English Channel. Breakfast included in the tariff. Reservations necessary for lunch and dinner. Open year-round. Many diversions available nearby. Mr. and Mrs. R. Leonard, Proprietors. (See Index for rates.)

Directions: From London, take the M3 and the A33 to the A31, which goes to Poole. Find the Quay and Thames St. on the left. Parking is at the rear of the building.

THE PRIORY HOTEL
Wareham, Dorset

The strife, fire, and bloodshed that have wracked Wareham in its 1,000-year history have passed into oblivion, leaving only a trace here and there in this now quiet little market town in the Purbeck Hills. There are prehistoric burial mounds and some evidence of Roman occupation. In the 9th century, King Alfred fought off the Vikings, throwing up huge earthen walls as fortifications, which still exist today. Religious and civil wars and fires wreaked their havoc, and in 1762 a great fire wiped out nearly all the buildings of the town. Most of the oldest buildings now date from that period.

Situated on the River Frome and close to Poole Harbour, Wareham was an obvious target for Viking raids. The Priory (now the Priory Hotel), originally a nunnery founded in the 8th century, was particularly vulnerable, being just a few steps from the river. The convent's treasure was sacked and the fate of the nuns can well be imagined. The great Church of Lady St. Mary, with which the Priory was connected until the dissolution of monasteries in 1536, has a fascinating history. A very fine history of the town is available in a little 36-page booklet, complete with a map and photographs of the historic buildings.

I was sorry to have missed the brothers Turner, Stuart and John, when I dropped in at the Priory Hotel, but their receptionist gave me a whirlwind tour of this interesting early-16th-century brick building. The first floor has very much the cloistered feeling of a monastery, with thick stone walls and a dim hallway. The guest rooms are prettily decorated with antiques and attractive fabrics. They all have private baths, with hair dryers and scales, as well as telephones, clock radios, and color TV. There are four very luxurious suites in the Boat House, across the garden and right on the river.

The drawing room is pleasant and comfortable, with a fireplace and a baby grand piano, and french doors leading out onto a patio or terrace with a grape arbor. The gardens are beautiful and the lawn slopes down to the river. There are moorings where boats can tie up.

The Priory menu offers three choices for a main course, with such items as fillets of spring lamb with sweetbreads and a port and orange sauce, breast of chicken filled with avocado pear and prawns on a light pink peppercorn sauce, or escalopes of baby salmon in a puff pastry served with a chive and vermouth sauce. The sweets trolley features homemade desserts and there is a selection of cheeses.

Sitting on the little swing under a tree and gazing out over the river could be a perfect way to end a busy day. As an unknown author has observed, behind the garden walls "one captures the feel of monastic quiet; amongst the flowering shrubs and roses . . . peace reigns."

THE PRIORY HOTEL, Church Green, Wareham, Dorset BH20 4ND. Tel.: Wareham 2772 and 51666. A 19-guestroom (private baths) 16th-century converted priory and boathouse in a small market town on the River Frome. Breakfast included in tariff. Breakfast, lunch, and dinner served to the public. Open year-round. Sailing, fishing, golf, and many cultural and historic attractions nearby. John and Stuart Turner, Proprietors. (See Index for rates.)

Directions: From Southampton, take the A35 to the A351, which is signposted for Wareham. In Wareham, from the main street, turn left at St. John's Hill, bearing to the right. At the green, in front of Lady of St. Mary Church, turn right and park to the right of the church beside the hotel.

MARSHWOOD MANOR
Bettiscombe, Bridport, Dorset

Mrs. Shakeshaft was showing me her capacious kitchen, and I was admiring the results of her morning baking—two golden-crusted pies, one blackberry and one apple, and a tray of equally golden choux buns (which I would call cream puffs) ready to be filled. Two deep soup kettles were bubbling with split pea and chicken soup.

"We have a choice of starters, such as homemade soup, eggs mayonnaise, or prawn cocktail. One of our main dishes could be pork fillet with mushroom sauce, chicken in lemon sauce, and another dish we do is lamb cutlets, served with red currant sauce, and all sorts of roasts. We have vegetables from the garden."

At this point, Mr. Shakeshaft intervened. "One of our guests once counted eighteen different vegetables during their stay." Mrs. Shakeshaft continued her recitation. "Yes, and we do a selection of sweets, followed by coffee in the main lounge, and we change our menu weekly. Our eggs come from free-range local chickens and we have spring water."

I had been driving along one of those meandering tiny country lanes, bordered on both sides by tall hedges, when I spied the sign for Marshwood Manor and decided to have a look. I turned into the dirt road and passed some farm buildings before coming upon an Edwardian brick manor-farmhouse. I thought it looked a bit rough around the edges; however, an English couple were just packing up their car and I asked how they had enjoyed their visit. "Very nice, very pleasant and clean and the owners are very friendly." As he shut the boot, the gentleman added, "And the food is very good, too."

I could see what he meant after a visit to Mrs. Shakeshaft's kitchen. This would be a great place for children. The atmosphere is relaxed and informal. The guest rooms, although simply furnished, are very large and many of them have double and single beds. Some of them have as many as three beds, and I saw one made up with a fourth bed.

It's a very natural country place, with all sorts of things to do outdoors. The swimming pool is mainly for children, and there are games, such as pool, ping-pong, and darts in a room that used to be the milking parlor. The putting green and croquet lawn, while not your clipped and manicured country club variety, can be a lot of fun. With two acres of copse with a stream running through, where there are wildflowers, birds, and deer, nature walks could be delightful. And of course there are some good beaches at Lyme Regis and Chideock nearby.

The Shakeshafts are indeed a friendly and accommodating couple, and I'm sure they do everything in their power to make their guests comfortable and happy.

By the way, while you're staying there, be sure to stop by the Shave Cross Pub—it's a delightful little place with a great fireplace and cozy nooks.

MARSHWOOD MANOR, Bettiscombe, Bridport, Dorset DT6 5NS. Tel.: Broadwindsor (0308) 68442 or 68825. A 9-guestroom (private and shared baths) country manor-farmhouse in the Vale of Marshwood deep in Dorset countryside, a few miles north of Lyme Regis. MAP or B&B by arrangement. Sun. dinner at 1 p.m. Light lunch can be arranged. Closed at Christmas. Wheelchair access. Swimming pool, croquet lawn, putting green, games room, nature walks on grounds. Beaches, great houses, parks, and sightseeing nearby. No credit cards. Personal checks accepted. Terry and Tricia Shakeshaft, Proprietors. (See Index for rates.)

Directions: From London, take the M3 to Basingstoke and then the A30 past Salisbury, Shaftesbury, and Yeovil to Crewkerne. From Crewkerne take the road to Lyme Regis. In Birdsmoorgate at the Rose and Crown Pub, turn left on Bridport Rd., and turn right at crossroads for Bettiscombe. Continue approx. 1½ mi. to entrance.

SUMMER LODGE
Evershot, Dorset

I had been able to join another solo traveler at dinner, and now we were both enjoying coffee and a delectable chocolate morsel in the drawing room, while our host, Nigel Corbett, gave my new-found friend all sorts of ideas where she might go to paint. Having been a painting teacher for many years, she was now on a painting holiday for herself. Nigel, a tall, curly-haired gentleman, was saying, "There's a spectacular view of the south coast from the cliff, and you could walk to Golden Cap, the highest point on the coast. On a clear day you can see for fifty miles, from Portland Bill to Start Point. Or you could walk over to Melbury Osmond, a very pretty little thatched village. There are literally miles of footpaths, several of which go through the deer park at Melbury House. And, of course, there is Tess of the D'Urbervilles cottage at the end of High Street, right here in the village."

I knew this was Thomas Hardy country, but hadn't realized that one of his characters actually lived in the village of Evershot. "Oh yes," Nigel told me, "Hardy called the village 'Evershead' in his novel. By the way, Hardy drew the plans for this wing of the house. He was also an architect, you know." (The cover of this edition shows a view of the village of Evershot and Tess's cottage.)

Looking around appreciatively, I noted the nobly proportioned fireplace, the floor-to-ceiling windows, the high ceiling, the serene aspect of the room. "Yes," I said, "I can see a fine intellect behind the design of this room." The discreet colors of the comfortable furnishings, the soft glow of the lamps, the many interesting paintings, books, magazines, and fresh flowers all formed a most agreeable background for the various conversations Nigel carried on with his guests, as he moved around the room.

Summer Lodge feels very British. There is a certain reserved air about the English guests. Couples murmur quietly between themselves and scrupulously respect the privacy of others. Margaret Corbett told me that when Americans come here, they tend to stimulate more group conversations. "Actually," she says, "they sometimes make such good friends that they've arranged to meet here the following year."

Margaret took some time away from her little workroom behind the office, where she puts together all the beautiful flower arrangements I noticed throughout the house, to show me the guest rooms. They were all very pleasing, with Laura Ashley wallpapers, harmonizing curtains and bedspreads, and with welcome views of gardens, fields, sloping meadows, and the thatched roofs of the village. Much of the furniture is cane, and adds to the light, airy feeling of the rooms.

Summer Lodge, until ten years ago, was part of the estate of the Earl of Ilchester, whose main abode is Melbury House. It was the dower house where the Earl's heirs would live until it was time for them to take the title and move into the big house.

The house is surrounded by lawns and gardens and lovely old trees. In a little walled courtyard garden that leads through a gate right onto the main street of the village, the wisteria was bursting into beautiful lavender blooms.

Meals in the very pleasant, many-windowed dining room tend to be simple and good, served by cheerful and attentive young people. The night I was there, the main course was one of my favorites—steak and kidney pie, with a starter of smoked haddock roulade. The main course was followed by a fresh green salad and a choice of sweets, including a combination of lovely fresh fruits.

Dinner is included in the tariff, and some of the other menu offerings might be a starter of fresh local asparagus, mushroom and parsley soup, or smoked salmon and scrambled eggs. Some of the main courses are beef Wellington with béarnaise sauce, roast pheasant, chicken marinated in lime juice with hollandaise sauce, baked local rainbow trout, and roast sirloin of beef with Yorkshire pudding.

The next morning, after a good night's sleep and a hearty breakfast, as I said my goodbyes, I saw my painter friend, paint box under her arm and wearing a pair of Wellies, making off for a day in the lush Dorset countryside.

SUMMER LODGE COUNTRY HOUSE HOTEL, Evershot, Dorset DT2 OJR. Tel.: Evershot (093583) 424. A 12-guestroom (private baths) country house hotel deep in Thomas Hardy country, midway between Yeovil and Dorchester. Breakfast and dinner included in tariff. Lunch and dinner served to public; reservations necessary. Open mid-Jan. to mid-Dec.; weekend minimum of 2 nights. Swimming pool, grass tennis court, croquet lawn on grounds. Golf, horseback riding, fishing, 20 mi. of footpaths, including cliff walks, hunting, beaches, sailing in Lyme Bay nearby. Wheelchair access. Children over 8 accepted. Nigel and Margaret Corbett, Proprietors. (See Index for rates.)

Directions: From London, take the M3 to A303, the A359 to Yeovil, and then the A37 from Yeovil, going toward Dorchester. Watch for sign to Evershot.

THE OLD RECTORY
Shaftesbury, Dorset

The Old Rectory is situated near the bottom of a very steep village street with houses closely lining its edges. This is Gold Hill in Shaftesbury.

It is here that Rose Marie de Crespigny and her husband, Anthony, have made their home, turning it into a very warm, comfortable, and sophisticated guest house.

I say sophisticated because it becomes obvious to the visitor that the de Crespignys have many interests in life, including music and art and history. Anthony goes up to London every Sunday evening, where he is involved with academics, and Rose Marie tends to the needs of weekday guests, enticing them with her Cordon Bleu cookery. The furnishings reflect the fact that the de Crespignys have traveled widely, living in the United States, Australia, and South Africa.

The Old Rectory is a wonderful Georgian house, with an earlier section built during the 17th century, and a later section added around 1724. Just across the village street from St. James Church, it served as the church rectory for many years. There is a very pleasant garden.

The house is informal, as one might expect when there are three children. There are two guest rooms, each with its own private bath.

At breakfast, I pressed Rose Marie for some of the typical dishes she serves for the evening meal. "I tend towards roasts when we have both rooms occupied," she said. "Things like stuffed loin of lamb and roast beef, and I'm fond of doing little extra things like smoked salmon mousse."

The Old Rectory provides a very pleasant and natural stay with an interesting family in an old town of Saxon origin. There's a splendid view from the escarpment in the middle of the town's shopping center.

THE OLD RECTORY (Wolsey Lodges), St. James, Shaftesbury, Dorset. Tel.: Shaftesbury (0747) 2003. A 2-guestroom village guest house, within half a mile of the center of Shaftesbury at the bottom of St. John's Hill. Open all year except first 3 wks. in Aug. Dinner available upon request. All of the many Dorset and West Country cultural and recreational attractions nearby. No credit cards. Anthony and Rose Marie de Crespigny, Proprietors. (See Index for rates.)

Directions: From Shaftesbury town center, take B3091 south about ½ mi. down St. John's Hill. At the bottom, you will find the house on the right opposite St. James's Church. Parking space is located opposite the main entrance to the house.

For room rates and last time for dinner orders, see Index.

THE WEST COUNTRY
Counties of Wiltshire, Avon, Dorset, Devon, Somerset, and Cornwall

Wiltshire has pleasant lofty downlands with rivers and meandering streams. It is a place of prehistoric monuments, the most famous of which is Stonehenge on the Salisbury Plain. Among its great buildings are the Salisbury Cathedral, the Malmesbury Abbey, and Lacock Abbey.

Avon is a new county in England, created on the first of April 1974, and it includes part of Gloucestershire, North Somerset, and the city of Bristol.

Somerset is the home of cider and cheddar cheese. There are some fine beaches and open countryside. Christianity in England is said to have its earliest roots in Somerset. This is also the romantic land of Lorna Doone and where King Arthur held court at fabled Camelot and Alfred sought refuge at Athelney.

Devon is one of Britain's leading holiday counties. It has sandy beaches, high-banked lanes, lush green valleys, rolling hills, and a mild climate. There are also wide open spaces like Dartmoor and Exmoor.

Cornwall is at the far southwest end of Britain and has a 300-mile coastline. The mild climate and semi-tropical foliage of the south coast has earned it the title of "Cornish Riviera." There are picturesque harbors crowded with fishing boats, many unusual villages and small towns with cobbled lanes. This is a photographer's and artist's paradise. Cornwall, as well as Devon, is famous for creamed teas.

THE WEST COUNTRY

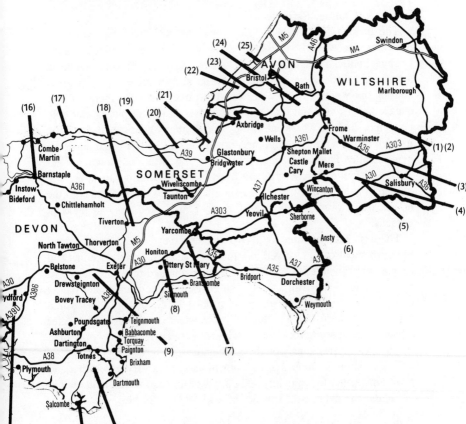

DUNDAS LOCK COTTAGE
Monkton Combe, Bath, Avon

The turning for Dundas is just down the A36 from the American Museum, and while I was getting a petrol refill at the Monkton Combe Garage, I noticed a sign that said "Dundas B&B." A small lane led down a dirt road through an archway of trees, and imagine my surprise at coming upon not just one waterway, but three! Actually, there are two canals and a river, and this is one of those wonderful places that only happen in England where one of the canals actually goes over the river on its own bridge and then continues down the valley. The canal aqueduct here is called Dundas, hence the name of this little sandstone cottage.

Here, I found the cheerful and fresh-faced proprietress most accommodating and quite willing that I should see all of the bedrooms in the house, which overlook the river, the canal basin, and the very pleasant gardens.

There is a little bit more to this than meets the eye, because Wendy and her husband also are involved in arranging canal trips on the Kennet and Avon canals aboard the *John Rennie*. She explained that on Friday and Saturday nights they run a three-hour cruise that includes dinner on the boat. There seemed to be many more plans in the offing, and I would suggest that if this sounds interesting, readers should write ahead for advance information. Incidentally, I know these cruises are very popular, so advance reservations would be necessary.

The location of Dundas Lock Cottage makes it a very interesting and rewarding center for enjoying the delights of this part of England, and in particular the delights of the city of Bath. It's really fun!

Reader Comment: "Absolutely smashing! Best place in your book."

DUNDAS LOCK COTTAGE, Monkton Combe, Bath, Avon BA2 7BN. Tel.: (022 122) Limpley Stoke 2292. A 2-guestroom (shared baths) canalside guest house near Bath with a few extra touches. Breakfast is the only meal served, but Fri. and Sat. night canal cruise dinners are offered with advance arrangements. Boats for hire. Write for brochure. Open from Apr. 1 to Oct. 31. Near the American Museum and the city of Bath. No credit cards. Mr. and Mrs. T. Wheeldon, Proprietors. (See Index for rates.)

Directions: From Bath take A36 (Warminster/Salisbury Rd.) through Claverton. About 1 mi. beyond, you will come to the Monkton Combe Garage (you have just overshot the entrance). Turn around, going north about 100 yds. and look for Dundas B&B sign on right.

HOMEWOOD PARK
Hinton, Charterhouse, Bath, Avon

If the reader will take a moment to look on the page with the map of the West Country, he or she will note that distances are very short, and it's possible, using Bath as the hub, to visit points in Somerset, Avon, and Wiltshire. I would suggest staying in one place for two or three nights; they are all excellent and somewhat varied in price.

The Homewood Park Hotel, recommended by Richard and Annie Skipwith at the Old House Hotel in Wickham, is a short, pleasant drive from Bath to the east.

The first thing I saw was a croquet lawn bordered by extensive gardens. The main house is a very old building with the entrance through an attractive flower-bedecked patio.

The reception area and the other rooms on the first floor were bright and cheerful with a mixture of modern and traditional furnishings.

I had telephoned ahead and introduced myself as a friend of the Skipwiths, and I must say that Stephen and Penny Ross were most gracious, even though they were hosting a very large wedding party. I am sure I couldn't have chosen a more inopportune time; however, their good humor and excellent manners prevailed. As it turned out I was very glad to see this lovely family-run country house hotel at its brightest and most inviting, with the happy, celebrating guests all gathered around a fabulous buffet table.

There are fifteen bedrooms individually decorated, each with private bathroom and lovely view.

Stephen, who is the chef, explained that the menu is a combination of French and country cooking. "Mildly influenced," he added, "by the new style. We would never admit to being *cuisine nouvelle,* but our approach has the light touch."

Penny chimed in quickly, "I think we are running a country restaurant with comfortable bedrooms. Most people coming here have very high expectations, so we cannot relax in the kitchen when people are expecting to find the food interesting."

I could readily see that both of them had to attend to their guests and so I wandered about, both indoors and out, admiring the gardens and tennis court, and enjoying for a moment the idea of sharing in a real English country wedding party. It was delightful.

HOMEWOOD PARK, Hinton, Charterhouse, Bath, Avon BA3 6BB. Tel.: (022122) Limpley Stoke 3731. A 15-guestroom (private baths) country house hotel near Bath. Breakfast, lunch, and dinner served daily. Closed Dec. 24 to Jan. 14. Located near the American Museum and all of the delights of the city of Bath. Good countryside walking and touring. Stephen and Penny Ross, Hoteliers.

Directions: Follow A36 south from Bath for 5½ mi. Turn left for Sharpstone, then first left for Homewood.

BISHOPSTROW HOUSE
Warminster, Wiltshire

I was sorry to have missed Mr. and Mrs. Kurt Schiller, but an unexpected visit on my way to Bath found them away on that Sunday afternoon in May. I would very much have liked to meet the people who had turned their private home, a very beautiful and elegant Georgian mansion, into such a special small hotel.

Sara Thornborough, a most winsome and obliging young lady, who was "on tap," as she put it, told me that Mr. and Mrs. Schiller wanted to keep the hotel very much as it was when they lived there, and I would have to say that with all its somewhat formal elegance, it definitely has a lived-in feeling, which only adds to its charm. At the same time, they offer the kinds of facilities and amenities that are found in the best resort hotels. Without reservations, I can say their indoor swimming pool is one of the most beautiful I've ever seen. Romanesque in feeling, with pillars, black and white Italian tile and marble bordering the somewhat asymmetrical pool, and a row of tall arched windows looking out on a garden, the room itself is really spectacular. There are also an outdoor pool, full-sized, hard-surface indoor and outdoor tennis courts, and a sauna and a solarium.

Sara, who was giving me a guided tour, took me through one exquisite room after another, and my overall impression was of refinement and taste, which was Mrs. Schiller's, I learned from Sara. The colors were mostly muted blues, grays, mauves, soft peaches, beiges, and creams.

The fabrics were velvets, satins, silks, brocades, and damasks—sometimes used as wall coverings, too. Wall-to-wall carpeting was overlaid with Persian carpets, which, Sara told me, "travel." Along with her attention to the decor, plantings, and fresh flowers, Mrs. Schiller likes to move the Persian carpets around. There were many, many beautiful French and English antique pieces and oil paintings.

I could write a paragraph just about the sumptuous bathrooms—I'll mention two. One has a *trompe l'oeil* painting behind a huge circular whirlpool bathtub and the other has a cloth sunburst canopy over the large circular tub. They are both fully carpeted and have potted plants and thick, soft towels.

I particularly liked the rather Victorian conservatory dining room with a sliding glass roof, where Sunday lunches are served on sunny days. It has arched windows all around and a trellis with sweetpeas. The tables have lace tablecloths.

The main restaurant looks out on the swimming pool and lawn and is a most pleasant room. Sara said the cuisine is traditional English. Some of the menu choices are calf's liver gently cooked, with avocado and Madeira, Wiltshire duck roasted with caramelized pears, rack of lamb with rosemary and garlic, fillet of pork roasted in fresh herbs with a puff pastry in a port wine sauce, and veal sweetbreads served on rice with a shellfish sauce. There are always some specials, which depend on what the chef finds at the market.

The desserts looked pretty sinful to me: gateau of chocolate with meringue served on a caramel sauce, iced apricot parfait on a fresh mango sauce, dark chocolate mousse with cream on a coffee bean sauce, and fresh strawberries and cream.

Snacks are available at any time, and if you were so inclined, you could have homemade soup with a roll and butter, a platter of smoked salmon, a sandwich, scrambled eggs with smoked salmon, or a slice of homemade cake. There is, of course, afternoon tea.

All of this luxury and elegance is placed in the middle of pastures where cattle graze, and—a humorous touch—as you come around the hairpin-curved driveway there is a pen with goats in it. Mildred and George, Sara told me, are for the children to feed.

BISHOPSTROW HOUSE (Relais et Chateaux), Warminster, Wiltshire BA12 9HN. Tel.: Warminster (0985) 212312. Telex: 444829. A 26-guest-room (private baths) luxurious country house hotel midway between Salisbury and Bath. Continental breakfast included in tariff. Lunch and dinner served in restaurant daily. Open all year. Indoor and outdoor swimming pools, indoor and outdoor tennis courts, solarium and sauna, fishing on the River Wylye, garden and country walks on grounds. Golf, many great houses, gardens, and ancient villages nearby. Within a half hour of Bath with all its cultural and historic attractions. Mr. and Mrs. Kurt Schiller, Owners. (See Index for rates.)

Directions: From London, take the M3 to Junction 8 at Basingstoke. Take A303 toward Andover to A36. Continue on A36 toward Warminster. Watch for signpost for Bishopstrow, and just beyond a sharp left curve (100 yds.) is the entrance on the right.

THE LAMB
Hindon (near Salisbury), Wiltshire

When I asked Walter and Elizabeth Lillie, my Canary Islands friends who live in Mere, to suggest a small inn near Salisbury and Stonehenge, they unhesitatingly recommended the Lamb, in an off-the-highway village about ten miles from Stonehenge — the kind of a place that a meandering traveler might find, but the person in a hurry would miss.

Mr. Alastair Morrison, the proprietor of this residential English country pub, proved to be very pleasant and accommodating and showed me his typical inn-guest rooms, most of which had private baths. We sat down in the main parlor with its low ceiling and cheery fireplace and he explained that although rather a small place, the Lamb is quite popular for lunch and dinner.

Roast pheasant and grilled Avon trout almondine are on the menu

frequently, as well as roast duckling and scalloped veal. The desserts were all homemade, including apple and raspberry pie, which I sampled. Scrumptious.

The Lamb, like the Kenmore Hotel in Scotland, the Pheasant in the Lake Country, and the Royal Oak near London, are typical, traditional English inns, most of them quite old, probably having enjoyed a career as a post house at one time. They have retained the atmosphere and traditions of old England and are open throughout the year.

According to my tariff sheet from the Lamb, the cost of bed and breakfast also includes dinner (see Index for rates and times of last order for dinner).

THE LAMB, Hindon (near Salisbury), Wiltshire SP3 6OP. Tel.: Hindon (074-789) 573. A very pleasant 16-guestroom (9 with baths) traditional village inn 16 mi. west of Salisbury. Open all year. Breakfast and dinner included in tariff. Breakfast, lunch, dinner served to non-residents. Convenient for Salisbury, Stonehenge, Stourhead House and Gardens. Riding, walking, fishing, and shooting available nearby. Alastair Morrison, Proprietor. (See Index for rates.)

Directions: From London take M3 to A303. Continue until 10 mi. past Stonehenge, then look for turning to left, signposted "Hindon."

CHICKLADE LODGE
Chicklade, Hindon, Salisbury, Wiltshire

Bronwen Nixon of Rothay Manor first introduced me to Peter and Audrey Jerram when they had a small farmhouse in the Lake District. Now they had moved to the south of England to the 19th-century gatehouse of a Wiltshire estate set amidst a lovely countryside in an area of outstanding natural beauty. It is ideally situated on the Wiltshire–Dorset border for a painting or touring holiday. During my visit, as we all were having a cup of tea in the garden, Audrey pointed out that painters would find many interesting subjects, not only in the garden itself, but in the hamlet of Chicklade and in the nearby villages with their thatched-roof cottages.

"We feel that a painting holiday is an informal one," Audrey commented. "We don't have any formal courses, and people are free to paint where and when they like. I believe that painting is a very individual activity, and painters should be encouraged to develop their own personal style. Of course, I'm here every day to talk with and help our guests."

Audrey left to replenish the teapot, and Peter explained that she has a great deal of experience in painting and teaching and is exhibited widely.

Audrey returned with more of her cookies, and said, "Things are basically the same as they were in the Lake Country. I prepare breakfast, and the evening meal consists of starters, main courses, and sweets. We serve coffee in front of our fireplace, where there is a fossil in one of the stones. Our facilities are similar to those at Low House, with the addition of tea- and coffee-making facilities in each room."

"Non-painters enjoy us, too," Peter said. "We have wonderful walks here, including the one up the road next to the house and through the villages in the Wylye Valley, and along the Roman Road. Shaftesbury is only seven miles, while Warminster and Stourhead House and Gardens are a bit farther. Stonehenge, Salisbury, Bath, and the Dorset coast are surprisingly near."

A painting holiday in England can also be enjoyed at Dedham Hall in Dedham, Essex, mentioned elsewhere in this edition.

CHICKLADE LODGE, Chicklade, Hindon, Salisbury, Wiltshire SP3 5SU. Tel.: (074789) 389. A 3-guestroom cottage (shared baths) ideally situated in painting country near Shaftesbury and Salisbury. The room rate includes breakfast and dinner. Open year-round. Splendid footpaths and excellent back roads lead to an endless variety of scenery as well as cultural and recreational attractions. A car is not necessary; guests can be collected at Tisbury Station, with regular services from Waterloo (London). Peter and Audrey Jerram, Proprietors. (See Index for rates.)

Directions: Chicklade is on the A303 (Andover–Exeter) and about 15 mi. west of Salisbury. It's the last house on the right leaving Chicklade going west.

HOLBROOK HOUSE HOTEL
Wincanton, Somerset

The village of Wincanton is situated on a hill only a few miles from the East Somerset border. The surrounding country is well-wooded hill and vale with splendid views of the neighboring counties of Dorset and Wiltshire. All around are beautiful villages with historic churches, mellowed stone cottages, and gracious mansions, many of which, with their lovely gardens, are open to the public.

This is Camelot country, and nearby Cadbury Castle is one of the reputed sites of King Arthur's last battle. Within a thirty-mile radius lie Salisbury, Bath, Wells, Glastonbury, Dorchester, the coasts of Dorset, and North Somerset.

The word that comes to my mind when I think of Holbrook House Hotel is "comfortable." It is situated in a rather large grove of cedar, beech, elm, ash, and rose trees, and I noted many familiar flowers as well.

Over half of the spacious guest rooms had their own bathrooms. The menu has some typical Somerset dishes, including pork cooked with apples and cider, chicken garnished with a mead and honey sauce, and a number of dishes with cheddar cheese, whose origins are just a few miles away.

There are two unusual recreational features at Holbrook House. I found both grass and hard-surface tennis courts, and also squash courts—I didn't see many of those in Britain. There's also a heated outdoor swimming pool.

"Holbrook" is not a family name, but is derived from the Old English *holbroc,* meaning "stream in a hollow." The property dates approximately to 1350, and some of the earlier owners lost their heads because of some injudicious political leanings. One family owned the property for nearly three hundred years.

It has been well preserved, and the conversion to a hotel by its present owners has been planned with care, taste, and wisdom.

HOLBROOK HOUSE HOTEL, Holbrook, Wincanton, Somerset BA9 8BS. Tel.: (0963) Wincanton 32377. A 20-guestroom (14 with private bath/ shower) country house hotel, 2 mi. west of Wincanton. Open all year. Breakfast, lunch, tea, and dinner served to non-residents. Convenient to Stonehenge, Stourhead Gardens, and many famous houses in the Somerset countryside. Grass and hard tennis courts, squash court, croquet, and heated swimming pool on grounds. Golf and fishing nearby. Mr. and Mrs. G. E. Taylor, Owners. (See Index for rates.)

Directions: From London, take M3 to Basingstoke, then A303 to Wincanton Bypass. Take exit signposted "Wincanton and Castle Cary." Follow signs to Castle Cary Rd.; 2 mi. beyond, on A371, is gate entrance.

WOODHAYES
Whimple (near Exeter), Devon

For at least six months before my arrival I had been looking forward to visiting Woodhayes. For one thing, I had met John Allan, the proprietor, when he was with an excellent country house hotel in Scotland. Then on two separate occasions he had journeyed to America to take part in innkeepers' conferences. So, besides being a first-time visitor to a highly recommended small country house hotel, I had the opportunity to see John once again.

We all would like our friends to be happy and successful, and as soon as I pulled up to the front of the house and walked through the entrance, I knew that both happiness and success were John's. He looked exactly the same, a very cordial, smiling, English face, as soft-spoken and considerate as ever. He beamed with pleasure as I commented on how handsome the house looked and how pleasantly it was situated.

"Thank you very much," he replied. "I've tried to preserve the original Georgian architecture and at the same time provide accommodations that would be exactly what I would like to find."

This is a simple Georgian house (as opposed to an opulent Georgian manor). The exterior could be described as plain, but the interior has an understated elegance. There are two drawing rooms on the first floor, both with a fireplace. The seven guest rooms are all centrally heated and have very comfortable and appropriate furnishings. As John pointed out, they aren't really authentic Georgian pieces because Georgian isn't that comfortable.

Over dinner that evening he explained that the house was probably built for a squire; perhaps built by the lord of the manor for one of his sons. "We made some changes to accommodate bathrooms and, in fact, when we came here, some of the rooms had been considerably altered from the original, so we put it back to rights again."

Food is given prime attention in the hotel, and John went to some trouble to explain that the local food in Devon is quite as good as one can get anywhere. Lamb and beef are from the region, as are the fish, with both the north and south Devon coasts just a short distance away. Preparation and presentation have also been given much thought. "We try not to overwhelm our dining room guests," John said with a faint smile, "but to provide them with just enough to make them feel comfortable."

After dinner, over coffee in front of the low fire, we discussed the fact that it really was an excellent first- or last-night stop for anyone using Heathrow Airport. It's about three-and-a-half hours on the Motorway via the M4.

WOODHAYES, Whimple (near Exeter), Devon EX5 2TD. Tel.: (0404) Whimple 822237. A 7-guestroom (private baths) elegant Georgian country house just a few miles from Exeter. Open every day; closed Jan. Dinner served to resident and non-resident guests. Most conveniently situated to enjoy Devon countryside and the north and south coasts. John Allan, Proprietor. (See Index for rates.)

Directions: Whimple is a small village located to the north of A30. Look for signpost for Whimple a few miles west of Honiton.

Rates for a room for two people for one night with breakfast, except where noted, are included in the Index of this book. They are not to be considered firm quotations, but should be used as guidelines only.

COMBE HOUSE HOTEL
Gittisham (near Honiton), Devon

Dusk had fallen on the A30. A scant twenty minutes earlier I had left Exeter and was now anxiously looking for the signpost for Gittisham. Ah, there it was. I turned into a truly ancient village with cob and thatched cottages and a babbling brook. There was a parish church that enshrined 500 years of the community's history.

A gate at the end of the village led to a narrow road that wound its way through the meadows of an extensive country estate. I parked in front of a large three-story stone building with many towers and windows, surrounded by beautiful hedges and flowers.

In the impressive main hall I found no reception desk or porters in white jackets, but rather a large, imposing man, his face wreathed in smiles, who said, "Welcome, Mr. Simpson, to the Combe House Hotel."

This was my introduction to John Boswell, who, with his wife, Thérèse, is the proprietor of this remarkably well-preserved Elizabethan mansion house, which possibly dates as far back as the 13th century. Standing at the head of a secluded valley, it commands extensive views over the hills where there are beautiful walks and a sublime serenity.

The Boswells came to Combe a number of years ago and found this old country house in a very dilapidated condition. John, whose early Scottish ancestors included the famous James Boswell, author of *The Life of Samuel Johnson,* had previously worked for a shipping organization in the Far East. Thérèse attended the Cordon Bleu School at Winkfield, and lived in France for some time.

"The improvements we made are not of the obvious sort," John commented. "We've reelectrified the house, got the water works right, and have done a lot to the inside, including adding more bathrooms and other such essential things. We now have telephones in all the guest rooms!

"The gardens were in an almost hopeless condition, and it pleases us when people enjoy all the flowers. In addition to our kitchen garden, where we grow our own peas, tomatoes, lettuce, french beans, radishes, brussels sprouts, corn, chinese lettuce, artichokes, and broccoli, there are several farms on the place."

There are twelve spacious, rather elegant guest rooms, each with its own bathroom.

The passage of time has left many noteworthy relics of Combe's illustrious owners. Antique lovers will enjoy the fine architecture, furniture, and decor that echo their taste throughout the centuries. John and Thérèse have added considerably to the atmosphere with their own cherished furniture, books, and pictures from Auchinleck House in Scotland, the ancestral home of James Boswell.

Dinner that evening in the sedate candle-lit dining room, included Dover Sole Mère Recamier, which Thérèse explained later was deep-fried with the backbone removed and filled with shrimps, prawns, and cream. Other specialties include Veal Escalope Vallée d'Auge, and fresh local lobster, cooked in a special cream sauce.

I spent the remainder of the evening talking with John, who is a superb conversationalist, learning about the history of Combe House and being shown the many oil portraits of its famous and infamous past owners.

On a more immediate note, Thérèse told me that nearby Honiton is becoming an antique hunter's "paradise."

I was delighted on my return visit to Gittisham to discover that nothing had really changed since my first visit. But, after all, nothing has changed in Gittisham village for upward of 500 years, so that really wasn't so surprising.

COMBE HOUSE HOTEL (Pride of Britain), Gittisham (near Honiton), Devon EX14 OAD. Tel.: (0404) Honiton 2756. U.S. reservations: 800-323-3602. A 12-guestroom country house hotel dating to Norman times. Breakfast, lunch, tea, and dinner served daily. Closed early Jan. to late Feb. Fishing and croquet on grounds; riding, swimming, squash, tennis nearby. Located a short distance from theaters and museums in Exeter, and many houses and gardens of historical interest, including Forde Abbey, Powderham Castle, and the Roman baths and Georgian architecture in Bath. John and Thérèse Boswell, Resident Proprietors. (See Index for rates.)

Directions: From Honiton take the A30 (Exeter road); after approx. 1 mi., turn left at the signpost for Gittisham. This road leads to Combe House.

GIDLEIGH PARK
Chagford, Devon

It was morning coffeetime on the terrace of Gidleigh Park. The sun, in addition to burning off the morning fog, was also warming up the temperature on this rather brisk autumn morning. Earlier, moving across the terraced lawns, replete with rosebeds, I had strolled down to the banks of the North Teign River where some adventurous birds sailed forth from the beech forest into the magnificent fifteen-foot-tall rhododendrons.

Now, two guests from Buffalo, New York, joined me over coffee for a moment or two, and we talked about the joys of traveling in England and the prospects of playing tennis on a real grass court for the first time.

"We drove out from Heathrow Airport two days ago," one said. "I think it's so exciting to be in a place like this. It's our first stay in England."

Meanwhile, Paul Henderson, the proprietor, joined me. "It's going to be a bully day," he said, with a twinkle in his eye. Paul and his wife, Kay, are Americans and met at Purdue University in Indiana, and have lived in Europe for the past fifteen years. I knew that he was pulling my leg, playing the British innkeeper, with his remark about a "bully" day.

"What we're aiming for here is to be one of the best of five or ten country house hotels in England. We try to treat our guests as if they are in our own home. Kay supervises the cooking and occasionally prepares some of the main dishes herself. She is the first American woman to get a 'star' from Michelin. (There are only thirty-five Michelin-starred restaurants in Britain.)

"We are continually adjusting to the needs of our guests," he went on. "For example, we are now offering a three-course lunch and guests are welcome to stroll in the garden. Dinner is a five-course experience, either à la carte or a full meal. A table is automatically reserved for each houseguest."

The house is Tudor-style and is set in thirty acres of gardens and forests in Dartmoor National Park. There are twelve guest rooms, each with its own bath.

In reply to my question about guest activities, Paul replied, "The walking around here is magnificent. There are literally hundreds of footpaths. You can walk off onto the moor, which is wild and open country, or down through the valley along the riverside, or perhaps up to the pastures. There's really great exploring. We also have two croquet lawns.

"The north and south Devon coasts are within an hour's drive, but Dartmoor is the real attraction. Within five miles of the hotel you can discover prehistoric megaliths that are similar—although smaller—to those at Stonehenge and Avebury. There are even Stone Age hut circles and villages, and several delightful 15th-century churches.

"As you might expect, there's good fishing and golf nearby, and also horseback riding or pony trekking on the moors."

Chagford, Devon, is a long way from Lafayette, Indiana, but it's very obvious that Kay and Paul Henderson have found in this extremely sequestered, almost idyllic, corner of England, one of the best of all possible worlds.

GIDLEIGH PARK (Relais et Chateaux), Chagford, Devon TQ13 8HH. Tel.: (06473) Chagford 2367; 2225. A 14-guestroom country house hotel on the edge of Dartmoor. About 4 hrs. west of London; ½ hr. from Exeter; and ¾ hr. from Plymouth. Breakfast, lunch, tea, and dinner served daily year-round. Tennis, croquet, fishing, riding, and golf available. Not particularly suitable for children. Paul and Kay Henderson, Proprietors. (See Index for rates.)

Directions: From the M5 take the A30 toward Okehampton. At Whiddon Down take A382 towards Chagford and follow signs to Chagford Square. Turn right on Mill St. at Lloyds Banks. After 200 yds, take right-hand fork. Follow lane downhill to the crossroads. Straight across, then 1½ mi. up to the end of the lane. (Is this the longest 1½ mi. in the world?)

BUCKLAND-TOUT-SAINTS
Goveton, Devon

Take a moment to look at the map of western England and you will note that at Exeter the main roads to Cornwall split, going around Dartmoor National Park to the north and south. There are roads through Dartmoor, principally B3212; however, the average visitors to Britain want to get to Cornwall as quickly as possible, so they usually opt for A30 to Okehampton or A38 going south toward Plymouth. It is to this second road that I would like to call your attention.

This peninsula, extending down into the sea and including Dartmouth, Salcombe, and Kingsbridge, is known as South Hams, so-called for the excellent quality of the native porkers. It is one of the holiday areas of the well-informed Briton.

Kingsbridge is a key turnoff for the village of Goveton, which I'm sure is only on the most specific of maps. I have been very specific about directions, but I'm certain that before you reach Buckland-Tout-Saints, just outside of Goveton, you will be convinced that you are totally lost. The sunken lanes are so deep and the hedges on top are so high that they are almost double the height of the car.

Regardless of whatever problems you may encounter, this exceptional Queen Anne mansion, part of which dates back to the 12th century, will be worth any motoring anxieties.

The hotel derives its name from the French-Norman family of Tout-sants, who held this manor after the Norman conquest of 1066. Today, it is a country house hotel of great dignity and grace in a delightful and remote park.

Ashburton marble fireplaces, 17th- and 18th-century molded plaster ceilings, intricate oak foliage scrollwork, and mahogany-and-gilt doors are just some of its characteristics. The main guest rooms are lofty and luxurious with tasteful furnishings and very choice views of the surrounding countryside. It has an excellent reputation for food.

The gardens are exceptional and feature, among other things, a species of New Zealand fern that demands subtropical conditions, shelter from the winds, and constant attention.

This particular part of South Devon is known to many servicemen from WW II, because it was used as a training area previous to the Normandy landings. Many have returned just to revisit the countryside.

Buckland-Tout-Saints was a complete surprise and a delight to me, and I think it provides an excellent reason to stop off on the South Devon coast.

BUCKLAND-TOUT-SAINTS, Goveton, Kingsbridge, Devon TQ7 2DS. Tel.: (0548) Kingsbridge 3055. U.S. reservations: 800-528-1234 or Josie Barr, 800-323-5463. A 12-guestroom (private baths) palatial country house hotel near the South Devon coast. Breakfast, lunch, and dinner served every day. Open all year. Most conveniently located to enjoy all of the recreational advantages of the south coast. Golf courses, fishing, and shooting nearby. The Shephard Family, Proprietors. (See Index for rates.)

Directions: From London take the M4 and M5 to Exeter; the A38 to Buckfastleigh. From there take A384 to Totnes, then A381 for Kingsbridge and look for hotel signs beyond Halwell. It is reached by a single passage road through the fields.

SOUTH SANDS HOTEL
Salcombe, South Devon

A few years ago when I wandered into the spotless kitchen of the South Sands Hotel, Peter Hey was cooking breakfast, and members of the staff were bustling around getting ready for the chores of the day. He served up scrambled eggs, hot smoked mackerel, and Lancashire pork sausage.

"Actually," he said, in the way that only the British say it, "Salcombe is one of the few places where it is still possible to get away from it all. I guess we are a bit difficult to find, but when you get here it's worth it. Directly on the beach, we are a haven for yachtsmen, fishermen, families with children, and just plain sun-worshipers. In the spring the wildflowers must be seen to be believed. Being the most southerly spot we get exceptionally warm and sunny weather.

"Yet we're within easy reach of the shops and entertainment in Plymouth or Torbay. Dartmoor is only an hour distant and you can walk on the moors or have a day's pony-trekking."

It happens that I have seen Peter and Elisabeth Hey several times since my original visit to meet them when they owned a small traditional inn in Lancashire. They have visited America at least twelve times and attended five meetings of innkeepers and hoteliers who are included in *Country Inns and Back Roads, North America* as well as *Country Inns and Back Roads, Britain and Ireland;* this year they hosted a party of American innkeepers in return.

We last saw each other at Rancho de los Caballeros in Wickenburg, Arizona, where they both buttonholed me with news about how the South Sands Hotel had been increased in size, scope, and service.

"You'll just love the things that have been going on," quoth Elisabeth. "Peter and I are both history and art enthusiasts, and two years ago we got the idea that it would be especially appropriate if we could put something of ourselves into each of our hotel guest rooms. I have always loved needlework and pottery and generally restoring things, so we started the task, and we are well on the way to having an individual piece of handiwork in each room—sometimes a wallhanging, a piece of needlework, hand-embroidered pillows, handmade rugs, a piece of stripped pine furniture, and so forth. Now we have 'homey bedrooms' and not just 'any' bedroom."

"Our car park is nicely landscaped now," Peter said, "and we have a garden with our own Devonshire apple trees, from which we hope to make our own cider. We were both very much against having a modern-day Olympic-type swimming pool, so we have built it in a sunken, old-fashioned rose garden, complete with the old brick walls, pebble paths, and a potting shed, which is really to hide the steam room, solarium, and changing rooms. All are indoors, and looked down upon from the new lounge and entrance via a cottage bow window. We commissioned a huge, twenty-foot-high mural, depicting a woodland grove with waterfalls, deer, and children playing that gives a really magical effect."

They both went on to say that they've added quite a bit to the old hotel, and, as Peter says, "It's always been our aim to have the facilities that help to make our season a year-round ongoing operation, combined with small conference facilities and personal service.

"We now know that we have a lovely family hotel in a perfectly wonderful part of England, and as the years go by more and more of your countrymen just seem to find us!"

SOUTH SANDS HOTEL, Salcombe, South Devon TQ8 8LL. Tel.: (054-884) 3741. A 27-guestroom waterside hotel on the picturesque and inviting South Devon coast. Breakfast, lunch, and dinner served daily. Open all year. Most conveniently located to enjoy all of the year-round natural, cultural, and scenic attractions nearby. Exceptional beach. Children most welcome. Deep-water moorings available with prior reservations. Peter and Elisabeth Hey, Hoteliers. (See Index for rates.)

Directions: A38 is the road from Exeter to Cornwall. After Exeter, look for A381 for Totnes and Kingsbridge and then Salcombe. The river estuary will be on the left; continue straight on with a lot of multi-colored row houses on your left. You will come to a 3-way junction, signposted Town Centre, Bennett Rd., and Sand Hills Rd. Take the latter, which is the extreme right fork, and you'll drop down to the harbor. Continue through North Sands to South Sands, with the hotel on the left.

FOX'S EARTH, LEWTRENCHARD MANOR
Lewdown (near Okehampton), Devon

I had to find out where that name came from and Greg Shriver told me: "We quite literally felt as if we'd been 'hounded to earth,' and we thought Fox's Earth was the perfect name for this place." Greg was talking about how he and Mary Ellen Keys had decided to give up their hectic lives as computer consultants and take up the life of innkeepers at this beautiful manor house in West Devon.

It may seem a bit paradoxical that two breezy Americans should be taking over as "lords of the manor" on this truly baronial estate, but from the looks of it, they have a real feel for the role.

Set in rather spectacular grounds that include walled gardens, lovely walks, a two-acre trout lake, and a sixty-foot waterfall, Fox's Earth is actually part of a 1,000-acre estate made up of farms and woodlands.

The manor house was built in 1620 and purchased by the Baring-Gould family, which retains title to it to this day. The most famous occupant was Sabine Baring-Gould, a prolific author and folklorist and composer of the hymn "Onward Christian Soldiers." "He was a real Renaissance man," Mary Ellen said. "He traveled widely and was a compulsive collector. He was probably most responsible for the richly carved ceilings and moldings and other decorations in the house."

Although this house reeks of baronial splendor, I could see that Mary Ellen and Greg give it a wonderful touch of informality and ease with their own special brand of relaxed hospitality. They get a lot of help from their English sheepdog, Michelin, who is always happy to accompany guests on walks.

Comfortable sofas and chairs, log fires in the huge fireplace, fresh flowers, and attractively draped stone-mullioned windows all contribute to the atmosphere of well-being in the public rooms. The upstairs gallery, which must be at least twenty feet wide, is a showplace with oriental rugs, heavy, Renaissance-style furnishings, an antique square piano and ancestral oil paintings. "We found this in the barn among a number of fascinating things," Mary Ellen told me when I exclaimed over an antique instrument. "It's an old hurdy-gurdy, which is something like a lute."

Mary Ellen and Greg are busily engaged in a program of redecorating and refurbishing the guest rooms, and although there were some very special antique pieces in the guest rooms and they were all attractive and replete with a number of amenities, I'm sure when the redecoration is completed they will be quite elegant.

But with all of this, "Our food is what is special at Fox's Earth," Greg says. "Our head chef trained at the Inn on the Park in London and our second chef is from Grosvenor House, and they present what we would call a modern international cuisine." The setting for dinner is in an impressively paneled room with a carved ceiling, leaded windows, and a large fireplace. A particularly fascinating feature is the border of medieval paintings on wood around the top of the walls, which depict figures that seem to represent various virtues.

Their menu features various treatments of fish, beef, lamb, veal, and pork—loin of pork in an orange and ginger coating with an orange and green peppercorn sauce, saddle of English lamb with Madeira, tarragon, and cream sauce, English veal in a light Stilton and basil sauce. Some dessert selections are pears in pastry with ice cream and strawberry coulis, a hazelnut tart with a fruit coulis, and flamed fruit crêpes with an orange and lemon sauce.

This is certainly a place where one could enjoy a feeling of being "to the manor born."

FOX'S EARTH, LEWTRENCHARD MANOR (Pride of Britain), Lewdown, Okehampton, Devon EX20 4PN. Tel.: (056 683) 256 or 222. A 10-guestroom (private baths) splendid country house hotel in a lush West Devon valley midway between Exeter and Plymouth. Continental breakfast included in tariff. Full English breakfast and lunch available to houseguests. Restaurant is open daily for dinner and Sun. lunch. Reservations necessary. Open year-round. Two-day minimum on holiday weekends. Croquet lawn, clay pigeon shooting, rough shooting, rough fishing on the River Lew, 2-acre trout lake, lovely walks on grounds. Ideal for touring Dartmoor and Cornwall. Horseback riding, golf, swimming, tennis nearby. Greg Shriver and Mary Ellen Keys, Hosts. (See Index for rates.)

Directions: Lewtrenchard is ¾ mi. from the village of Lewdown off the A-30.

THE OLD SCHOOLHOUSE
Veryan (near Truro), Cornwall

Let's begin this story by explaining that the Old Schoolhouse, owned by Mr. and Mrs. J. W. Baseley, is a private house that has a twin-bedded apartment with a full kitchen for rent on a weekly basis. I've included the telephone number, but please arrange for accommodations in advance by letter.

Now, for the story.

I had discovered, with some chagrin, that my portable radio was broken. St. Mawes was behind me, and when I saw the sign for the village of Veryan, I turned off the main road hoping to find a repair shop. Veryan proved to be a tiny hamlet with a few snug homes tucked behind their gardens. Coming toward me was a hearty-looking man wearing a brown corduroy coat, smoking a pipe, and accompanying a dog on a brisk midmorning walk. When I stopped to inquire about an electronics shop, he smiled and said, "Well, we have no such thing here, but let me take a look at it."

It took him about five seconds to decide, "I can do that in my little workshop. Just drive around the corner to my garage and we'll see what we can do."

While he worked on my radio, I learned that he was John Baseley, formerly a Midlands businessman, who had, with his wife, moved out to Cornwall a few years ago to open up a tea shop.

Well, one thing led to another, and after deftly connecting the radio's errant wires, he invited me inside to meet his wife, Katie, and to have a cup of tea. Before I knew it, I was seated in a very comfortable little parlor talking about Cornwall creamed teas and the joys of Cornwall in general. I soon discovered that John and Katie had some limited accommodations available at the Old Schoolhouse.

"We have people who come to us every year," said Katie, handing me another cup of tea. "This is one of the most beautiful parts of Britain. We're just a mile from the water in two directions. Our little village with its thatched roofs and stone houses and public footpaths is just perfect for a quiet holiday."

They assured me that if any of our readers gave them a ring and they were booked, they would try to refer them to other similar places in the area. "We would prefer to have people contact us by mail, well before the start of the season," said John.

The village of Veryan is distinguished by having four ancient, completely round buildings, two of them at each end of the village. In olden times, these were supposed to protect the villagers from evil spirits who could not live in a round house because there are no corners where they could hide. A cross on the top of each building was supposed to keep them away from the village altogether.

If any of our readers stop at the Old Schoolhouse, I would be most grateful if they would extend my warmest greeting to Mr. and Mrs. Baseley.

THE OLD SCHOOLHOUSE, Veryan (near Truro), Cornwall. Tel.: (087-250) 1440. A vintage Cornish thatched private house, having for let a twin-bedded apartment annex with a full kitchen. Located in the Roseland peninsula just a few miles from St. Mawes. Please arrange for accommodations in advance by letter. Mr. and Mrs. J. W. Baseley, Proprietors. (See Index for rates.)

Directions: A few miles east of A3078, Veryan is on the St. Mawes-Tregory road.

THE LOBSTER POT
Mousehole, Cornwall

Please note: As we went to press we learned that The Lobster Pot has closed.

The very first time I stopped to ask for directions to Mousehole, a good-natured Cornishman set me straight as to the correct pronunciation: "It is not Mouse-hole," he said, repeating my original pronunciation, "it is Mao-zil." I practiced saying "Mao-zil" assiduously for several miles as I passed through the town of Penzance on Route 3315. Penzance, by the way, is the very one featured by Gilbert and Sullivan, and it is a most pleasant town located on a broad bay with a good view of St. Michael's Mount, a castle on an island in the bay.

Mousehole is somewhat similar to Camden, Maine, having much the same aspect with all types of watercraft in the harbor and also behind the quay. Signs have many references to smuggling and pirates, and several restaurants and pubs derive their names from these Cornish traditions.

The Lobster Pot is a very attractive inn overlooking the quay and sheltered by the sea wall. Major John Kelly has been its proprietor for over forty years and has built the place up from almost nothing. The guest lounges, restaurant, and tiny little bar all have completely enchanting views of the harbor. I noticed many, many books on the shelves, and some loose-leaf folders with quite a number of brochures with information on local attractions. There were also several water colors of St. Michael's

Mount, just up the coast, three miles off Penzance. In both the public and guest rooms, there were a great many flowers.

The bedrooms all appeared to be quite comfortable and are equipped with tea- and coffee-making facilities, color TV, telephone, and other amenities. Most have their own private bath. Prices vary considerably, depending upon the location of the rooms.

Among the culinary treats at the Lobster Pot are shellfish, particularly lobster and crawfish. Helford oysters may be ordered year around.

Dylan Thomas has an interesting association with the Lobster Pot and Major Kelly was kind enough to send me a copy of a letter written by Thomas in July, 1937, which, among other things, mentions that he had been married just a few days earlier in the Penzance registry office. Evidently, the Lobster Pot was a honeymoon haven for this well-known poet.

As I was leaving, I saw the attendant for the town car park leaning on the windowsill of his little booth watching the youngsters in kayaks skimming about in the harbor. "Ever been in one of those?" I asked. He replied, "No, and I ain't bloody likely to be in one, either."

THE LOBSTER POT, Mousehole, Cornwall. Tel.: Penzance (0736) 731140. A 24-guestroom (21 with private bath) waterside inn in one of Cornwall's most fetching small villages, about 3 mi. from Penzance. Breakfast, lunch, tea, and dinner served daily. Open from early March to early Jan. Just short drives to Land's End, the Minack Theatre, and all of the other attractions on both the south and north Cornish coasts. Shark and sea fishing available. Golf about 10 mi. away, as well as tennis, squash, and horseback riding. No credit cards. Major John Kelly, Proprietor. (See Index for rates.)

Directions: Mousehole ("Mao-zil") is about 5 hrs. driving time from London. Use either the M4 or the M5, and then either A38 via Plymouth or A30 via Bodwin. Follow Rte. 3315 from Penzance.

THE WEST COUNTRY

The West Country could well be called a "Kingdom of Legends." Not only does it hold many of the great national legends of Britain that are a part of a centuries-old heritage—the Arthurian Legends, the search for the Holy Grail, and the Glastonbury stories—but it is full of stories of giants and saints, supernatural happenings, ghostly ships, holy places, wreckers and smugglers, pixies and witches in such a profusion as to give the whole of the area a touch of magic.

PORT GAVERNE HOTEL
Port Gaverne, Port Isaac, North Cornwall

"A chap by the name of Ken Duxbury, when he was writing a book about the area, found the signals, the number of lights they showed, to let the smugglers know if it was safe to come into Port Gaverne or if they had to go on to Boscastle with their contraband."

Fred Ross told me this as he showed me the little back room that was part of the original inn, built in 1608 with timbers and spars from ships that had wrecked on the rocky Cornish coast.

A few minutes earlier I had parked in a small area overlooking the narrow fishing cove across the street from the Port Gaverne Hotel and walked past an ice-cream stand toward a knot of people sitting in the sun around the front door, talking animatedly. A rather courtly gentleman detached himself from the rest and greeted me with an outstretched hand. It was Fred Ross, the owner of this interesting small hotel in the tiny fishing village of Port Gaverne, cheek by jowl with the larger 16th-century Port Isaac.

The hotel, with its cozy and interesting pub, is clearly a community gathering place for local folks and fishermen. But it betrays a more cosmopolitan character with the many, many paintings, watercolors, etchings, and fascinating artifacts collected by Fred and Midge Ross over their twenty years as proprietors here. Among other objects of interest were a beautiful early clock in a glass case, a 1628 John Speed map of North and South America, many antique ship and fishing implements, and some tiny dioramas of the original village of Port Gaverne and the cove, with models of sailing ships that brought in coal and limestone and took out the Delabole slate that has been quarried locally since time immemorial.

Mr. Ross took me all around the hotel, up and down twisty stairs, through corridors, and around corners, showing me room after attractive room, all pleasantly furnished and with nice, clean bathrooms. Some of the rooms in the older section had original beamed ceilings; others in a more modern addition were off airy, white-painted, windowed corridors, decorated with plants and paintings. All the rooms had books and magazines, paintings, and TV, and looked most comfortable and agreeable. There are some brand-new suites across the road with completely equipped kitchens, and the residents' lounge and TV room are nicely furnished.

I was surprised to learn that Mr. Ross was originally from Cedar Rapids, Iowa. He met his English wife in New York, and in the mid-fifties took her back to England, where they have been living ever since. "Living in Port Gaverne is an Edwardian kind of life," he says. "The village makes its own entertainment. Everybody knows everybody."

He told me about the nearby Saint Enodoc golf course, on the grounds of which is a church where poet laureate Sir John Betjeman is buried. Tintagel Castle is just up the coast, and there is a coastal hiking path that runs for 300 miles.

The busy dining room of course features local fish, as well as locally grown beef, lamb, and fresh garden produce. The set menu changes daily, with a choice of three dishes for every course. The food is good, simple, home-style, with such local specialties as roast Cornish lamb stuffed with apricots and honey, grilled John Dory, and sautéed sliced duck breasts with green pepper sauce. A very nice feature for families is an early sitting for children, along with smaller portions and menus.

This is the sort of place where you can get a real sense of the daily life of a tiny fishing village, and at the same time enjoy the comforts and conveniences of a very attractive and interesting hotel.

PORT GAVERNE HOTEL, Port Gaverne, Port Isaac, North Cornwall PL29 3SQ. Tel.: Bodmin (0208) 880244. A 19-guestroom (private baths) village hotel on a fishing cove on Port Isaac Bay on the north Cornish coast, south of Tintagel and 6 mi. from the market town of Wadebridge. Restaurant serves breakfast, buffet lunch, and dinner. Open from March to mid-Jan. Offshore and deep-sea fishing, 300-mi. coastal path, swimming, surfing, sailing, golf, backpacking, bicycling, pony trekking nearby. Fred and Midge Ross, Resident Proprietors. (See Index for rates.)

Directions: From A30 to Bodmin, continue to Wadebridge and follow signs to Port Isaac. From Port Isaac, continue on coastal road B3267, going down the hill to the right to Port Gaverne and the hotel.

THE OLD RECTORY
Martinhoe, Parracombe, Barnstaple, North Devon

Tony Pring, the proprietor of the Old Rectory, and I were talking about the North Devon coast. "It's a most interesting area," he observed, "one that is quite neglected by American travelers. It is possible to wander around by car on the country roads and better still, to enjoy excursions on the footpaths. The vistas are magnificent, with great farmlands and occasional views of Bristol Bay."

Tony and I were sitting in the conservatory of the Old Rectory, a trim little Georgian house, built in the early 1880s, adjacent to an 11th-century church. It is surrounded by well-maintained gardens and a small stream that crosses the garden in a series of waterfalls.

All of the guest rooms are rather elegantly furnished, and there are various combinations of twins and doubles, all with private bathrooms. The atmosphere is pleasant and relaxing with nice views of the countryside.

The dining room has some lovely antiques, and Tony assures me that local fresh vegetables, meat, fish, eggs, and cream help to provide dishes such as stuffed and baked rainbow trout, kidneys in sherry sauce, roast lamb with rosemary stuffing, and fresh fruit pies. Picnic lunches are available, if requested the previous evening.

Although rates in the Index are for bed and breakfast, Tony assures me that most of the guests also take the evening meal.

THE OLD RECTORY, Martinhoe, Parracombe, Barnstaple, North Devon. Tel.: (059 83) Parracombe 368. A 19-guestroom (private baths) hotel on the attractive North Devon coast, adjacent to Lynmouth. Breakfast included in tariff; dinner available. Open from April until the end of Oct. Conveniently situated to enjoy all of the Devon cultural, scenic, and recreational attractions nearby, including Exmoor National Park. Not suitable for children under 12. Tony and Elizabeth Pring, Proprietors. (See Index for rates.)

Directions: Turn north off A39 at Martinhoe Cross (look for the hotel signpost); go across Martinhoe Common for about 1½ mi. to the village sign. The entrance to the Old Rectory is immediately on your right.

THE RISING SUN HOTEL
Lynmouth, North Devon

The Sunday afternoon journey from Glastonbury eventually had found me on the A39 through Minehead, then Porlock, where I had a choice of roads to Lynmouth. One is a toll road and, remembering some earlier advice, I elected to pay the few pence and was glad I had, because it afforded a panoramic view of the Bristol Channel, with Wales on the other side. This road rejoins the A39 at the top of the cliffs, and it's only a few more miles to Lynmouth.

The many buildings of the Rising Sun—one of which, by the way, Shelley is supposed to have stayed in—enjoy a splendid view of the ever-changing harbor. At the time of my arrival the tide was out and the sailboats and working boats were on their sides on the mud flats.

Upon checking in I was immediately shown around by the proprietor, a very personable gentleman named Mr. Jeune. Because the building is quite ancient, the hallways and staircases are rather narrow and twisty, and some of the rooms might be described as "snug." Most have views of the harbor.

One of the surprises is a very pleasant, protected garden, carefully designed and manicured, with many types of blooms and a view of the Bristol Channel. During this tour I learned that the novel *Lorna Doone* was somewhat inspired by this inn.

That evening in the low-ceilinged dining room I, appropriately enough, had excellent lamb chops, Devon being well known throughout England for its lamb. The room had a most congenial atmosphere, and I struck up a conversation with a couple from Tampa, Florida, who were enjoying their stay very much.

In the morning, the little harbor was again filled with water almost to the top of the wall, and the boats were bobbing merrily on the waves. The Devon cliffs and the town itself (which reminds me of Portofino, Italy) is very, very pleasant and the prospect of walking on the tops of the cliffs was most inviting. I learned that it is quite crowded in July, August, and September, so plan to visit during other months.

THE RISING SUN HOTEL, Lynmouth, No. Devon EX35 6EQ. Tel.: (0598) Lynton 53223. A 17-guestroom (15 private baths) smugglers' inn overlooking the Lynmouth Harbor in North Devon. Breakfast, lunch, and dinner served daily. Open all year. Most conveniently situated to explore and enjoy the wonderful walks, the Exmoor National Park, and the Lorna Doone country. Sailing, fishing, horse-riding, and golf nearby. Hugo F. Jeune, Proprietor. (See Index for rates.)

Directions: A39 is the main road traversing North Devon, occasionally providing wonderful glimpses of the Bristol Channel and Wales. Outside of Porlock, take the Toll Road, which rejoins A39 and continues on to Lynmouth and Lynton. Hotel is on the harbor.

BICKLEIGH COTTAGE GUEST HOUSE
Bickleigh (near Tiverton), Devon

Stuart and Pauline Cochrane and I were strolling on the banks of the River Exe in the grassy garden in front of the Bickleigh Cottage Guest House. We were talking about what for me was a new discovery: Devonshire cream.

"For one thing, it is a very thick cream," explained Pauline. "It is not runny, it is thick and solid. The cream here is different from the kind served farther west, and one of the things that determines the quality of the cream is the type of cow.

"Our cream is scalded and left to settle. Then, it is skimmed off leaving the thin milk underneath. This 'skimming off' in large pans occurs several times." I soon learned there is nothing quite like thick, buttery Devonshire cream served on scones with fresh fruit jam.

At thatch-roofed Bickleigh Cottage, Stuart and Pauline are carrying on a family tradition that started almost fifty years ago. "The cottage dates back to 1640," explained Stuart. "It was originally two cottages used by the Bailiff of Bickleigh Castle. In recent years, we have made some improvements and additions, and now have a total of nine guest rooms, four of which have private baths. The other rooms all share three bathrooms."

As we paused to look up the river toward the historic bridges reputed to be haunted on Midsummer's Eve, I caught the quick flash of a kingfisher diving in the water.

Pauline laughed and said, "That's one of Stuart's principal competitors. You see, he catches the salmon we use for dinner right here in the river. We also specialize in roast meats, including lamb, beef, steak and kidney pie, and other traditional dishes. Our set menu at night includes home-grown fruits and vegetables. We have our own vegetable garden. We always have pies and crumbles, which our guests seem to enjoy very much." They offer a full English breakfast with cereals, fruit juice, bacon and eggs and sausages.

We stepped inside one of the two dining rooms, whose windows overlooked the pastoral scene of the river and the meadows beyond with the ever-present sheep. There was a little fireplace in the low-ceilinged room, and lots of brass, copper, and pewter, with a rush matting on the floor. Its comfortable and homey aspect certainly would invite a visitor to stay on indefinitely.

Bickleigh is one of many British inns with a twin inn in the United States. The innkeepers of Bickleigh's twin inn, Gary and Sue Mansfield of the RiverSong in Colorado, recently visited Stuart and Pauline at Bickleigh.

The good news from Bickleigh is that an old inn on the other side of the road has been purchased by the Cochranes and includes four extra guest rooms plus two cottages and ample restaurant facilities.

BICKLEIGH COTTAGE GUEST HOUSE, Bickleigh (near Tiverton), Devon EX16 8RJ. Tel.: (08845) Bickleigh 230. A 15-guestroom (4 private baths) riverside country cottage, between Tiverton and Exeter. Bed and breakfast offered from April 1 to Oct. 15; dinner served from May to Sept. Fishing, golf, riding, nearby. Many museums, castles, theater, cinema, and other natural attractions within a short drive. Mr. and Mrs. Stuart Cochrane, Proprietors. (See Index for rates.)

Directions: Use Exit 27 from M5, follow signs to Tiverton. At Tiverton, follow A396 (signposted: Bickleigh) for 4 mi. Bickleigh Cottage is on the left, adjoining the Trout Inn Car Park.

It's not that the distances are very long in the British Isles, it's the many diversions along the way that sometimes make it impossible to estimate traveling and arrival times. Last order times for dinner are included in the Index so that you can see what time you must arrive in order not to find the kitchen door locked. If you are going to arrive later, call ahead—there isn't a hotel/inn listed here that will not make some provision to feed you if they know you can't make it before the kitchen closes.

THE CASTLE HOTEL
Taunton, Somerset

The Castle has a fascinating history that is cloaked in the mists of time. The earliest written record indicates that there was a castle on the site in A.D. 710. There have been three castles since, the present building having stood for the past 300 years. But I leave you to discover the drama and romance surrounding this historic edifice. Be sure to see the 12th-century garden with its ancient moat wall and castle keep.

Tucked away in the center of a bustling market town, the Castle isn't easy to find. The town crowded in around it, seeming to want to huddle close to its protective walls. My first view as I drove around the corner on a narrow street was of the Green and indeed of a castle, with crenellated battlements and great stone turrets on either end. It formed an oasis of quiet in its busy surroundings. The facade was covered with magnificent wisteria blooms, which obviously had to be pruned back around the many stone-mullioned windows.

Poring over the really impressive map that came in the Castle's very useful packet of information in my room, I was struck by the sheer wealth of historic places in the region. The Chapman family has put together an excellent map with careful annotations, which shows the locations of ancient ruins, castles, cathedrals, wildlife preserves and parks, historic houses, and many other points of interest within easy driving distance. They have also outlined several motor tours with directions to such places as the "picture postcard village" of Winsford; Oate Church, where Lorna

Doone was shot; and Lyme Regis, the setting for the film *The French Lieutenant's Woman*.

I had been in correspondence for over a year with Kit Chapman, the second-generation proprietor, planning but never quite managing to pay him a visit. Unfortunately, my itinerary and his schedule did not work out, and I was sorry to miss meeting him. However, he left me in the very capable and friendly hands of David Prior, his general manager.

David and I chatted over a cup of tea in the Rose Room, and when I commented on how much it resembled a very elegant living room in someone's home, he told me that Kit's mother, Etty Chapman, had done all of the decorating in the hotel. She has been dubbed "Director of Aesthetics." Peter Chapman, Kit's father, is head of the company and is still actively involved in the business. His principal passion, David said, is their fine wine list.

A feeling for aesthetics is very evident throughout the hotel. I very much enjoyed my room, with its high casement windows overlooking the town. There were all the amenities of a big-city hotel, with room service (extremely prompt and cheerful), remote-control color TV, towel warmer, huge wraparound bath towel, terry cloth robe, and all the attendant goods and services.

David gave me a tour of the guest rooms, and each is done differently, with great taste and very pleasing color schemes. There are canopied beds, brass beds, quilted beds; some rooms have a traditional feeling, while others have a more contemporary look. Some rooms have figured fabric wall coverings that match the draperies and bedspreads; some walls are covered with grass paper; others are painted in soft hues. Every room has comfortable chairs, pleasant lamps, handsome desks, paintings, plants, and fresh flowers. There is a new section of very luxurious suites overlooking the historic gardens.

As to the food at the Castle, after hearing that a writer for *À la Carte* claimed that the chef might well be a genius, I was eager to see for myself. I felt instant approval upon seeing, in addition to the main restaurant menu, presented in straightforward English, a dinner menu for "guests who may prefer a more simply cooked meal." Having dined rather richly for several previous nights, I appreciated the simply but nicely grilled lamb Barnsley chop with crisp straw potatoes and rosemary béarnaise. The chef also cautions that "vegetables are prepared 'al dente.' Please let us know if you prefer them cooked a little longer."

My meal, topped off with an apple mousse served with glazed apple, struck just the right note for me. Some other dishes on the main restaurant menu were sea bass mousseline garnished with asparagus tips wrapped in salmon on a light lemon and chervil butter sauce; roast lamb with a mint and green peppercorn crust, served with a poached currant sauce; and fillet of venison with celeriac rosti and glazed apples. The desserts looked utterly mouth-watering—I'll mention one—fresh pineapple mousse layered between two meringue biscuits topped with glazed pineapple slices on a plum coulis. There was also homemade prune and rum ice cream, a plate with three kinds of chocolate desserts, and a hot orange soufflé.

"Kit Chapman is an absolute perfectionist," David declared. "He wants his hotel to be one of the best, if not THE best, in the country." He told me that among other illustrious guests, they have entertained the Queen Mother, Princess Margaret, and the Duchess of Kent—not to mention a queen of another realm—Joan Collins.

THE CASTLE HOTEL (Prestige Hotels), Castle Green, Taunton, Somerset TA1 1NF. Tel.: (0823) 272671. U.S. reservations: 800-223-5581. A 35-guestroom (private baths) luxury castle hotel in a busy market town in the Vale of Taunton Deane. Continental breakfast included in the tariff. Dec. 24–27 full board only. Breakfast, lunch, and dinner served daily. Open year-round. Close to King's College, Queen's College, Taunton School, and Millfield School. Surrounded by many historic and literary points of interest. The Chapman Family, Proprietors; David Prior, General Manager. (See Index for rates.)

Directions: Follow signs to town center and continue toward Wellington and Exeter. Go straight through 2 sets of pedestrian lights and after about 150 yards, turn right immediately after the medieval municipal building signposted to the Castle Hotel. This will bring you to the Castle Green and the hotel on the right.

MEADOW HOUSE
Kilve, Somerset

"This is quite literally our home—with all of the advantages and limitations that involves—we don't pretend to be a hotel. We have a maximum of six couples at a time, which creates a very informal, friendly atmosphere." David MacAuslan, a tall, amiable chap, and I were strolling around the lawn and gardens of the pristine, Georgian-style Meadow House. David was telling me how he and his wife, Marion, had decided to forsake their rather frenetic lives in London for the tranquility of country innkeeping. David had been involved with the music record business and Marion was an interior designer.

Originally the rectory for the church down the road, the oldest part of Meadow House dates from 1650, and the walls were built with rocks from the beach, some of which contain prehistoric fossils. Exploring coastal rocks and tidal pools for fossils along the beach, ten minutes away, is one of the reasons many people come to this area.

The Meadow House is down a narrow country lane bordered by hedges, thatched cottages, and beautiful laburnum trees hanging over the road. There are old oak trees and sheep grazing on the surrounding hills and meadows. Across the lane from the Meadow House is a stream and a waterfall.

In this immaculately kept, very attractively furnished house, the eclectic tastes of the owners are displayed in the contemporary paintings, the extensive and varied record collection, books, plantings, and fresh flowers. Guests can relax in the very pleasant drawing room and the study or entertain themselves at the snooker table in the billiards room.

The guest rooms are of generous size and outfitted most completely, including "the biggest, fluffiest towels we could find," David told me.

Marion's cooking tends toward a Cordon Bleu style, although she says it's not exactly French. She does light, delicately flavored sauces and often gathers herbs and vegetables from their garden about an hour before dinner. She presents a four-course *prix fixe* dinner, which includes a starter and a main course. Some of her menu items are a gateau of smoked salmon and lemon sole, a soufflé of sweet corn and prawns, sliced breast of Barbary duck with honey and lemon sauce, and fillets of the new season's lamb with onion and mint purée and red currant gravy. I'm sorry I couldn't stay for dinner, which is served in the attractive pink and rose dining room with tall windows and french doors looking out on the garden. A very dramatic oil portrait of Lady Gwendolyn Churchill hangs on one wall.

David, it turns out, is something of an authority on wines, and his extensive cellar won an award for the best wine list in 1986–87. He told me that wine afficionados come to visit for the express purpose of sampling his cellar.

MEADOW HOUSE, Sea Lane, Kilve, Somerset TA5 1EG. Tel.: 027 874 546. A 6-guestroom (private baths), including a small cottage, serene and gracious home near the rocky coast of northern Somerset on the Bristol Channel, 12 mi. northwest of Bridgwater. Breakfast is included in the tariff. Dinner is served by advance reservation only. Open year-round except for Christmas and New Year's holidays. Advance reservations absolutely necessary. Croquet lawn and billiards on premises. Horseback riding in the Quantock Hills; wooded walks and streams in the Exmoor Hills, a National Trust preservation area; walks along the coast nearby. Children over 12 welcome. No pets. No smoking in dining room. David and Marion MacAuslan, Proprietors. (See Index for rates.)

Directions: From the M5 take the A39 toward Bridgwater and Minehead. Kilve is 12 mi. from Bridgwater. In the village, turn right on Sea Lane, just before the pub. Meadow House is ½ mi. on the left.

THE GEORGE & PILGRIMS HOTEL
Glastonbury, Somerset

Although there is a lot of smiling and joking on the subject of ghosts at various castles and ruins in Britain, I got the feeling that the ghost at the George & Pilgrims Hotel has been taken much more seriously than your average British ghost.

I think that even a ghost would feel easy at this truly ancient hostelry, because it's been providing comfort and hospitality to visitors for more than five hundred years. It was *rebuilt* in 1475, and pilgrims and visitors to Glastonbury have taken shelter here since before Columbus discovered America.

Major Jack Richardson and his wife, Elzebie, make certain that behind the ecclesiastical stone frontage and mullioned windows are found good food, modern service, and comfortable lodgings. In spite of the age of the building, bathrooms are private, and guest rooms have direct-dial telephones.

The entrance is through a flagstoned hallway with oak paneling and heavy furniture. Old timber beams adorned by carved angels and guarded by death masks of monks lend a very special character to the first-floor public rooms. There are many Cromwellian and Glastonbury chairs.

Many of the bedrooms have canopied beds and half-timbered walls. At one point during a major renovation in 1951, the original mud-and-wattle plaster was discovered, and a section has been preserved to show some heather and mud as a good example of the old construction methods.

The top floor has some of the most interesting guest rooms, including the Abbot Whiting Room. He was hung, drawn, and quartered at the time of the Reformation. There is still another small bedroom that was once the confessional of the monastery.

Jack and Elzebie are two very lively and friendly people who are obviously having a wonderful time running the George & Pilgrims. I believe they see it as far more than just a wayside hotel. Jack put it this way:

"Glastonbury is the center of the Arthurian legends, and we have the tomb of King Arthur and Queen Guinevere in the Abbey. Both Anglicans and Catholics are drawn here because it is the origin of Christianity in England. Joseph of Arimethea planted his staff on Wearyall Hill, and this holy thorn still blooms at the time of the Nativity, when we cut a sprig for the royal Christmas table.

"We also have the Guy Fawkes Carnival every year. Miracle plays are staged in the Glastonbury Abbey ruins. The actors are our townspeople. Tor Fair has been held every September for the last eight hundred years." The menu at the George & Pilgrims includes game soup made from local wild meats, homemade bread, poultry cooked in cider, delicious cheddar cheese, and a creamy trifle for dessert. During my noontime visit, there were some enthusiastic tour-bus patrons enjoying lunch in this atmosphere of antiquity.

Did you think I had forgotten about the ghost? The Richardsons assured me that he's been seen about three times in the last two years, and parties of ghost-hunters have visited the hotel. This apparition is apparently one of the monks who lived here before the shameful sacking of the Glastonbury Abbey by Henry VIII.

Reader Comment: "This is a popular hotel, especially with the motor coaches. The area is well worth a visit."

THE GEORGE & PILGRIMS HOTEL, Glastonbury, Somerset BA6 9DP. Tel.: (0458) 31146. A 14-guestroom village inn (private baths) in one of England's most historic areas. Within walking distance of the famous Glastonbury Abbey. Breakfast, lunch, tea, and dinner served daily to non-residents year-round. Jack and Elzebie Richardson, Proprietors. (See Index for rates.)

Directions: Glastonbury is about 25 mi. from Bath and Bristol. Use Exit 23 from M5 to A39 and follow Glastonbury signs (13 mi.).

THORNBURY CASTLE
Thornbury (near Bristol), Avon

It is indeed a happy circumstance that Maurice Taylor and Thornbury Castle have found each other. Mr. Taylor, a distinguished-looking gentleman with a Van Dyke beard, is an art collector who has a fine appreciation for the history and character of this really superb Tudor castle. He is in the process of bringing into clearer focus the neo-Gothic origins of the castle, with his Renaissance tapestries, paintings, chandeliers, and other appointments. He has stonemasons working full time restoring the stonework in some of the towers.

While Mr. Taylor was engaged in an animated conversation with some guests, I read an inscription in a painted panel over the seven-foot-high fireplace in the Hall. It read in part: "This castle was built in the reign of King Henry VIII, A.D. 1514, by Edward Stafford, Duke of Buckingham, Earl of Stafford. . . ."

"Henry VIII might very well have stood right where you're standing now," Mr. Taylor said, returning from his duties as host. "He had appropriated the castle when the Duke was executed for treason. Public records in London show that he spent ten days here with Anne Boleyn in 1535. However, Mary Tudor, who lived here for some years, returned the castle to the Duke's descendants in 1554."

I noticed that the legend over the fireplace went on to declare that the interior of the castle had been restored in the reign of Queen Victoria, which accounted for the heavy Victorian dark wood paneling and other Victorian touches.

The Hall, which I would call the drawing room, has a two-story-high ceiling, colorful heraldic shields, and stained-glass windows, which are really unique. Mr. Taylor explained it to me while we were outside in the Privy Garden, where I could see the towerlike structure. "There are only two sets of windows like these in England, and the other one is in Windsor Castle. There are five banks with 704 curved panes of glass in the upper sections, and the lower windows are in a star-shaped structure."

The furnishings of the castle are luxurious, with deep, comfortable sofas, oriental rugs, fine antiques, beautiful fabrics and draperies, and many huge oil paintings. Mr. Taylor pointed out a portrait of Mary Tudor and a couple of other royal personages.

I liked the warm feeling of the cozy library with all the books, where soft music was playing and there were little nooks for reading.

Mr. Taylor led me up into a tower, going around and around on old stone steps, into the truly regal bedroom once occupied by Henry VIII and Anne Boleyn. The four-poster bed was canopied and curtained in a beautiful rose damask. The room is hexagonal with a carved wood crest in the ceiling and beams radiating out from the center. A settee is in front of the working fireplace, and a curtained and canopied standing wardrobe resembles a medieval tournament tent. This is a spectacular room, with stone mullioned windows and lovely views of surrounding farmlands and the hills of Wales.

Other guest rooms of various sizes in the tower and main section of the house are beautifully furnished. They are all replete with telephones, television, private bathrooms, and other amenities.

I had mentioned the Privy Garden, which was the Duke's private garden. It lies between the castle and the 14th-century Norman church next door. Protected by a high crenellated wall on the front, it's a place for peaceful contemplation, and I could imagine the Duke walking along the paths, enjoying the camellia tree and the ivy and wisteria climbing the castle walls, checking the flowering fruit trees, and perhaps pondering the outcome of his trial for treason. There are actually four enclosed formal gardens, with sculptured hedges, flowers, walks, a vineyard, and little shelters where one can sit and meditate.

I would be remiss not to mention the food. Some of chef Colin Hingson's dishes include calf's sweetbreads with a ginger wine sauce, salmon poached with saffron and sorrel, breast of free-range chicken stuffed with avocado and smoked bacon, and a vegetarian dish of cannelloni with a tomato, aubergine, and basil filling. I understand the wine cellar is extensive and first-rate.

When I asked Mr. Taylor what his aims for the castle were, he replied, "When people come to a castle, they expect a great deal, and I feel they will not be disappointed. It is a very unique place where they will feel at home and comfortable." I think he's being very modest.

THORNBURY CASTLE (Prestige Hotels), Thornbury, Bristol BS12 1HH. Tel.: Thornbury (0454) 418511 or 412647. U.S. reservations: 800-223-5581. A 14-guestroom (private baths) restored Tudor castle, in the Vale of Severn, 5 mi. from the Severn Bridge on the edge of the Cotswolds. Continental breakfast in room or full breakfast in dining room included in tariff. Lunch and dinner served daily. Closed Christmas week. Croquet lawn on grounds. Clay pigeon shooting, fishing on private beat, horseback riding, ballooning, and many natural, cultural, and historic attractions in Bristol, the Cotswolds, Wye Valley, and South Wales nearby. No children under 12. No pets. No smoking in dining rooms. Maurice and Carol Taylor, Proprietors. (See Index for rates.)

Directions: From London, take the M4 to Exit 20. Go 3½ mi., turn left onto B4061 to High Street in Thornbury. Keep left at the village pump, going down a gentle hill. At the bottom a large gate beside the parish church leads to the castle.

STON EASTON PARK
Ston Easton, Chewton Mendip, Somerset

Those who watched the winter series on public television "Treasure Houses of Britain," hosted by John Julius Norwich, will no doubt be well prepared in advance for a visit to Ston Easton Park. At the time I was writing this portion of the book, the series had not been completed and Ston Easton might well have been included.

A Palladian mansion of great distinction, it contains some of the most exceptional architectural and decorative features to be found in Britain's West Country. The house was completed in 1791, and still retains the core of an earlier Tudor house and its Queen Anne additions within the present structure. For 400 years it was the home of the Hippisley family, and more recently it is the home of Peter and Christine Smedley.

On each of my visits I have been tremendously impressed with the 18th-century decorations and the appointments and furnishings of the guest rooms, all of which overlook the romantic parklands. Several rooms have four-poster beds of the Chippendale and Hepplewhite periods.

The menu is English and French, and in 1982 Ston Easton Park was honored with the Egon Ronay Gold Plate Award for the Hotel of the Year.

STON EASTON PARK (Pride of Britain), Chewton Mendip, near Bath, Somerset BA3 4DF. Tel.: (076 121) Chewton Mendip 631. U.S. reservations: 800-323-3602. A distinguished great house of Britain, now a country house hotel, 11 mi. from Bath and Bristol. Open year-round. Breakfast, lunch, and dinner served daily. Convenient to visit Bath, Wells, Stonehenge, Wilton, Castle Combe, Lacock, and Dyrham Park. Peter Smedley, Proprietor. (See Index for rates.)

Directions: Ston Easton is on A37 between Bristol and Shepton Mallet, 6 mi. from Wells and 11 mi. from Bath and Bristol.

In Britain, acceptance of a hotel booking by telephone or in writing is generally regarded as a legally binding contract. If it's necessary to cancel, advise the hotel immediately. If they are unable to re-let the room, the hotel may be entitled to claim compensation—usually two thirds of the agreed price—and any deposit would be included as part of this payment.

HUNSTRETE HOUSE
Hunstrete (near Bristol), Avon

April in Avon is like late May in Stockbridge, and I could feel the bright sun already turning this incredible land into a veritable green Eden, warming my face and vivifying my spirits. Here in the sunshine at Hunstrete House, with clouds (if I may say so) of daffodils and fleecy real clouds in the sky, birds calling to each other, and many other reminders of spring in England, I felt as if I were enjoying some very special moments.

Hunstrete House is a sedate greyish-white stone Georgian house set against a glorious background of gracefully swaying green trees. It is completely surrounded by fields and parkland.

Like a number of other country house hotels in Britain, it has vines growing on the outer walls, particularly on the west side. It is indeed a country house hotel of considerable and deserved merit. There is a beautiful lawn with a big croquet layout, and on one side a high hedge with beckoning arches separates the lawn from one of the most magnificent gardens I've ever seen, outside of those that I have found in grand, great houses in England.

Now, my first bumblebee of the season, after circling me a couple of times and obviously finding that I wasn't quite sweet enough for his liking, started pursuing the daffodils growing in profusion on the lawn.

There are twenty-one most stylish guest rooms, named after birds that can be seen at various times from the windows. Each guest room has its own bathroom, telephone, and television.

On the grounds just a few steps away are the swimming pool and tennis courts.

The owners are Thea and John Dupays, whom I met quite a few years ago on my first trip to Britain. Thea is an artist, and the lounge displays a permanent small collection of paintings by her and two associates.

The cuisine includes venison, breast of chicken, sweetbreads, and other good old English fare. These main dishes are all enhanced during a great many months by vegetables from the extensive garden and provender from the rich local farmlands.

The location of Hunstrete House makes it an excellent place from which to tour England's West Country and possibly even Cornwall in the west.

HUNSTRETE HOUSE (Relais et Chateaux de Campagne), Hunstrete, Chelwood (near Bristol), Avon BS18 4NS. Tel.: (07618) Compton Dando 578. Telex: 449540. A 21-guestroom country house hotel, approx. 8 mi. from both Bath and Bristol. Breakfast, lunch, tea, and dinner served daily. Closed first week Jan.; open Christmas. Tennis, swimming, croquet, deer park on grounds; riding nearby. Exquisite garden. No children under 9. John and Thea Dupays, Proprietors. (See Index for rates.)

Directions: From Bath take A4, then A39 toward Wells. At Bences Garage in Marksbury, follow A368 toward Weston-super-Mare and Bristol Airport. Go 1½ mi. to first turn on right, signposted for Hunstrete; 200 yds. down that lane is the driveway to the hotel.

SOMERSET HOUSE
Bath, Avon

Once again, I was indebted to Bronwen Nixon for introducing me to some really lovely people who are the proprietors of a small hotel in Bath that can only be described as "super."

"Oh, you'll like Jean and Malcolm Seymour very much," Bronwen exclaimed. "They used to be restaurateurs in the Lake District, and now they have Somerset House, a lovely hotel in a quiet residential area of the city."

First, let me tell you about Somerset House. It is a classical Regency house, built in 1829, and because it is a listed building nothing has been allowed to harm its Georgian elegance. The rooms retain their original and comfortable dimensions, and by careful adaptation the Seymours have been able to provide all of the guest rooms with their own bathroom or shower. There are two lounges, a large, quiet garden that features an ancient Judas tree, and a car park within the grounds.

It is about a twelve-minute walk from Bath Abbey, the Pump Room, and Roman Baths.

Bed and breakfast are offered and dinner is on an optional basis, but I would suggest to everyone that they include dinner at the Somerset House during their stay. "If guests only take breakfast with us," Jean declared, "they cannot really appreciate the 'family house' atmosphere, and we don't get to know each other."

When I pressed Jean about the nature of some of the main dishes, she commented that because the standard of produce in the West Country is so superior, their menus have a great many homegrown items such as game, meat, fish, and farmhouse cheese and cream. "Just along the canal bank, we have our own allotment garden where we grow most of the fruits and vegetables served. In our kitchen we make everything that is possible to make. All cakes, pâtés, soups, ice cream, and yogurts are homemade, and almost all of the bread, using stone-ground flour from the mill at Priston."

Besides all of this, I think the special-interest and activity weekends, arranged autumn through spring, provide some fascinating reasons to visit Somerset House. I cannot list them all here, but let me give you a soupçon. There are opera weekends at various times, combining a stay in Bath with visits to the best of British opera outside London. There are Georgian Bath weekends and the opportunity to examine the architecture and see the city through the eyes of famous figures in Bath's past, including Beau Nash, Jane Austen, and John Wood. Visits are arranged to Stourhead Garden nearby and also include an escorted city sightseeing tour. There are other special-interest weekends as well, and I hope that readers will write for an excellent descriptive folder.

To me, Somerset House is a perfect complement to a visit to Bath and I urge everyone to plan ahead on at least a two-night stay, because to see the important points of Roman and Georgian Bath takes at least half a day. Also the cathedral cities of Wells, Salisbury, and Stonehenge, Tetbury and Cirencester, Castle Combe and Bradford-on-Avon are all within an hour's drive away.

SOMERSET HOUSE, 35 Bathwick Hill, Bath, Avon BA2 6LD. Tel.: (0225) 66451. A 9-guestroom (private baths) beautiful classic Georgian house at the lower end of Bathwick Hill. Dinner, bed, and breakfast offered throughout the year. Special-interest weekends available. Especially suitable to enjoy all of the many attractions in the city of Bath and the surrounding countryside. Not suitable for children under 12. No smoking permitted. Jean and Malcolm Seymour, Proprietors. (See Index for rates.)

Directions: Once having arrived in Bath, locate Bathwick Hill on the southeast side of the city and drive about a quarter of the way to the top. Somerset House is at the corner of Bathwick Hill and Cleveland Walk and is readily identified by its garden, which is most unusual for a Georgian house.

Rates for a room for two people for one night with breakfast, except where noted, are included in the Index of this book. They are not to be considered firm quotations, but should be used as guidelines only.

It's not that the distances are very long in the British Isles, it's the many diversions along the way that sometimes make it impossible to estimate traveling and arrival times. Last order times for dinner are included in the Index so that you can see what time you must arrive in order not to find the kitchen door locked. If you are going to arrive later, call ahead—there isn't a hotel/inn listed here that will not make some provision to feed you if they know you can't make it before the kitchen closes.

THE COTSWOLDS AND THE HEART OF ENGLAND
Counties of Gloucestershire, Hereford, Worcester, and Warwickshire

Sometimes known as the West Midlands, this area extends almost the full length of the Welsh border and spreads eastward to include the counties at the very heart of England.

Here is the land of Shakespeare, the Cotswolds, and the Shropshire Lakeland.

In Gloucestershire, which embraces the largest portion of the Cotswolds, are restful landscapes and gentle hills, clear rivers, shallow trout streams, and houses built of butter-colored limestone. It includes Cheltenham, Cirencester, Stroud, Chipping Campden, and Stow-on-the-Wold.

Herefordshire lies against the Welsh borders and has lush green meadows, apple orchards, hop fields, manor houses, castles, and an excellent collection of Elizabethan timber-framed buildings. This is excellent walking country.

The peaceful towns of Shropshire were once outposts on the grim frontier with Wales. Now ponies and grouse share the lonely heather-cloaked heights, and walkers carry A. E. Housman in their kit bags.

Stratford-upon-Avon, in Warwickshire, Shakespeare's birthplace, attracts thousands of visitors every year.

THE COTSWOLDS AND THE HEART OF ENGLAND

RECTORY FARM
Woolstaston, Church Stretton, Shropshire

The road over the Shropshire hills from the Old Rectory Hotel in Worfield to Rectory Farm in Woolstaston was a joy. It was a quiet Saturday afternoon and there was hardly another automobile on the road, most of which winds across the tops of limestone ridges. There are dozens of ways to make this trip and rather than get too involved, I'll just say that even if you get lost, it's a pleasure. Incidentally, I found in many years of traveling in Britain that some of the most common directions include making turns at one or another of the many well-known pubs.

This part of Shropshire is really lovely and is just a few miles east of Wales. I came upon the sign for Woolstaston, pointing west from A49. It is half-concealed by bushes, so have a care. I turned up the narrow-passage road and I must say I had some misgivings when I passed a few piles of red gravel along the side of the road, presumably to be used in case of icy conditions. It was a sunken road, centuries old I'm sure, and I had the feeling of traveling in a sort of green tunnel, open at the top, similar to the sunken roads in Dorset and Devon. The afternoon rain had given way to fluffy white clouds and I soon arrived at the village. I quickly found Rectory Farm, a beautiful, half-timbered house with a splendid view of the rolling countryside. It has a very attractive garden with surrounding fields where Hereford beef cattle and Friesian milking cows graze.

I knocked, stepped inside, and hearing voices in the distance, called out in what I hoped were well-modulated, but carrying, tones. Mrs. Davies soon appeared, and she remembered Mrs. Jane MacDonald, who had recommended Rectory Farm to me originally.

There followed a splendid tour of this long farmhouse with suites and bedrooms overlooking the landscape. The house was built in 1620, and there is a definite slant to some of the floors and stairways; I was pleased to see the exposed timbers and the wonderful, pristine white plaster.

The common room, occupying one end of the house, has a cathedral ceiling with exposed beams, very pleasant furnishings, a friendly fireplace, and a television set.

Rectory Farm was just as Jane MacDonald described it: "A fantastic, super, wonderful farmhouse run by a terrific woman named Mrs. Davies. She is young, energetic, lots of fun, and her house is gorgeous. We had our own wing, complete with mahogany antiques, needlepoint, brass and copper everywhere, and tea and biscuits served at 10 p.m."

RECTORY FARM, Woolstaston, Church Stretton, Shropshire SY6 6NN. Tel.: (069-45) Leebotwood 306. A 4-guestroom (private baths) bed-and-breakfast home on a farm in the lovely Shropshire country. Breakfast, the only meal served. Open from Mar. to Oct. Splendid walking country. Within a most convenient distance of the many recreational, cultural, and scenic attractions in Shropshire and Wales. Not suitable for children under 12. Mrs. J. A. Davies, Proprietress. (See Index for rates.)

Directions: On the A49 between Shrewsbury and Hereford, look for signpost pointing west to Woolstaston; continue (as above) 1½ mi. to Rectory Farm.

THE OLD VICARAGE HOTEL
Worfield Bridgnorth, Shropshire

Christine and Peter Iles and I were enjoying a cup of tea in front of the fireplace in the drawing room of the Old Vicarage Hotel. Although I had visited Shropshire fleetingly on an earlier visit, this was the first time I had been able to talk with anyone acquainted with its many virtues. There was one prime question in my mind and I put it to them. "What is the Ironbridge Gorge Museum?"

Peter stirred another half lump of sugar into his tea and his eyes took on the look of a man fascinated by history.

"Actually, the Severn Gorge was the scene of the remarkable breakthrough that led Britain to become the first industrial nation and workshop of the world," he declared. "Here the iron master Abraham Darby first smelted iron using coke as fuel. This paved the way for the first iron rails, iron bridges, iron boats, iron aqueducts, and iron-framed buildings. The museum itself has actually been created around a unique series of industrial monuments, and spreads out over six square miles of the Gorge.

Ironbridge Gorge has been awarded "World Heritage Site" status by UNESCO.

"It actually takes more than half a day to really see and understand everything, but as an educational and entertaining experience it compares with almost anything in its class. Most of our guests take the time to visit it."

In the course of my short visit with Peter and Christine I found that the entire area had much to recommend it, with a wealth of museums, castles, historic houses, abbeys, archeological sites, and associations with such famous people as Charles Darwin and Charles Dickens.

The Old Vicarage provides an excellent base for both the tourist and the businessman visiting the West Midlands. It is a very handsome Victorian house, built around the turn of the century on two acres of well-cultivated grounds. It is on the edge of a conservation village that has changed little since the 13th century.

I was quite taken with the elegant good taste of the guest rooms, named after the local Shropshire villages, and the warm hospitality of the house.

We talked extensively about the dinner menu, which features, among other things, roast duckling, turbot steak, casserole of wild hare, and lamb cutlets. Some appetizers are crab mousse with prawns and avocado pâté.

The British Tourist Authority, in commending the Old Vicarage, speaks of it as "a good, well-run hotel which offers very good standards of comfort and service. The cuisine is excellent and the period furnishings enhance the peaceful, welcoming atmosphere."

THE OLD VICARAGE HOTEL, Worfield Bridgnorth, Shropshire WV15 5JZ. Tel.: (07464) Worfield 498. An 11-guestroom (private baths) country house hotel located in the Shropshire countryside. Breakfast, lunch, and dinner available. Open all year and all holidays. Most conveniently situated to enjoy the cultural, historical, and recreational attractions of the Severn Gorge, the Clee Hills, Shrewsbury, Ludlow, and Hereford. Also convenient to visit nearby Wales. Peter and Christine Iles, Proprietors. (See Index for rates.)

Directions: First locate Bridgnorth, west of Birmingham. Avoid going to Birmingham and Wolverhampton, and take the other roads to Bridgnorth. The hamlet of Worfield is north on A454, which runs between Bridgnorth and Wolverhampton; turn north at the Wheel Pub. Take the first left fork and go to top of hill.

For room rates and last time for dinner orders, see Index.

THE FEATHERS
Ludlow, Shropshire

I'm sure that many of our readers have seen photographs of the facade of the Feathers Hotel. It was featured for a few months on the television commercials for a popular credit card. In fact, its half-timbered, ornate, Jacobean exterior is one of the best-preserved examples in all of the United Kingdom.

The lobby and reception area have the wonderful patina of antiquity and the public rooms, some named after former reigning monarchs, have carved mantelpieces, stone arches, outstanding paneling, and exceptional decorations.

The hotel has a history dating back to 1603 and, like the town of Ludlow, has had many periods of feast and famine. It is the site of the Ludlow Festival, held during the last part of June through the first ten or eleven days of July, with concerts, quartets, jazz bands, popular entertainers, and theater. I doubt very much if one could get a room at the Feathers at that time without reserving at least a year in advance.

Behind the facade and above the first floor, the Feathers resembles a contemporary American city hotel or motel. The furniture is much the same and the amenities include color TV, glass tops on the dressing tables, and serve-yourself-coffee with non-dairy creamer. I'd describe some of the bedrooms as conventional, but certainly comfortable.

THE FEATHERS, Ludlow, Shropshire SY8 1AA. Tel.: (0584) 5261. A 37-guestroom inn (all private bathrooms) near the border between England and Wales. Open all year. Breakfast, lunch, and dinner served. Quite convenient to enjoy excursions into the Shropshire and Wales countryside. Reservations needed considerably in advance for stays during the Ludlow Festival, late June and early July. Mr. and Mrs. Peter Nash, Managers. (See Index for rates.)

Directions: Ludlow is located on A49 between Shrewsbury and Hereford.

CALCOT MANOR
(Near Tetbury) Gloucestershire

First impressions are important and lasting, aren't they? My first impression of Calcot Manor on a rather chilly morning in April was a cheery log fire in the lounge and lots of comfortable chairs and many interesting magazines. The colors were beige and tan, with other harmonizing tints filling in. The interior has a very contemporary feeling, but looking outside, I realized that the buildings were really ancient. A 14th-century tithe-barn is among the oldest in Britain. It was once part of

Kingswood Abbey, founded by the Cistercians in 1158. (Almost everything in Britain is old.)

Calcot Manor is owned and managed by the Ball family, Brian and Barbara and their son, Richard. Brian began his career with training in Switzerland and is well known in England as one of the leading figures in the hotel profession. Richard is one of the new generation college-trained hoteliers, with experience in London, Paris, and Oxford, and his mother, Barbara, is a most gracious hostess.

Calcot is in the heart of the Cotswolds and is perfect backroading country. You can have a delicious picnic hamper and many sight-seeing suggestions if you like. Or you can have lunch in the light, airy restaurant or on the terrace overlooking the countryside.

Richard speaks of dinner as being "a civilized affair with a consistently delightful menu." The atmosphere is formal, but relaxed.

I am happy to report that since my last visit Calcot Manor has received a Michelin star. Among the main dishes are a prime beef fillet with a red wine and shallot sauce served with crisp veal sweetbreads in a puff pastry case, slices of fresh salmon on a bed of braised onion with tarragon and a wild mushroom sauce, and veal liver and kidney in puff pastry with a port wine and grain mustard sauce. A very enticing dessert is the iced honey and muesli parfait layered between a light hazelnut pastry and served on a fresh apricot sauce. There's a very extensive Sunday lunch here as well.

Each of twelve guest rooms has its own private bathroom and individual decor. There are very attractive wallpapers and matching fabrics and many handcrafted mirrors and flowery chintzes.

Calcot Manor is situated to enjoy the delights of the Cotswolds and generous helpings of England's West Country, including Bath and its environs.

CALCOT MANOR (Pride of Britain) (near Tetbury), Gloucestershire GL8 8YJ. Tel.: Leighterton (066 689) 355/227. A 12-guestroom former manor-farmhouse, now a comfortable country house hotel in the heart of the South Cotswolds. Breakfast and lunch served daily. Dinner is served daily except Sun., when a cold supper is served to houseguests only. Open year-round. Heated swimming pool and croquet on grounds. Convenient to all of the lovely Cotswold countryside. The Ball Family, Hoteliers. (See Index for rates.)

Directions: From the M4 take A46 toward Stroud, turning at A4135 toward Tetbury. Keep a sharp lookout for the entrance, about 150 yds. on the left side amongst a lot of very old Cotswold barns. From the M5 take A4135 for Tetbury as above.

BACKROADING IN THE COTSWOLDS

Some of the best English roads are not on the map, and don't even have numbers. These can be the most exciting, with surprises like pheasants in the fields, foxes—a blur of fur streaking across the road in front of the car—and flocks of birds swooping down to settle in the trees.

It's May in the Cotswolds, and on a sunny day the great rolling fields are separated by hedgerows and trees, and the greenness of the fields is blended with the blue-green of the sky. Ah, the skyline . . . sometimes a row of trees, sometimes a solitary tree . . . or the chimneys and roofs of an old Cotswold farmhouse.

Now, a family playing badminton without a net . . . a weekend mason mending his stone wall. . . . Here and there frequent picnickers.

At the crossroads there's always a pub, a B&B, and stopped automobiles with people bending over maps and peering at signposts. . . .

THE SWAN HOTEL
Bibury, Gloucestershire

Colin Morgan, a rather large man with a genial disposition to match, is the perfect picture of a debonair Cotswold innkeeper. He possesses a very keen wit and is a man who laughs quite easily. I became acquainted with him under rather unusual circumstances.

I had driven to Bibury from Malmsbury on a Saturday morning and upon arrival in the village, I was immediately enchanted by the arched bridge over the Coln River. The Swan's handsome inn sign directed me to its vine-covered buildings and to innkeeper Morgan.

Introductions over, Colin explained that he was on his way to the market

at Cheltenham, about three-quarters of an hour away, and suggested that I might enjoy the trip, which would give us a good opportunity to talk. So, off we went.

After about an hour or so of the attractions of Cheltenham on a pleasant Saturday morning, we returned to the Swan and Colin showed me through the hotel. Then we strolled in the garden across the road, talking about the joys of innkeeping in general.

"I think I'm a very fortunate person," he said. "I have an extremely comfortable inn in one of the beauty spots of Britain and the staff is friendly and courteous. It's like entertaining in my own home."

At this point, we were joined by Bob, a lovable English sheepdog, whose size made him a perfect companion for his master. "In addition to all that," he continued, patting Bob on his woolly head, "here I am situated on the bank of this lovely river in the center of one of Britain's prettiest villages. We are just a few miles of very pleasant driving from Cirencester, Chedworth, Cheltenham, and all of the picturesque villages of the Cotswolds."

Our stroll took us to one end of the gardens to a trout pool fed by a spring. We walked up to the very edge. "These are our own trout," he said. "The guests like to look at them because the water is so clear. Later, they appear on our menu either poached or grilled and served with a special cucumber sauce. I do hope that you'll come next time for our Sunday lunch, when we always have a large sirloin of beef that I carve at the table. It's the time when many residents from the surrounding area join us."

The public rooms and lodging facilities at the Swan are done in quiet good taste, and I could see that Colin has an appreciation for the prints of Hogarth and Thomas Rowlandson. The Swan is a beautifully mellowed old stone building set against a low hill with swaying trees. Most of the guest rooms look over the river and gardens to the adjacent wildlife refuge.

Yes, I quite agree with Colin Morgan. He is, indeed, a very fortunate man.

THE SWAN HOTEL, Bibury, Gloucestershire GL7 5NW. Tel.: (028 574) 204 or 277. A 24-guestroom Cotswold inn, 8 mi. from Cirencester. Breakfast, lunch, tea, and dinner served every day in the year. All of the many scenic and cultural attractions of the Cotswolds are within a short distance. Fishing on the grounds; golf and other sports available nearby. Colin Morgan, Innkeeper. (See Index for rates.)

Directions: From London take the M4 motorway to Exit 15 (Swindon). Follow A419 to Cirencester, then A433 to Bibury.

THE GREENWAY
Shurdington, Cheltenham, Gloucestershire

While I was sitting in the attractively furnished drawing room at the Greenway, looking out of the impressive floor-to-ceiling windows over a portion of the garden with its beautiful sculptured hedges, I happened upon an article in the British magazine *Country Life* dealing with the origins and perhaps some of the meanings of this manor house. The Greenway takes its name from the historic 4,000-year-old walkway running alongside the hotel up onto the Cotswolds. This walkway, the "Green Way," was the original drovers' road through the lowlands.

The house was built in 1584 as a private manor house by the Lawrence family. In the mid-17th century, William Lawrence created special gardens with statuary and decorative structures, all designed as a memorial to his recently deceased beloved wife and only son.

Today, the Greenway is expertly guided by Tony Elliott, who is among a growing number of hoteliers in Great Britain who are preserving the integrity and usefulness of former country manor houses by converting them into country house hotels.

Before relaxing in the drawing room, I had strolled around the extensive gardens in which, on this Easter weekend, some beautiful fruit trees were already in blossom and daffodils and other English spring flowers were in bloom. The extensive lawns and gardens are separated by a brick wall and some handsome hedges. On the front, the lawn stretches right out to the road, and many, many birds make their homes in literally dozens of beautiful old trees. There is a splendid old English oak that may date back to the early 1700s.

My bedroom was on the third floor with a marvelous view through the mullioned windows of the lily pond and the gardens. Each of the guest rooms is individually decorated and furnished with fine antiques, and also with the amenities that today's travelers have come to expect, including a bathroom en suite, direct dial telephone, and color television.

The coach house and stable block date from 1816 and, long before Tony's enthusiastic remodeling, had fallen into what he describes as "a totally derelict state." "We spent months and months restoring them, using all of the original beams, bricks, and so forth, and have created eight very, very large double bedrooms. They have a spectacular view over the walled garden and the hills."

Other innovations at the Greenway include a hot-air balloon service from the front door for those guests who would like a gentle and quiet flight over the Cotswolds; a ride in an 8-seater 1934 Phantom II Rolls Royce; and a two-hour trip around the Cotswolds in an open horse-drawn carriage, which, as Tony explains, "is a particularly delightful thing to do in the early part of the evening. The traffic on the roads has thinned out considerably."

The Greenway is a lovely place to stay for a holiday in the Cotswolds.

THE GREENWAY (Pride of Britain), Shurdington, Cheltenham, Gloucestershire GL51 5UG. Tel.: (0242) 862352. U.S. reservations: 800-323-7308. An 18-guestroom former manor house in the Cotswolds. Lunch and dinner served daily. Restaurant closed for lunch Sat. and bank holidays; Sun. evenings available to residents only. Closed Dec. 28 to Jan. 11. Conveniently situated to enjoy the cultural, recreational, and historical attractions near Blenheim Palace, Stratford-on-Avon, Broadway, Oxford, and the dozens of unspoiled Cotswolds villages. Golf and horseback riding nearby. Children over 7. No pets. Tony Elliott, Managing Director. (See Index for rates.)

Directions: From Heathrow take the M4 to Exit 15 (Swindon) and the A419 to Cirencester. Here, ignore the sign to Cheltenham and continue on A419 to Gloucester. At roundabout just beyond Bridlip, turn left at Air Balloon Pub down hill to A46. Turn right to Cheltenham. The Greenway is at Shurdington, 2½ mi. from roundabout on right-hand side.

LOWER SLAUGHTER MANOR
Lower Slaughter, Gloucestershire

There are various explanations of the word "slaughter." Some say it derives from the Saxon word *sloh,* meaning "marshy place." Others say it is a corruption of the name of a Norman knight, Philipe de Sloitre, who was granted this land by William the Conqueror. All agree it does not refer to some terrible scene of carnage.

"Idyllic" is a better word for this enchanting tiny village. A little stream runs beside the narrow winding street, lined with stately old yew trees, and there are low walls and ancient houses of that soft honey-colored Cotswold stone. I understand it has been described as the most beautiful village in the Cotswolds, and I wouldn't argue with that.

Right in the middle of this village stands Lower Slaughter Manor, behind an imposing wrought-iron fence and beyond a broad lawn with flowers and clipped hedges.

In my conversation with Eric Roby, the new owner of the Manor, I discovered that it has quite a fascinating early history, having been a convent for several centuries before being taken over by Henry VIII when he broke with the Pope. From 1608 until 1964, the descendants of Sir George Whitmore, High Sheriff of Gloucestershire, lived here. During that period there were various reconstructions and remodelings; however, there are still traces of the original building, which dates back to the

1400s. There is a two-story dovecote at the back of the grounds, the largest in Gloucestershire, which is said to have provided food for the nuns.

Eric and his wife, Narney, are dedicated to making this into one of the most beautiful country house hotels in England. Narney, who has worked with well-known chefs, aspires to being one of three women chefs in England to receive a Michelin award. The other two women are restaurateurs, so if she attains her goal, she will be the first woman chef of a country house hotel to receive such an award.

How, you may ask, will she accomplish this lofty aim? Well, I'll mention just a few of the items I noticed on one of her very impressive menus. Among a choice of five starters was a hot mousse of hare with an orange and beetroot sauce served with warm peeled grapes, a panache of fish in a white butter sauce, and a tartlet of duck livers and fois gras served with a port wine sauce. There were five possible main courses, among which were a fan of salmon and brill with baby leeks in a vermouth and fresh basil sauce and julienne of vegetables, roast pigeon with raspberry vinegar and bitter chocolate, and medallions of beef fillet in a cepes sauce with glazed baby onions and light garlic sausage. Some of her sweets included a strawberry tart filled with pastry cream, glazed and served with strawberry sauce and thick Jersey cream, a dark chocolate marquis on a vanilla and cream sauce, and a tulip of banana ice cream with a rich raspberry sauce. Am I making you hungry? There is also a very long list of cheeses and a whole book of wines with relevant literary quotes along with various notations and suggestions.

I would say this is a place where the gourmet might think he had died and gone to heaven.

Everything has been done with style and taste here. The furnishings are eclectic, with many beautiful antiques, fresh flowers everywhere, and lots of books and magazines. I believe a feeling for the comfort of their guests was uppermost in the Robys' considerations.

The guest rooms are all beautifully appointed, and have private bathrooms, color television, radios, telephones, complimentary wine, fresh fruit, and homemade shortbread.

Eric and Narney are a young and enthusiastic couple who aim for the top. I applaud their aspirations and wish them well.

LOWER SLAUGHTER MANOR (Relais du Silence), Lower Slaughter, Gloucestershire GL54 2HP. Tel.: Cotswold (0451) 20456; Telex: 437287 SHARET G. A 21-guestroom country house hotel in a charming, serene tiny village in the Cotswolds, close to Bourton-on-the-Water. Continental breakfast included in tariff. Lunch and dinner served to the public by reservation only. Open year-round. Indoor heated swimming pool, hard-surface tennis court, croquet lawn, and private trout fishing on grounds. Golf, fishing, riding, country walks, and all of the attractions of the Cotswolds nearby. Children over 10 welcome. Eric and Narney Roby, Resident Proprietors. (See Index for rates.)

Directions: From London, take the A40 past Oxford to A429 toward Stow-on-the-Wold. Just past Bourton-on-the-Water, look for signs to Lower Slaughter.

COLLIN HOUSE HOTEL
Broadway, Worcestershire

"I believe we are here to entertain people and to offer them a whole experience, and I don't like to impose my ideas of food on anyone. We try to offer our guests a selection of food that I hope they will find interesting and enjoyable. After all, everyone has different tastes and, therefore, many things have to be taken into consideration. I take my time seeking out good food, including the duckling, excellent steak, fresh vegetables, and I develop a menu from that point. I would describe our cuisine as very English in character. We have an impressive dessert menu. But underneath it all, the only thing that I would hope to achieve is meals that are reasonably well balanced—main courses not loaded with cream; and I deliberately keep a fairly large selection of what I call 'light meals.'"

Judith Mills of the Collin House was explaining some of her deeply felt convictions about not only cuisine, but also hospitality. We were in a very snug sort of tavern room with a large inglenook fireplace and, along with other diners, were making our menu selections before going to dinner. This was my second visit to Collin House, and I must say that the proprietors, John and Judith Mills, have really done a marvelous job of establishing a lovely country house hotel. It is a 300-year-old Cotswold farmhouse on eight acres, and lots and lots of gardens and a swimming pool. All of the guest rooms include bathrooms and are furnished with a lighthearted air. The rooms have been named after plants and flowers.

Although at the time of my visit the beautiful fireplace was flanked with flowers, during many of the other months a large fire blazes here and makes it even more cozy.

One of the engaging things about Collin House is the unusual art collection assembled by John Mills, who has quite a bit of experience in this field. John has prepared a very useful directory of castles, manor houses, bird sanctuaries, walking tours, and back road drives for the guest. His knowledge of such things is incredibly wide.

"What plans do you have for tomorrow?" John asked with a twinkle in his eye.

"Well, you're an expert on the Cotswolds and I was going to put myself entirely in your hands."

"That's a pleasure," he said, and immediately produced a wonderful map of the Cotswolds that included all of the famous villages and attractions. "By the way, you might tell your readers that this is a lovely place to visit in the off-season and we are open every day except Christmas and Boxing Day. Now, do you want to go by car or will you try the walking route?"

A walk in the Cotswolds. It's hard to imagine anything more idyllic.

Reader Comment: "Very friendly staff, even though owners were not there. One of the few places that helped with our bags."

COLLIN HOUSE HOTEL, Broadway, Worcestershire WR12 7PB. Tel.: (0386) 858354. A 7-guestroom (private baths) farmhouse-cum-inn in the heart of the Cotswolds. Breakfast, lunch, and dinner served except for Christmas and Boxing Day. Open all year. Swimming pool. Conveniently located to enjoy all of the scenic, literary, and recreational attractions of the Cotswolds. Many palaces, castles, and glorious countryside drives and walks nearby. Mr. and Mrs. John Mills, Proprietors. (See Index for rates.)

Directions: On A44, 1 mi. from Broadway toward Evesham. Turn right at signpost for Willersey. Entrance 300 yds. on right.

Rates for a room for two people for one night with breakfast, except where noted, are included in the Index of this book. They are not to be considered firm quotations, but should be used as guidelines only.

LYGON ARMS
Broadway, Worcestershire

Guests at the Lygon Arms are presented with a brochure that offers a brief history of the inn since 1535. I mention this to emphasize just how much history has taken place in this inn over the centuries.

The brochure makes fascinating bedside reading, and I am certain that many guests at the inn find it most interesting. For several centuries Lygon Arms was known as the White Hart Inn, and as the brochure notes, "It is of interest that in a four-foot-thick wall in one of the old bedrooms there is a fireplace that appears to be 14th-century work, and one of the mullioned windows in another bedroom has dates from 1586 to 1640 cut in it."

There is a room on the first floor in which Oliver Cromwell is said to have slept before the Battle of Worcester, which took place on the 3rd of September, 1651. It has a carved Elizabethan fireplace and an early 17th-century plaster-enriched ceiling and frieze. There were other manor house ceilings in this part of England that were also decorated in the same manner and so it is believed that a group of traveling artisans did the work on their way through.

Another room has the original 17th-century oak paneling and oak spiral staircase. Charles I, who is known to have passed through Broadway at least five times, may have met some of his local supporters at the inn.

A somewhat modern touch is the bell of the *USS Hunter*, which was given to Britain during World War II and renamed the *HMS Broadway*. The new year is rung in with this bell at midnight on January 1.

Today, the Lygon Arms is a large country hotel with many luxury features. The atmosphere, particularly in the front part of the inn, is definitely "old world." Low ceilings, lots of well-polished wood beams and panels, old fireplaces, canopied beds, and antique wooden chairs and tables are a thrust backward in time.

Every room in this section has an individual color scheme and fine antique furniture. I'm told that this is one of the finest collections of Old English furniture in England.

Because the Lygon Arms and Broadway are very popular with American tourists, guest rooms have been added in new wings at the rear of the building. I would prefer to stay in the old part of the inn, but the new rooms are quite satisfactory.

When I was there in the height of the season in August, the main street of Broadway, on which the inn is located, was a very busy place. Therefore, the garden area in the rear, including some very natural fields and orchards, was most welcome. There was also a good tennis court.

LYGON ARMS, Broadway, Worcestershire WR12 7DU. Tel.: (0386) 852255. U.S. reservations: 212-535-9530. A luxurious 67-guestroom hotel in Shakespeare country, about 40 mi. from Birmingham. Breakfast, lunch, tea, dinner served to non-residents. Open all year. Royal Shakespeare theater, many stately homes or gardens, golf course, fishing, and riding nearby. Adjacent to attractive Cotswold villages and countryside. (See Index for rates.)

Directions: From London take A40 through Oxford to Burford. Follow A424 through Stow-on-the-Wold to Broadway.

MANOR HOUSE HOTEL
Moreton-in-Marsh, Gloucestershire

Moreton-in-Marsh is an ancient Cotswold town situated on the Roman Road (Fosse Way) that runs from Seaton to Lincoln. It's an attractive place with a wide main street lined with shops and houses, built for the most part of the pleasant local stone. The Market Hall and Curfew Tower date back to Tudor times.

Near at hand are the delightful Cotswold villages, including the Swells, the Slaughters, Bourton-on-the-Water, and the towns with their "wool churches," built and enlarged by merchants over the centuries.

The Manor House Hotel is from three to five hundred years old and new additions have been made with great care to match the colors and textures of the original mellowed stone. As in the Mermaid Inn in Rye, there is also a priest's hiding hole, a secret passage, and a bedroom reputed to be haunted.

The guest rooms in the old building are furnished in traditional style with some canopied beds, but with modern services.

English people all love gardens and the Manor House garden is really exceptional. The buildings of the inn and the long high walls keep the noise of the outside world from intruding into its tranquility. There are many varieties of flowers, including roses, and a considerable number of happy songbirds. The old church in Moreton-in-Marsh is off one corner of the garden, and the ancient font, which was used in the church, is now the center of a sunken garden.

On my most recent visit, I was delighted to find that there are many new diversions for enjoying a longer stay at the Manor House Hotel, including an indoor swimming pool, a spa bath, a sauna, and new all-weather tennis court.

MANOR HOUSE HOTEL, Moreton-in-Marsh, Gloucestershire GL56 OLJ. Tel.: (0608) 50501. Telex: 837151. U.S. reservations: 800-223-9868. A 40-guestroom in-town hotel on the main street of a bustling Cotswold village, 27 mi. from Oxford. Open all year. Breakfast, lunch, and dinner served to non-residents. Tennis court, indoor swimming pool, spa bath, and sauna on premises. Excellent walking and splendid backroading nearby. A short distance from Stratford-upon-Avon. Mr. and Mrs. M. H. Fentum, Proprietors. (See Index for rates.)

Directions: From Oxford take the A34 to Woodstock and then on to Chipping Norton and Moreton-in-Marsh on the A44.

EASTNOR HOUSE HOTEL
Stratford-upon-Avon, Warwickshire

This is a very small bed-and-breakfast hotel, modest and simple, but very clean and quite comfortable. The Everitts are most friendly and Graham Everitt is an obliging chap who seems eager to help his guests find their way around Stratford. He directed me to the post office and showed me how to get to the Royal Shakespeare Theatre. He also gave me excellent directions on how to avoid the heavily traveled auto bridge and instead walk on a much more pleasant footbridge over the River Avon.

The bedrooms are simply furnished and are very large and roomy; in fact, several of them are able to accommodate up to three beds. One room could even take a fourth made-up bed. So, this is really an excellent place for families, and at the time of my visit, Mr. Everitt was planning to install en suite bathrooms for five of his rooms.

The Everitts serve an English breakfast in their little red and white breakfast room, and there is a parlor across the hall where guests can relax and get acquainted.

Being on the edge of the town center makes this an extremely convenient place at a modest price for all of the attractions of Stratford-upon-Avon. There is parking space in front and in back of the hotel.

EASTNOR HOUSE HOTEL, Shipston Rd., Stratford-upon-Avon, Warwickshire CV37 7LN. Tel.: Stratford (0789) 68115. An 8-guestroom in-town tiny private hotel a stone's throw from the River Avon. Full English breakfast included in tariff. Open all year. The Royal Shakespeare Theatre within walking distance. Cultural, historic, and recreational attractions nearby. Margaret and Graham Everitt, Resident Proprietors. (See Index for rates.)

Directions: From Oxford on the A34, continue to the intersection of Clopton Bridge. Eastnor House is on the left across from the Shell gas station.

In Britain, acceptance of a hotel booking by telephone or in writing is generally regarded as a legally binding contract. If it's necessary to cancel, advise the hotel immediately. If they are unable to re-let the room, the hotel may be entitled to claim compensation—usually two thirds of the agreed price—and any deposit would be included as part of this payment.

GRAFTON MANOR
Bromsgrove, Worcestershire

Little did I realize when I turned off the M5 to follow the byways and lanes to Bromsgrove that this manor house had such an extensive and exciting history.

Grafton Manor has been closely associated with many of the leading events in English history—Jack Cade's Rebellion, the War of the Roses, the Battle of Bosworth, the Gunpowder Plot, the expulsion of the Stuarts, and the establishment of William of Orange.

Nestled in a hollow off the Bromsgrove–Droitwich Road, Grafton Manor was one of a parcel of estates in the heart of England doled out to members of his family by no less than William the Conqueror. A short, illuminating history of the house points out that the Grafton estate then extended to about 400 acres, every one of which "sheltered resentful tenants and Saxon serfs."

During the second half of the 17th century, there ensued a scandal and an encounter on the field of honor that would make popular American TV evening soap operas seem pallid indeed.

There's much more to all of this, but for further and absolutely entrancing details, I commend you to June and John Morris, who have lived at Grafton Manor since 1945 and have now turned it into a small, stylish country house hotel. Set in twenty-six acres of Worcestershire countryside, the manor offers a peaceful experience in the heart of England.

This architecturally splendid house has been painstakingly restored and furnished in a traditional and elegant style. The guest rooms are complete with such modern comforts as private bathrooms, color television, clock radios, and telephones. Some have their own open fires.

Beautiful scenery abounds, including six acres of well-tended gardens and a tranquil water garden bordering the lake. The large, formal herb garden has been laid out in a decorative chessboard pattern with over one hundred herbs, which are in regular use in the restaurant kitchen.

As the chef, John takes a personal interest in the herbs and vegetables grown in the garden, as well as all other aspects of the cuisine. He told me that he has developed a number of original dishes and lighter sauces. The menu has many enticing items, including gravlax salmon, served in a mild mustard sauce, and marinated leg of lamb, cooked on charcoal and served with lemon butter. A whiskey steamed pudding is always on the menu.

To me, June and John Morris, along with their daughter and two sons, represent a new spirit in British hospitality. They have preserved not only the history of this truly impressive manor house, but also its many beautiful architectural features. They offer their guests what may be the best of England, both past and present.

GRAFTON MANOR (Pride of Britain), Grafton Lane, Bromsgrove, Worcestershire B61 7HA. Tel.: Bromsgrove (0527) 31525 or 37247. U.S. reservations: 800-323-7308. Telex: 254461. An 8-guestroom country house hotel in the Cotswolds and within a short driving distance of Stratford. European plan. Open year-round. Breakfast, lunch, and dinner served daily. Fishing, croquet on grounds. Many other recreational, historical, and cultural activities nearby, including the Royal Shakespeare Theatre in Stratford. No children under 5. The Morris Family, Proprietors. (See Index for rates.)

Directions: Grafton Manor is just off the M5. After leaving the motorway, follow A38 from Bromsgrove to Grafton Lane.

It's not that the distances are very long in the British Isles, it's the many diversions along the way that sometimes make it impossible to estimate traveling and arrival times. Last order times for dinner are included in the Index so that you can see what time you must arrive in order not to find the kitchen door locked. If you are going to arrive later, call ahead—there isn't a hotel/inn listed here that will not make some provision to feed you if they know you can't make it before the kitchen closes.

DERBYSHIRE

My interest in Derbyshire centered around the Peak District, comprising all of the North Derbyshire uplands. The Peak District National Park makes grand walking-and-touring country, easily explored from centers such as Buxton, Bakewell, Melbourne, and Ashbourne.

The region is characterized by many small villages with limestone houses and tiny greens. It is also the home of one of the great houses in England: Chatsworth, the home of the Dukes of Devonshire, which stands in the wide valley of the Derwent River. I think the best way really to enjoy the Peak District is to settle at one of the places I have suggested in the following text. The distances are not very far and the rewards are many. You might find it interesting to stay in one place for two nights or more and take lunch or dinner at the others.

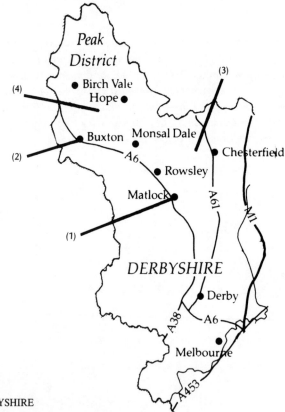

DERBYSHIRE

RIBER HALL
Matlock, Derbyshire

Riber Hall, on the borders of the Peak District, has many things to recommend it. Not necessarily in order of importance are the really auspicious views of the valleys and high, flat moors ending in dramatic cliffs, called "edges." There is also the house itself, dating to Elizabethan times, and so ancient that in 1668 seven generations of the same family had inhabited it. The latest addition (before 1970) was in 1661.

Certainly near the top of the list of its virtues is the wonderful walled garden, dominated by a great copper beech tree. In this garden I was allowing myself to be carried away with the entire Riber Hall atmosphere—being carried away was very easy with the wonderful English blue sky and fleecy clouds, the flittings of white-feathered birds, the green lawns, and beautiful flowers. The phlox and other spring blooms had made the garden their very own, and I can well imagine that some most romantic scenes have been played here ever since the 1400s.

The entrance area is through what was once a dovecote, and the little passages where the doves would fly in and alight are still visible. Beyond the reception area, dominated by flowers, the way leads down some well-worn stone steps into a cozy lounge area, where there was a nice fire burning on the second day of June. I could see out over the valley through a little courtyard. It is obvious that this is a favorite gathering place for Riber Hall guests in the late afternoon and evening.

The dining room is especially interesting, with decor that reflects different periods in the history of Riber Hall and is enhanced by fine period furniture and fireplaces.

There is one guest room in the Hall itself, and the staircase leading to it is lined with some diverting photographs and prints, along with several examples of stitchery.

Most of the guest rooms have been created in one of the stone outbuildings, just a few paces from the main hall. The building is of heavy wall construction and the low ceilings have exposed timbers. There are four-poster beds in most of the guest rooms, and the furnishings would make an antique collector green with envy. Several of the private bathrooms have whirlpool baths.

I arrived just after lunch had been served, but I studied the evening menu with care and noted that among other offerings were medallion of lamb with a port and orange sauce, fillet of turbot served in a light citrus sauce, as well as pork fillets served in a lemon-butter sauce.

Over and above the view, the integrity of the old house, and the enticement of the menu, I think I remember Riber Hall most of all for that truly impressive walled garden. It has a wonderful tranquility and the opportunity for introspection so dear to the hearts of Britishers everywhere.

RIBER HALL (Pride of Britain), Matlock, Derbyshire DE4 5JU. Tel.: (0629) 2795. U.S. reservations: 800-323-7308. A 12-guestroom (private baths) Elizabethan country house hotel on a high hill in the Peak District. Breakfast, lunch, afternoon tea, and dinner. Open all year. All-weather tennis court on grounds. Adjacent to Riber Castle. Conveniently located to enjoy all of the recreational, cultural, and scenic attractions in the Peak District. Alex Biggin, Proprietor. (See Index for rates.)

Directions: Leave the M1 at Exit 28 and continue to A38 toward Matlock for 3 mi. Turn off on A615, signposted Matlock, for 7 mi., at the end of which you come to a very long hill into the village of Tansley. Continue to bottom of hill and about 20 yds. on your left there is a UK filling station. The road to Riber runs on the near side of the filling station on your left-hand side. Continue on 1 mi. to the top of the hill.

THORN HEYES
Buxton, Derbyshire

If, by some chance, you have not heard of the Peak District, much less visited it, I can assure you that in the process of traveling throughout the U.K. I have met many Britons who have yet to visit it.

I have explained the virtues of Derbyshire elsewhere, but a visit should be made to the spa town of Buxton, which was discovered by the Romans. It nestles in a natural bowl surrounded by high moors at a thousand feet above sea level.

The town has many interesting buildings, including the famous Crescent; the Old Hall, where Mary Queen of Scots stayed; and the restored Opera House, the focal point, with the Pavilion Gardens, for the annual festival, held during July and August each year.

Built in 1860 of local stone, Thorn Heyes was a gentleman's residence, and its architecture is quite in harmony with the Victorian elegance of the town.

It is a very quiet, rather conservative accommodation, where the traveler would be more likely to meet Britons than visitors from other countries. There are several other so-called private hotels in Buxton of the same size and demeanor, but I found the rather low-keyed atmosphere maintained by David and Pat Green quite appealing.

They offer bed, breakfast, and the evening meal on request. The dining room looks out over the very pleasant garden, as do many of the bedrooms.

The main dishes at the evening meal feature home-cooked food and include soups, meat pies, roasts of beef, lamb, and pork. A vegetarian meal is also available. As Pat Green explains, "We try to be friendly, clean, and give good value at the table."

THORN HEYES, 137 London Rd., Buxton, Derbyshire SK17 9NW. Tel.: (0298) 3539. A conservative 7-guestroom (private baths) private hotel on the outskirts of Buxton. Open every day. Breakfast is included in the room rate. An optional evening meal is also served. Quite conveniently located to enjoy all of the many recreational, cultural, and scenic attractions of the Peak District. Pat and David Green, Resident Proprietors. (See Index for rates.)

Directions: Locate Buxton on your map; note that it is about 45 min. from the M1, M6, and Ringway Airport (Manchester). Thorn Heyes is on A515 coming from Ashbourne.

CAVENDISH HOTEL
Baslow, Derbyshire

The British have a wonderful expression: "Good value for the money." I think that describes the many virtues of the Cavendish Hotel.

In the heart of the Peak District National Park, it is set in the Chatsworth Estate, owned by the Duke and Duchess of Devonshire. The Cavendish Hotel is actually within a very short walk of Chatsworth, one of England's most beautiful and best-loved "great houses" and one of the many reasons to visit the Peak District.

A very imposing, two-story stone building with extensive lawns, gardens, and terraces, the Cavendish is situated so that all of the public rooms, dining rooms, and bedrooms overlook the valley of the Derwent River.

The furnishings, some of which enjoyed an earlier career at Chatsworth House, are entirely in keeping with the subdued yet casual atmosphere, and great taste and care are evident throughout the hotel. There are open fires, oak beams, fresh flowers, lovely views, and a friendly staff.

It is my understanding that originally there was an inn, called the Peacock, here for so long it is uncertain when it was built. The Peacock was the property of the Duke of Rutland and served the turnpike between Chesterfield and the spa town of Buxton. It became the Duke of Devonshire's property about 1830, and in the early 1970s was rebuilt as the Cavendish, with decor and furnishings selected by the Duchess herself.

The hotel has all of the amenities the British are very fond of, including breakfast any time in the morning; lunch served either formally in the Paxton Room or in the bar or gardens or even as a picnic; dinner is served very late (until 10 p.m.).

The menu for both lunch and dinner is lavish, much larger than I can cover here. For lunch I enjoyed the roast partridge with grape and Burgundy sauce.

Golfers will enjoy the putting greens and golf driving net, and fishermen will find the waters well stocked.

The Cavendish is a most unique experience—"Good value for the money."

CAVENDISH HOTEL, Baslow, Bakewell, Derbyshire DE4 1SP. Tel.: (024-688) 2311. A 23-guestroom (private baths) country house hotel in the heart of the Peak District. Open every day of the year. Breakfast, lunch, dinner, and tea served. A few moments from Chatsworth, one of England's most beautiful stately homes, with private art collections, state apartments, gardens, cascades, and fountains (open Mar. 27 to Oct. 30). Cavendish is ideally situated to enjoy all of the recreational, cultural, and scenic attractions of the Peak District. The Duke and Duchess of Devonshire, Owners; Eric Marsh, Manager (and tenant). (See Index for rates.)

Directions: From M1, use Exit 29 near Chesterfield; 2½ hrs. from London.

ROWAN HOUSE
Great Hucklow, Derbyshire

The village of Great Hucklow is high in the Peak District about twelve miles from the spa town of Buxton. Locating it and driving there is half the fun, although the directions I have included here should be adequate.

It is in many ways a typical, unpretentious, English B&B with two clean guest bedrooms, one with a wash basin, sharing a bathroom.

There is a small B&B sign at the front on a low stone wall, behind which is a very pleasant garden and some lawns.

As is the case with most B&Bs, the guests gather around the breakfast table. Here, Mrs. Susan Morgan serves a full English breakfast, and at the time of my visit there was lots of chatting about places we had all been, including the famous church at the nearby village of Eyam. There is also a comfortable lounge for guests and a good collection of literature, which would be useful in touring the Peak District.

ROWAN HOUSE, Gt. Hucklow (near Buxton), Derbyshire SK17 8QU. Tel.: (0298) No. Tideswell 871715. A 2-guestroom (shared bath) village B&B in the beautiful Peak District of Derbyshire. Dinner served on request. Open year-round. Ideal center for a sightseeing holiday. Near Chatsworth House, Haddon Hall. Mrs. Susan Morgan, Proprietress. (See Index for rates.)

Directions: From Buxton take A6 toward Bakewell; turn left on B6049 to Tideswell and through the crossroads at the Anchor Pub. After about 1 mi., turn right at the village of Windmill and follow signs to Great Hucklow and Gliding Club. In Gt. Hucklow look for B&B sign on the left opposite Unitarian Conference and Holiday Center.

LANCASHIRE
County of Lancashire

Lancashire is one of the most diversified areas in England. Along the coast are invigorating holiday resorts, such as Blackpool and Morecambe. It is a region of vast and beautiful estuaries, old-world villages, and wide recreational areas.

A great deal of my interest was centered in the fell country to the northeast of Preston, near the town of Clitheroe.

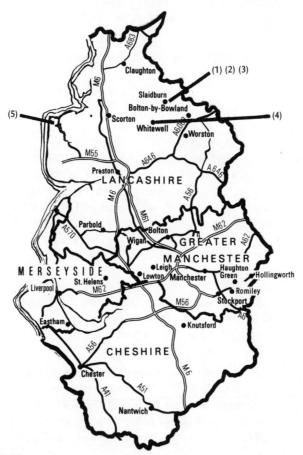

LANCASHIRE

HARROP FOLD COUNTRY FARMHOUSE HOTEL
Bolton-by-Bowland, Clitheroe, Lancashire

Let me share a portion of a letter I recently received from Victoria Wood, who, with her husband, Peter, and their two sons, is the proprietor of Harrop Fold.

"Harrop looks really lovely now—everything is at its best. The hawthorne blossoms are magnificent, weighing the branches down on the trees. Swallows and swifts are darting to and fro catching flies for their young. The hedgerows and fields are full of wild flowers, their growth has been encouraged by the wet spring, and now the warmth. Farming-wise we are waiting for the grass to thicken in leaf, and in about another ten days Daniel will be ready to reap. Before then he will start to clip the sheep—all 200 of them! We have had a good lambing time in spite of the weather, due largely to Daniel's expert shepherding—what a difference it has made to Peter to have him at home.

"The garden is looking super too—Andrew's patient care is paying dividends. His attentions have extended to keeping the common well under control (at great expense, I may add). Harrop has become home for a second-hand Montfield tractor that makes light work of grass cutting.

"However, Andrew has become our full-time chef, and his creativity in the kitchen has been warmly praised. He bakes all of our bread, quite a mammoth task, and it is so good. He has finally settled on a granary recipe and is swapping bread-rising stories with all the whole-food enthusiasts."

The farmhouse accommodations are rustic-elegant. They all have private bathrooms, very comfortable, firm mattresses, and such fetching names as Meadow Sweet, Forget-me-not, and Buttercup.

The old farmhouse lounge is comfortable and easy to relax in with the original oak beams and meat hooks and a mellow pine cupboard with brasses and interesting pieces. A log fire burns merrily in the evenings in the stone fireplace.

If all this sounds rather intriguing, may I suggest you write to Victoria Wood for a brochure about the farm.

HARROP FOLD COUNTRY FARMHOUSE HOTEL, Bolton-by-Bowland, Clitheroe, Lancashire BB7 4PJ. Tel.: (02007) 600. A 7-guestroom (all have private baths) guest house in the lovely farming country of Lancashire. Open all year. Breakfast and afternoon tea included in tariff. Evening meal available on request. Conveniently located to enjoy excursions into the Lancashire and Yorkshire Dales. Private trout and salmon fishing on the Hodder and Ribble rivers. Peter and Victoria Wood, Proprietors. (See Index for rates.)

Directions: Clitheroe, which is reached by taking Exit 31 from the M6 and continuing on A59, is the key to locating Harrop Fold. When you get to Clitheroe, telephone the farm for directions into the rural countryside.

PARROCK HEAD FARM
Slaidburn, Clitheroe, Lancashire

The coffee was hot and the cream was thick. Richard and Vicky Umbers, the proprietors of this guest house, and I were enjoying the marvelous euphoria that follows a satisfying dinner. It was quite natural for the conversation to turn to regional British cooking. Richard was unstinting in his praise of their kitchen, "We make the best roast beef and Yorkshire pudding I've ever had, and I'll put our Lancashire hot pot up against anybody's! Here on the farm we serve lots of local roast lamb with mint sauce, and also cheese and onion pie."

They were full of enthusiasm over what fun it is to keep a small country hotel and how they meet people from all over the world. "We try to keep our farm as natural as possible," explained Vicky, passing me another helping of a tasty tart. "Almost everything we have on the table is raised right here on the property. I love to cook and this makes it all the more fun. We keep our kitchen door open to the guests and many of them come out to visit with us while we're mashing the potatoes or basting the lamb."

Parrock Head Farm offers dinner as well as bed and breakfast. The guest lounge has a whole wall of books, a table with many maps and suggestions about all the things to be enjoyed in this part of Lancashire and nearby Yorkshire.

There are several combinations of suites and guest rooms, all with private baths.

Even as we talked, the sun went down behind the fells and the wonderful countryside was bathed in a golden light.

During the recent Christmas season I was delighted to receive a beautiful full-color "Lancashire Life" calendar. Among the photographs of the Lancashire Fells area there was one of a farm in the Trough of Bowland, not far from Parrock Head.

PARROCK HEAD FARM, Slaidburn (near Clitheroe), Lancashire BB7 3AH. Tel.: (02006) Slaidburn 614. A 9-guestroom small country hotel, 8 mi. from Clitheroe and about 1 mi. from Slaidburn, in the Bowland Fells area. Breakfast, lunch, and dinner served to houseguests. Open all year except Dec. and Jan. Conveniently situated for walking and driving trips in the Lancashire countryside. Golf and fishing nearby. Located just 30 mi. from the coastline, 35 mi. from the Lake District, and 35 mi. from the Yorkshire Dales. Richard and Vicky Umbers, Proprietors.

Directions: Leave motorway M6 at Junction 31. Follow A59 to Clitheroe, 15 mi. Turn left at Clitheroe roundabout to B6478. Continue to Waddington, Newton, and Slaidburn. Turn left at Slaidburn and after 1 mi., Parrock Head Farm is on the left-hand side and plainly marked.

THE HARK TO BOUNTY INN
Slaidburn (near Clitheroe), Lancashire

First the name. "Bounty" was the name of a hound owned in the dim past by a local squire who, sitting in the pub and hearing a pack of hounds baying in the distance, always insisted that he could separate Bounty's voice from those of the others. Hence, the term "Hark to Bounty!"

"It may sound farfetched," said Richard Holt, who with his wife, Patricia, are the innkeepers at this country hotel, "but it's as good a reason as any to name an English pub, and maybe better than most."

Richard and I were enjoying the bar lunch along with many other "locals" and travelers in this rather remote Lancashire residential pub. The bar lunch is an entirely British phenomenon, and all of the pubs and inns in Britain are very proud of the fact that they can provide many varieties of salads, pâtés, meat pies, and the like. Here at the Bounty, patrons were sitting around small tables. The conversations were lively, and the feeling was good.

I was surprised at the number of patrons, because Slaidburn, a very small, very ancient village, seemed so remote. Richard explained that the inn has an excellent reputation for food. "They come from miles around." Among the tasty temptations on the menu are roast guinea fowl, local trout, and tenderloin of pork.

Richard and his wife, Patricia, are just the type of people for whom an inn is an excellent setting. Both are very cheerful and energetic. "We serve food all day from breakfast time until 10 p.m. This is very popular because so many pubs close their doors when their bars are not open."

The Bounty dates back to the 13th century and like other traditional inns has served a number of other purposes over the years. On the second floor, there's a remarkably well preserved courtroom which was still in use as recently as 1937. It had been visited by traveling justices since the 14th century, being the only courtroom between York and Lancaster. This area was once famous for its witches.

There are eight very pleasant and comfortable bedrooms, most with private baths.

"Our guests not only have the advantage of being able to enjoy the Lancashire fells [hills], but we're also within very easy driving distance of the holiday resorts and beaches to the west. We don't see that many Americans, because they stay on the M6 headed north from Bath or Wales to the Lake Country. However, from Slaidburn we have several meandering secondary roads through the fells that offer splendid scenery and lead on to Kendall," remarked Richard.

The Bounty is very much the community center of this stone village and the scene of local celebrations such as weddings, rallies, and political gatherings.

"As you know we sold Parrock Head Farm to Richard and Vicky Umbers and we're finding it's quite different and great fun to be at a busy pub here in the center of downtown Slaidburn," exclaimed Pat, with a mischievous wink. Downtown Slaidburn probably doesn't have more than two shops beside Hark to Bounty.

THE HARK TO BOUNTY INN, Slaidburn, Clitheroe, Lancashire, England. Tel.: (02006) Slaidburn 246. An 8-guestroom traditional country inn located in a cloistered Lancashire village approx. 7 mi. from Clitheroe. Breakfast, lunch, tea, and dinner served to nonresidents. Open every day in the year. Slaidburn is located in the heart of the Forest of Bowland, an ideal center from which to explore the open moorland and quiet riversides. Several castles, recreation areas, and wonderful backroading and walking. Fishing, riding, grouse shooting, other sports available. Richard and Patricia Holt, Proprietors. (See Index for rates.)

Directions: Use Exit 31 from the M6 and follow A59 to Clitheroe. Take B6478 through Waddington to Slaidburn.

In Britain, acceptance of a hotel booking by telephone or in writing is generally regarded as a legally binding contract. If it's necessary to cancel, advise the hotel immediately. If they are unable to re-let the room, the hotel may be entitled to claim compensation—usually two thirds of the agreed price—and any deposit would be included as part of this payment.

A LANCASHIRE IDYLL

Some people take their dogs for a walk; I take my tape recorder. Such was the case in late May when I arose early and went for a walk in the Lancashire countryside. Here are a few of my impressions as I dictated them into my recorder:

"Beautiful stone walls on each side of the road leading past ancient farmhouses . . . Rippling waters of the brook mingling with the sound of early morning crows and the animals at the watering troughs . . . Milk already out on the platform waiting for the pickup . . . Trees getting well armed for their full leaf . . . The sheep ever placid, ever grazing, to be seen in all directions, and always turning to watch me as I pass by. I think they can hear me talking to the tape recorder. Here's a public footpath . . . continuing down into the meadow and over the rise into the forest . . . More black-faced sheep with lambs still at the nursing stage, and as the mothers move away from me their young charges plainly show their annoyance.

In front of me a rabbit disappears into the underbrush . . . down in the meadow, white birds dot the lush green grass . . . Now, near the crest of a hill, a bench with a small medallion that says simply: "Elizabeth, 1953." This is the simple country way of recognizing the Queen's coronation . . . A wooden bench has been placed on a concrete slab and is ideal for sitting

*and looking over the fells and the peaceful countryside, down into the
village of Slaidburn.*

*. . . Now along the side of the road, a huge oak whose center section
has been torn away by the elements—its two side branches still remain—
looking for all the world like some gigantic figure with its arms raised
imploringly to heaven . . .*

*Here, a herd of cows moving toward the barn . . . overhead, two birds
shrilly signal to each other . . . in the middle distance, a sheepdog
running through the fields . . .*

*Reluctantly turning back to the village . . . my presence is being
announced by feathery watchers calling back and forth . . . different calls
and different greetings to the morning . . .*

*Two or three errant sheep on the road, finding grass on the outside of the
fence sweeter than on the inside . . . there are always a few who seem to
find their way out of the enclosures. Across the valley, a man walking in the
field, approaching a herd of sheep . . . he seems to be searching for
something. I know not what.*

*Most of all, it is a refreshingly complete natural quietness, with the
pastoral accompaniment of the sounds of nature wafting up from the
valley—the occasional baa-ing of the sheep and the moo of the cattle.
These are the sounds that inspired the poets of the English
countryside . . .*

*Returning to town on the quiet road . . . the small garden area over-
looking the Ribble River . . . a wonderful view of its three arches. On one
of the benches, a small plaque, saying "Presented by the Ribble Valley
Borough Counsel to Slaidburn, the Best Decorated Village in the Queen's
Silver Jubilee Year, 1977."*

THE INN AT WHITEWELL
Forest of Bowland, Clitheroe, Lancashire

"Typically English"—how blithely we Americans use that term, and
yet as I went back over my notes on the visit to the Inn at Whitewell those
two words kept coming to the front of my mind. It is a real country-cum-
village hotel in a section of England that really has not yet been discovered
by the North American traveler. I think this inn is difficult to find, and if it
were not for the good offices of the innkeepers at Parrock Head Farm in
nearby Slaidburn, I never would have discovered it at all.

As soon as I saw the Inn at Whitewell one beautiful Saturday morning, I
knew it would be a special place. It was indeed a rather bustling hotel, as
evidenced by the numbers of English couples who were making use of the
reception room and lounge on a weekend holiday. Meanwhile, more

guests were coming in for that great English tradition, morning coffee, which has become almost as important as afternoon tea.

I was given a very courteous tour of all of the guest rooms, many of which look out over the Hodder river. The view is of the valley with the fells on each side. The large dining room has a big bow window that also overlooks the river. I was amused to see some interesting and colorful prints by Thomas Rowlandson.

The evening meal has four courses, including duckling, lamb, pork, and halibut as the main dishes.

Mention should be made of the parish church of Saint Michael, immediately adjacent, with a history dating back many centuries. Walking through the graveyard and into the church itself reminded me that my good friend, Rev. Robert Whitman in Lenox, Massachusetts, a fellow Anglophile, would indeed find it interesting and worthwhile. At the back of the church there was a reproduction of the list of disbursements made for the repair of the chapel in the year 1666, which came to 37 pounds 2 pence. I dropped a donation in the milk churn, which had been placed at the gate of the church; the coins bounced around on the bottom with a hollow, tinny sound. A recent note from Richard Bowman reports that he has added a gallery, which features contemporary artworks and some early sporting prints.

Visit Whitewell and stay overnight at the inn, or at least enjoy a bar lunch or dinner. I promise you'll never forget it.

THE INN AT WHITEWELL, Forest of Bowland, Clitheroe, Lancashire BB7 3AT. Tel.: (02008) Dunsop Bridge 222. A 10-guestroom (6 have private baths) traditional country inn situated in a most pleasant hamlet in the valley of the Hodder River in rural Lancashire. Breakfast, lunch, dinner, and bar supper served. Open all year. Most conveniently located for pleasant walks or drives into the Lancashire and nearby Yorkshire countryside. Richard Bowman, Innkeeper. (See Index for rates.)

Directions: The key once again is the town of Clitheroe, which is on A59 between Preston and Skipton. Once in Clitheroe, telephone the inn for further directions.

THE RIVER HOUSE
Skippool Creek, Thorton-le-Fylde, Lancashire

There is so much to write about concerning the River House, that I wonder just where to begin. It's situated on the banks of the River Wyre estuary, which is most attractive. The furnishings and decorations in the house deserve more than a passing mention. The same is certainly true for

the unusual menu. Furthermore, there are a few pieces of very small adult furniture actually used by General Tom Thumb, who was one of P. T. Barnum's prime attractions during the 19th century.

Proprietor Bill Scott, who is also a man of opinions and ideas, speaks of the River House food as being the principal reason for guests to make a visit. "We have been included in many of the U.K. country house hotel guides, as well as the Master Chefs' Guide. Both Carole and I are very proud of our growing reputation."

Whilst I was enjoying an extremely gratifying bar lunch at this Victorian house, built in 1830 as a gentleman farmer's residence, Bill explained some of his philosophy of cuisine:

"We cook each meal individually and all food is freshly cooked from top-quality produce. Incidentally, tables must be booked in advance.

"Our à la carte menu includes Dover sole stuffed with fresh salmon mousse, and other local seafood. We also serve our own home-cured gravaad lax, breast of duck with orange and green peppercorn sauce, eye of loin of lamb with garlic cream sauce, veal schnitzel, partridge, grouse. pheasant, and venison.

"We also have a few oriental dishes, including salmon sashimi and salmon Angelique. Also, we have a beautiful Scotch salmon served with a soy-based sauce. We may well be the only non-Japanese restaurant in the country serving Japanese food."

The guest rooms are very comfortable in a natural, relaxed way. I mentioned this to Bill during our little tour, and he responded, "We were once described in *Cosmopolitan* as being 'shabbily comfortable.' I took that as a compliment."

The dining room has a most attractive view of the River Wyre. The view is out over the lawn and the rose garden to the boats moored at the quaint little wooden jetties that go out from the road over the salt marsh to the mud bank. This is a tidal scene that changes almost every fifteen minutes.

There is much more to say about the River House, but Bill was particularly adamant about my being certain to feature their food as the real attraction. I just don't have space to explain the General Tom Thumb furniture, do I?

THE RIVER HOUSE, Skippool Creek, Thornton-le-Fylde, Lancashire FY5 5LF. Tel.: (0253) Poulton-le-Fylde 883497. A 4-guestroom waterside hotel just off the M6, south of Lancaster and east of Blackpool. Breakfast, lunch, and dinner served daily except for two-week staff holiday (please inquire). Pleasant amenities, including television, room telephones, and electric blankets. Fishing, golf, and boat hire nearby. Bill and Carole Scott, Proprietors. (See Index for rates.)

Directions: From M6 follow M55 to Exit 3; go north on A585, following signs for Fleetwood through three traffic lights to big roundabout, following signs to Little Thornton. On leaving roundabout, immediately follow sign to Skippool Creek (this is a very small road to the right, immediately before the Buccaneer Pub). This leads down to the River Wyre estuary. Look for a small sign pointing to the River House.

Rates for a room for two people for one night with breakfast, except where noted, are included in the Index of this book. They are not to be considered firm quotations, but should be used as guidelines only.

It's not that the distances are very long in the British Isles, it's the many diversions along the way that sometimes make it impossible to estimate traveling and arrival times. Last order times for dinner are included in the Index so that you can see what time you must arrive in order not to find the kitchen door locked. If you are going to arrive later, call ahead—there isn't a hotel/inn listed here that will not make some provision to feed you if they know you can't make it before the kitchen closes.

YORKSHIRE

Yorkshire is England's largest county, comprising two national parks, one hundred miles of coastline, and many attractive fishing villages. The county is centered around the ancient city of York with its four great gates, old streets, and world-famous York Minster, a church that contains over half the medieval stained glass left in England. The castle museum is another principal attraction with recreations of complete Victorian and Edwardian streets and old crafts workshops.

Yorkshire is divided into sections called "Ridings," a Scandinavian term meaning one-third. The North Riding is famous for its national park, its popularity with walkers, and its lavish display of heather. The West Riding contains the Yorkshire Dales National Park and is one of the most peaceful and unspoiled regions in Britain.

West Yorkshire is the land of the Brontë sisters, Charlotte and Emily. Many people make a literary pilgrimage to the village of Haworth, located in typical brooding Brontë country among the rolling moors and dark purple hills. It is situated between Leeds and Blackburn, south of Keighly. The Brontë parsonage has been reproduced to look as it did when the sisters lived there with their father.

YORKSHIRE

OLD SILENT INN
Stanbury (near Haworth), West Yorkshire

There are now two reasons to visit this part of Yorkshire; the first is to experience the Brontë presence and the other is to visit the Old Silent Inn.

The Brontë presence is experienced by visiting the Parsonage in Haworth; once the home of the Brontë family, it is now an intimate museum cared for by the Brontë Society. The rooms of this small Georgian parsonage are furnished as in the Brontës' day, with displays of their personal treasures, pictures, books, and manuscripts. Visitors can see where the writers of *Jane Eyre* and *Wuthering Heights* lived.

Now to the Old Silent Inn, a few miles out in the West Yorkshire countryside, which would be a curiosity no matter where it was located. As the story goes, Bonnie Prince Charlie, in his flight from Scotland, took refuge here, and because everyone kept silent about his presence, the inn was named "Old Silent."

It is jammed from top to bottom with knickknacks and photos and prints of the royal family, including the Queen and Duke of Edinburgh and the Prince and Princess of Wales. Around the inside of one of the dining rooms are display cabinets with wonderful collections of silver, while the walls are covered with handpainted dishes.

The guest rooms are traditional pub-inn rooms, all with private baths, telephone, television, and videotapes.

The menu is extensive, with everything from bar snacks to a full à la carte dinner, including soup, country pâté, individual dishes of home-made steak and kidney pie and chicken pie. There is also the Plowman's Brunch, with two cheeses, potatoes, a hard-boiled egg with pickles, lettuce, and tomatoes. And much, much more.

Children are welcome, and children's portions are available.

OLD SILENT INN, Stanbury (near Haworth), West Yorkshire BD22 8DR. Tel.: (0535) 42503. A 7-guestroom (private baths) country pub-inn in the heart of Brontë country in West Yorkshire. Breakfast included in room rate. Light lunches and evening meals also served. Closed from 3:00 to 6:30 p.m. Make arrangements ahead if checking in between these times. Conveniently located to enjoy all of the recreational, cultural, and scenic attractions of this section of Yorkshire, including a visit to the famous Brontë Parsonage. Open year-round. (See Index for rates.)

Directions: From London take the M1 north and M62 west to Bradford, then M606 to Bradford city center. Follow signs for Keighley. Haworth is signposted from Keighley. Follow main road to Stanbury.

WOODLANDS
The Mains, Giggleswick, North Yorkshire

Afternoon teatime at Woodlands. I was enjoying a splendid solitary moment on the terrace, allowing my eye to play the game of following the course of the seemingly endless stone walls that wind their way down into the valley of the Ribble River and continue on up the green, rugged countryside, now joining other walls and finally disappearing over the top of the fell into some kind of Yorkshire eternity.

A little earlier, coming from the Lake District, I turned off A65 and found my way to the top of the hill for my first glimpse of this Georgian-style country house, serenely master of all it surveys. The view is of wooded slopes and grassy fields dotted with sheep, the Ribble River rushing over pebble and rock, and the Dale itself dotted with stone houses and barns.

The house, built of local stone, was originally designed as a private estate around the turn of the century. The bedrooms and public rooms are well appointed and many helpful amenities, such as television, radio, and electric blankets, are provided by Roger and Margaret Callan, the hosts. Almost every bedroom shares this marvelous view.

There are many different plans available for the traveler, but by all means do arrange to have dinner at Woodlands. You must make your table reservations by noon that same day.

Woodlands is within easy driving distance of the Lake District, James Herriott country, Haworth (home of the Brontë family), and the city of York. The footpaths wind up the famous limestone fells and along the bank of the Ribble. The unspoiled Yorkshire Dales provide ample diversions for a two- or three-night stay.

WOODLANDS, The Mains, Giggleswick, Settle, North Yorkshire BD24 0AX. Tel.: (072 92) Settle 2576. A 9-guestroom (private and shared bathrooms) Georgian-style country house in the Yorkshire Dales district. Open all year except Christmas and New Year. Bed and breakfast; dinner also available. Most conveniently located for walking and automobile tours of this section of Yorkshire. Many castles, abbeys, halls, and distinguished houses nearby, as well as the Yorkshire Dales National Park. Margaret and Roger Callan, Proprietors. (See Index for rates.)

Directions: The A65 runs from Skipton northwest to the edge of Cumbria. Woodlands is actually located in the village of Giggleswick, next to the larger town of Settle. Once in Giggleswick, look for the signpost for the Mains. Continue to the top of the rise for Woodlands.

STONE HOUSE HOTEL
Sedbusk, North Yorkshire

The British love to unravel mysteries, whether they be literary or real. Witness the great success of the Agatha Christie books and Sherlock Holmes.

Enter now the *dramatis personae* of our mystery. They are P. G. Wodehouse, the very popular British novelist and creator of *the quintessence* of the English gentleman's gentleman; a man named Robinson; and a Yorkshire cricketer named Percy Jeeves.

And what has all this to do with a beautiful stone house in North Yorkshire, an ideal setting for a relaxing holiday in the heart of the Yorkshire Dales National Park?

We must now introduce the final member of the cast: Mr. H. A. Crallan, racehorse owner and cricketer. Mr. Crallan is important to us, because he was the man who built the Stone House in 1908.

According to my information, newspaperman Rowland Ryder determined that P. G. Wodehouse actually hired a butler from an agency in order to study him for the character in his book. However, this man's name was Robinson, which lacked the comic overtones for which Wodehouse was searching.

The ideal name was discovered by Wodehouse as he watched a man named Jeeves play in a cricket match.

Now for the final connection: It seems that in 1909 this selfsame Jeeves worked as a gardener on the grounds at Stone House for Mr. Crallan! Aren't you amazed! May I add that Jane and Peter Taplin, host and hostess at Stone House, have all the documentation to make this a jolly literary adventure. They also have many other things that make staying at Stone House a North Yorkshire holiday adventure, including this lovely, comfortable house with its garden, and their Yorkshire terrier.

There is also an impressive collection of miniatures, including pocket watches, thimbles, toys, and vintage automobiles. These are all carefully arranged to provide an enjoyable diversion for the viewer. The public rooms and guest rooms are all comfortable and accommodating. The evening meal emphasizes home-cooked, plain English food, such as roast beef and, of course, Yorkshire pudding. There are usually two main choices.

Incidentally, Stone House sits in the middle of the setting for the James Herriot TV series "All Creatures Great and Small." The area provides marvelous walking and motoring throughout the magnificent Yorkshire Dales.

STONE HOUSE HOTEL, Sedbusk (near Hawes), North Yorkshire DL8 3PT. Tel.: (09697) Hawes 571. A 12-guestroom (most with private baths) country house hotel in the heart of North Yorkshire. Breakfast and dinner served daily. Open March to Nov. Most conveniently located to enjoy many of the historic towns, castles, abbeys, waterfalls; bird watching, walking, and motoring through the nearby Dales. Tennis on grounds. This is James Herriot country. Jane and Peter Taplin, Hoteliers. (See Index for rates.)

Directions: A684 runs east and west between Kendall and A19. In Hawes, turn north toward Muker; follow the road over the bridge and make the first right turning. Continue about 500 yds. to Stone House Hotel.

THREE TUNS HOTEL
Thirsk, North Yorkshire

The more I traveled in Yorkshire, the more fascinated I became, and the more I realized just how many different faces Yorkshire presents to the world.

I originally journeyed to the town of Thirsk in hopes of getting a glimpse or even a word with James Herriot, the author of *All Creatures Great and Small* and several other books on his life in Yorkshire. I am a tremendous fan of the TV series, which has been playing on public television in North America for the last few years and have even seen some episodes three times, laughing and even crying at the same episodes more than once.

It was through my good friend Lou Satz that I actually received an introduction to Mr. Herriot and also learned about the Three Tuns. I think that even if James Herriot were not in Thirsk, the town and the small hotel would be worth a visit.

It sits in one corner of this traditional North Yorkshire market town. On market day the village becomes a blend of the past, the present, and the future as everyone gathers from miles around to buy and sell.

The Three Tuns belongs in just such an atmosphere. It was built in 1698 as a dower house for the Bell family of Thirsk. It started its public life in 1740, when it was converted into a coaching house. It has undergone several changes through the many decades, but still retains some of its original features and cozy atmosphere.

I learned a great deal about the Three Tuns while enjoying a cup of morning coffee with the owner, Mr. Ivan Redman. We sat in the lobby with Barney, his golden retriever, a most lovable dog, hospitably greeting old friends and new.

"I'd say we were unpretentious, but well intentioned," Ivan observed, with a twinkle in his eye. "We're open 365 days a year and we serve breakfast to our houseguests, as well as lunch and dinner. We have twelve guest rooms, eight of which have private baths, and the others have wash basins in the room. They are all equipped with color TV, radio, and telephone service."

While he excused himself for a moment, I could hear the ticking of the large, old clock from Paterson & Son hanging on one wall. It was obvious that the lobby was also a meeting place for townsfolk, because there were many tables and chairs, suggesting congenial gatherings of coffee or tea drinkers.

Glancing at the menu, I noticed that for the most part the Three Tuns serves traditional English food, including beef and roast duckling and the like. There were a few Continental dishes as well, because this part of Yorkshire also has quite a few visitors from the Continent.

I found both the Three Tuns and Ivan Redman a very warm and generous experience, and Thirsk, a Yorkshire town with a natural, un-affected feeling.

Now a word or two about James Herriot. Ordinarily, he is quite willing to see visitors at his Surgery, and if you arrive between 2:30 and 2:45 on either Wednesdays or Fridays, he's happy to have a word with you and perhaps autograph one of his books. I was fortunate to be there at the appointed time. We did have a very splendid, short talk as he explained, "I cannot guarantee that I am going to be here on those two days and I hope that no one makes a special trip. However, if I am here, I'm delighted to meet anyone. You see, I'm still very much a country veterinarian."

The Surgery is located on the little road off the square next to the Royal British Legion Club and the signs says, "Sinclair & Wight."

Reader Comment: "We stayed at the Three Tuns. The hotel, the people, the town, and the region were everything you said they would be. . . ."

THREE TUNS HOTEL, Market Place, Thirsk, North Yorkshire YO7 1LH. Tel.: (0845) No. Thirsk 23124. A 12-guestroom (8 with private baths) traditional town hotel overlooking the square. Serving breakfast, lunch, and dinner 365 days a year. An ideal center for touring the Yorkshire Dales, the North Yorkshire Moors National Park, and the city of York. Pony-trekking, gliding, fishing, golfing nearby. Market days are Mon. and Sat. Within walking distance of Dr. James Herriot's surgery. Ivan Redman, Proprietor, Hotelier. (See Index for rates.)

Directions: From south, take M1 and A1 to Dishforth; turn right on A168 to Thirsk. From York, take A19 direct to Thirsk. From north on A1, turn left on A61 at the Ripon/Thirsk intersection. Nearest railway station— Thirsk 1½ mi. Phone hotel to arrange transport.

MALLYAN SPOUT HOTEL
Goathland, Whitby, North Yorkshire

"Cozy" and "bustling" are two good words to describe the Mallyan Spout Hotel, in the heart of the Yorkshire moors. The note of coziness is underscored by the decoration and furnishings of all of the three spacious lounges that have welcome fires most evenings and wide windows overlooking the spectacular moorland.

I arrived at the end of a rather stormy day and was immediately taken in hand by Judy Heslop. She ensconced me in a room at the top of the house with an impressive view of the countryside, and after a welcome tub and a bit of rest, I joined her in the main lounge before dinner.

Again I was struck with the thought that inns and pubs in England provide an opportunity really to get acquainted with the people of the surrounding area. All around me were the sounds of distinctive Yorkshire accents and faces that seemed to be crinkled up in good humor much of the time. The hotel is an ivy-clad stone building that in some ways typifies British solidarity.

Because this part of Yorkshire is really not on the main tourist route, Judy pointed out that Americans are not readily apt to find their way here. "We love to see them," she said, "because there is so much to do out-of-doors here that appeals to the American 'get-up-and-go' spirit. Besides the moors, there's tennis, golf, horseback riding, and also some good trout and salmon fishing in the River Esk."

For dinner, I ordered grilled Whitby plaice, a local fish garnished with sliced bananas and served with a special sauce. Other dishes included Goathland broth, another local tradition, and moorland trout, of which I had two bites from Judy's plate. Super.

Judy told me that Castle Howard, where "Brideshead Revisited" was filmed, is just a short distance away.

I was up early the next morning for a brisk walk in the freshly washed moors, which today gave promise of being blessed with sunshine. Filled with American "get-up-and-go," I would have enjoyed several days at the Mallyan Spout.

MALLYAN SPOUT HOTEL, Goathland, Whitby, North Yorkshire YO2 2AN. Tel.: (094786) 206. A 22-guestroom (most with private bath-shower) traditional country inn, 35 mi. from York. Open all year. Breakfast, lunch, tea, dinner served to non-residents. Horse riding, golf, walking the Yorkshire moors, all within a convenient distance. Judith Heslop, Innkeeper. (See Index for rates.)

Directions: From York take A64 to Malton Bypass. At Malton take A169, signposted Pickering/Whitby. After passing Flying-Dales radar station, take first turning to Goathland. It is 3 mi. to hotel.

MORNING ON THE MOORS

I'm always an early riser and sometimes that's the very best time to take walks. On this Sunday morning I found myself wandering through a parish churchyard, considerably in advance of the eight o'clock service. It was located right across the road from the Mallyan Spout Hotel in a small triangular park where several roads all came together. Among the headstones in that churchyard was one marked 1695.

A signpost by the road said thirteen-and-a-half miles to Pickering and four miles to Egton Bridge, where the Roman Road is. Still another sign said nine miles to Whitby-on-the-Sea.

Dominating everything and stretching out into all distances are the low fells of the North York Moors, where the heather will bloom madly at the height of the season.

Carefully making my way among a flock of sheep, I climbed to the top of one of the fells, where I could see the splendid farms tucked into their own fields, now serenely verdant. I could imagine what it would be like here in January and February with the snow swirling, and the winds off the moors rattling the windowpanes and shaking the buildings—a time for sitting-by-the-fire.

These are not the dramatically deserted heaths of Northumbria, nor the gentler hills of Lancashire. Here, the earth is convoluted with twists and folds. Above a certain line, the shrubs are low, and the grazing meager.

The sun climbed higher and shone brightly off the wet surface of the road. I stopped to look at a plaque on a big chestnut tree behind a stone wall that announced "His Majesty's Manor of Goathland commemorates the Silver Jubilee of His Majesty King George V." The tree was planted by Captain Smalass on the sixth day of May in 1935. The fence around the tree kept the sheep from getting inside. I couldn't help but wonder what happened to the good Captain . . . did he see action at Dunkirk, or perhaps in the jungles of Burma? The peaceful years between wars were all too short.

On my way back, I passed in front of the Mallyan Spout Hotel and two young lads lying on a bench at the bus stop. I asked them if they were waiting for the first bus to Whidbey, and they said no, they were resting— they had been up all night at a party.

WHITWELL HALL COUNTRY HOUSE HOTEL
Whitwell on the Hill, York

I'd been told that Whitwell Hall was very impressive, but I never expected anything like this. It was almost as if some genii had rubbed his magic lamp and suddenly created a gracious and expansive country house hosted by a former Naval type and his beautiful wife. It was worthy of a motion picture setting.

Set in its own park at the end of a curving gravel drive, the front entry to the hall is made through a stately porte cochere and into a center hall with a cantilevered staircase and balcony framed by an elegant wrought iron balustrade. It is two-and-a-half stories high with a skylight that creates a gentle even glow. It all reminded me somewhat of Inverlochy Castle in Scotland.

Lieutenant Commander Peter Milner, formerly of the Royal Navy, turned out to be a very entertaining, voluble man with a keen interest in many different areas. He joined the Navy when he was seventeen and went to Dartmouth School, which also provided Prince Philip's naval training.

Both the Lt. Commdr. and Mrs. Milner obviously share a great interest in art, because the hotel is enhanced by many oil paintings, some quite heroic in dimension.

The furniture and decorations in the graceful, spacious drawing room have been chosen with care to blend with the numerous works of art.

"We actually like to feel that this is a real house party," he said, as we strolled through the gardens and grounds. "We have eighteen acres of grounds here, and if I do say so myself, we keep the gardens in fairly good condition. It is not easy, because at one time there were half a dozen gardeners; now we get along with just one. The Americans who come here enjoy our tennis court, indoor swimming pool, and sauna, as well as fishing and bicycling. Croquet is something we feel rather serious about, too."

Whitwell Hall is quite convenient to many of the beautiful natural attractions of Yorkshire, as well as being only twelve miles from the city of York. In fact, the famous tower of the Minister is visible from the terrace. In the adjacent woodland areas there are beeches, sycamores, and yews, and delightful walks overlooking the Vale of York. Close by are the River Derwent and Kirkham Abbey.

All the guest rooms have their own bath or shower, color TV, radio alarm, and direct telephone, and all overlook the gardens and spacious lawns.

For years I've been looking for the perfect place where I can stride into the drawing room in my white flannels and utter that inimitable line, "Tennis anyone?" I believe Whitwell Hall is the place.

WHITWELL HALL COUNTRY HOUSE HOTEL, Whitwell on the Hill, Yorkshire YO6 7JJ. Tel.: (065 381) 551. A 20-guestroom (private bath/ shower) country house hotel, 12 mi. from York. Open every day of the year. Breakfast, lunch, tea, dinner served to non-residents. (Please ring in advance.) Castle Howard ("Brideshead Revisited"), York, North Yorkshire Moors neaby. Tennis, indoor swimming pool, sauna, bicycles, croquet, and garden walks in grounds. Not suitable for children under 12. Lt. Commdr. and Mrs. P.F.M. Milner, Resident Owners. (See Index for rates.)

Directions: Exit A1 for York. Follow A64 bypass signposted "Scarborough." Leave A64 and turn into village of Whitwell on the Hill. Turn left in village at telephone box.

THE NATIONAL PARKS OF BRITAIN

It was while crossing the North York Moors and the Yorkshire Dales that I became aware of the National Park System, established in the 1950s by what is now the Countryside Commission and administered by local planning authorities who have the double duty of conserving the fine landscape and then ensuring that people can get there to enjoy it.

Fortunately, these parks will preserve some of the remaining forest lands of Britain, which over the past five centuries were all but decimated for the building of ships and for fuel.

In my journeys for this book, I have traveled in Dartmoor Park in Devon, the biggest area of elevated moorland and wilderness remaining in southern England; in Exmoor, with its wild red deer in Somerset; Brecon Beacons in Wales; Snowdonia, an unusually large park in North Wales containing high bleak passes and valleys that were scoured by glaciers; the Lake District, which contains England's highest mountains; and the North York Moors and the Yorkshire Dales.

There are National Park Information Centres throughout Britain. Extensive and valuable literature on each park is available.

It's not that the distances are very long in the British Isles, it's the many diversions along the way that sometimes make it impossible to estimate traveling and arrival times. Last order times for dinner are included in the Index so that you can see what time you must arrive in order not to find the kitchen door locked. If you are going to arrive later, call ahead—there isn't a hotel/inn listed here that will not make some provision to feed you if they know you can't make it before the kitchen closes.

Rates for a room for two people for one night with breakfast, except where noted, are included in the Index of this book. They are not to be considered firm quotations, but should be used as guidelines only.

CUMBRIA
The County of Cumbria

Cumbria, which includes all of the English Lake District, is one of the most sought-after tourist objectives in the U.K., although some of the roads through the fells and passes are narrow and quite steep. There are switch-back roads and tranquil lakes interspersed with majestic mountains and sweeping views.

Nearly every town or village in Cumbria has a literary association. The great Lake Country poet William Wordsworth was born in Cockermouth, went to school in Hawkshead, lived in Grasmere at Dove Cottage, now the Wordsworth museum, and then moved to Rydal Mount. He is buried in the churchyard in Grasmere. Matthew Arnold lived for a time in Ambleside, and Charlotte Brontë stayed there for a week visiting the Arnold family. Coleridge found a house in Keswick with a magnificent view and was in frequent contact with Wordsworth. Charles Lamb and Robert Southey also visited Coleridge. Coniston contains the Charles Ruskin Museum with a collection of drawings and letters. Nab Farm, on the shores of Rydal Water, provided a setting for a series of rather bizarre relationships involving Thomas DeQuincey (Confessions of an English Opium Eater) *and the Wordsworth family. It's worth investigating.*

I'm indebted to Bronwen Nixon, the proprietress of Rothay Manor, for an unusual overview of all the activities in the English Lake District. There are national parks, museums, forest, market days in various villages (usually Wednesdays and Saturdays), castles, gardens, festivals, sheep dog trials, boating, cycling, pony trekking, twenty-three different golf courses, crafts workshops, and all manner of Wordsworth memorabilia. There is summer theater, a wildlife center, and of course, that great Lake Country diversion, fell walking.

June, October, and November, are excellent months to visit, but please make reservations well in advance.

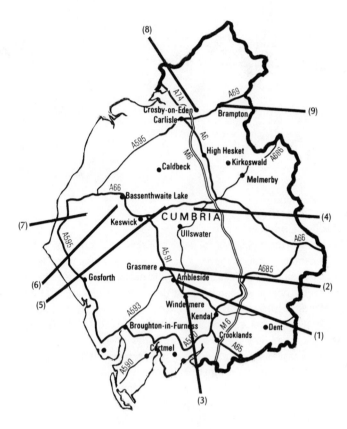

CUMBRIA

ROTHAY MANOR
Ambleside, Cumbria

Many of my most pleasant memories of this handsome country house hotel are centered around the very early morning walks that I took with Bronwen Nixon. We didn't stray too far and because the morning dew was always pretty heavy we stuck to the designated footpaths and country roads. Her dog, Hootie, was our advance guard and every once in a while he would scamper back, bark a little as much as to say, "Why are you lagging, there are so many wonderful things to see!"

On one occasion she shared some of her deep love of the Lake Country. "We move to a different rhythm than the world outside. To enjoy one's self it is sufficient to be here, anything else you may choose to do is a bonus. Walking is of course a natural choice. There is golf at Windermere, which is a very attractive and challenging course. There is a first-class stable nearby if you care to ride horseback. We have fishing here, both river and lake. There is the literary heritage of the lakes to explore as well as our 'industrial past.' You can enjoy a day of pure nostalgia, taking a motor launch down the lake and from the southern tip take a steam train to Haverthwaite and back."

"Looking after" is a wonderful English term that goes a long way in describing just how guests are treated at Rothay. There are separate dimmer switches and good reading lamps, bedside control of all other lamps in the room, bedside telephone, a hair dryer, a handsome wash basin set into a dressing table with plenty of space for cosmetics, shaving kits and the like, a bowl of fruit with a sharp knife for assuaging hunger before bedtime. The bathrooms are, as the British would say, "first rate." And, besides towel warmers, there is a rack folding out from the wall over the bathtub to provide a quick, ready method of drying those small items that may have to be washed.

Decorated in shades of brown with beige accents and with candles on each table, the dining room has a wonderful feeling of relaxed elegance. The menu includes an interesting combination of British and Continental cuisine. In addition to roast mallard, pheasant, venison, lamb and pork, there are gourmet dinners in the winter, each of which has a special theme, including cuisine from various regions of France.

Incidentally, many innkeepers from North America have visited Rothay Manor in the past few years and have conveyed to me enthusiastic praise for their experience. "We were really 'looked after,' " said Cliff Rudisill of the Village Inn in Lenox, Massachusetts.

Bronwen passed on over two years ago, but whenever I return to Rothay I go out for the early morning walks and can still hear some of her comments as she pointed out the many features of this gorgeous landscape. Under her sons Stephen and Nigel's direction, Rothay Manor continues.

ROTHAY MANOR, Ambleside, Cumbria LA22 OEH. Tel.: Ambleside (05394) 33605. U.S. reservations: 800-323-5463. An 18-guestroom country house hotel in the heart of English Lake District, 46 mi. from Carlisle. Open mid-Feb. to early Jan. Lunch, afternoon tea, dinner served to non-residents. Ambleside is in the center of the national park famous for its mountains, lakes, and rivers. The sea is 20 mi. away. Carlisle and Hadrian's Roman Wall, 45 mi. Wordsworth's Dove Cottage and museum, 4 mi. Rydal Mount, 2 mi. The Lake Country abounds in theater, museums, and galleries. Croquet on grounds, mountain and fell walking, pony trekking, sailing, boating, fishing, and golf nearby. The Nixon Family, Proprietors. (See Index for rates.)

Directions: From London leave M6 to Exit 36. Follow A591, 16 mi. Fork left on A593, signposted "Coniston and Langdales"; ½ mi. beyond, there's a black and white Georgian house. Follow Coniston signs again to get to front entrance.

WHITE MOSS HOUSE
Grasmere, Cumbria

"Yes, the house was once owned by Wordsworth, and that lake out there is called Rydal Water. Actually, we're midway between two other Wordsworth houses: Dove Cottage at Grasmere and Rydal Mount. It's possible to walk to either one of those."

Sue and Peter Dixon were telling me about the joys of innkeeping at the White Moss House, deep in the Lakelands District of England.

"Things have changed relatively little as far as the hotel is concerned since your first visit with my mother and father, Jean and Arthur Butterworth," Sue remarked. "We still have five bedrooms and Brockstone, an old Lakeland cottage. My mother and father furnished and decorated White Moss and, as you see, it has some lovely English touches, with fresh flowers, gay curtains and bedspreads."

"I think the highlight of any day is dinner," Peter declared. "I do all the cooking, and we are essentially English. Each meal is designed as a whole, so that the flavors and textures balance and complement each other. There is also a set menu for the soup, starter, and main course, and for dessert there is always a choice, including a 'proper' old-fashioned hot pudding. Of course we have lots of fine English cheeses."

"Peter's rack of lamb" Sue added, "with gooseberry mint sauce, as well as his crispy roast Lakeland mallard with sage and onion stuffing, are two of our most popular main dishes. The *London Times* described our meals as 'the best English food in the country.' As well as being a warm, hospitable, caring inn, we are also a top restaurant—perhaps the top 'English restaurant' in the country."

Now Arthur and Jean Butterworth have retired, and Susan and Peter are on hand to meet people, and to help out and make suggestions about Lakeland walks and drives. The atmosphere and the house are the same as they were on my first visit in the mid-seventies, with general redecoration and refurnishing.

Fishing permits are available for guests to fish on the river or on Rydal Water, and the Dixons have walked all over the Lake District mountains many times and can offer expert help and advice. Each room has, among other things, copies of eight different walks that begin and end at the house.

Advance bookings at the White Moss are normally taken for a minimum of three nights or, when mutually acceptable, one or two nights may be taken. In such cases, there is a small surcharge per night. I would suggest that an overseas telephone call directly to the White Moss is well worth the effort.

White Moss was one of the first inns that I visited in the Lake District, almost fifteen years ago. I am sure that Jean and Arthur Butterworth, who worked so diligently and sincerely to make it an outstanding experience, are very pleased with what Susan and Peter Dixon have done during the last few years.

WHITE MOSS HOUSE, Rydal Water, Grasmere, Cumbria LA22 9SE. Tel.: (096 65) Grasmere 295. A 7-guestroom country house hotel in the midst of the beautiful English Lake Country, approx. 14 mi. from Kendal. Modified American plan. Resident guests are served full English breakfast, and dinner promptly at 8:00 every night. Dinner served to nonresident guests by reservation only. Within easy driving distance of every point in the Lake District, including museums, historical and literary landmarks, and Wordsworth's cottage. Excellent center for some marvelous fell walks; fishing nearby. Commissions are not paid to travel agents. No children under 10. No pets. Susan and Peter Dixon, Owners. (See Index for rates.)

Directions: From the south: leave the M6 at Exit 36. Follow A591 through Ambleside. The hotel is at the head of Rydal Lake, 2 mi. north of Ambleside on the right side. From the north: leave M6 at Exit 40, follow A66 to Keswick, turn left on small country lane B5322. Turn left at A591 for 7 or 8 mi. Arrive at the Swan Hotel, Grasmere; carry on a mile farther. White Moss House is on the left at the head of Rydal Lake.

MILLER HOWE
Windermere, Cumbria

As far as Miller Howe is concerned, frankly, I don't know whether to talk about the fabulous view of the English Lakes from the bedrooms and the terrace, the highly acclaimed cuisine, or the Master of the House himself, John Tovey.

Let's take a few lines to discuss John Tovey, because it is his ideas and innovations that have gained such an excellent reputation in England and beyond.

He was in the British Colonial Service and then in the theater for ten years before acquiring Miller Howe in 1971. I first visited him two or three years later. As the owner-chef, he has ample opportunity to create original new dishes, many of which he demonstrates on television and has shared in his cookbooks. He visits the United States frequently, and has given English country house dinners and breakfasts in many places.

Since the evening meal (there is no lunch served, although a boxed lunch is available) plays an important role in any guest's stay at Miller Howe, it might be well to share a small inventory of some of his main dishes. These include Windermere Char with horseradish cream, turkey breasts with Cumberland sauce, cold leeks with sour cream, Scottish salmon, and, of course, Lakeland lamb.

John is particularly well known for desserts and sweets, including his apple and orange farmhouse pie, chocolate butterscotch shortbread tart, and homemade pistachio cream ice.

Guests gather for dinner at 8:30 in the bilevel dining room overlooking Lake Windermere. Everyone eats each course at the same time. There are no choices for the main course, but an alternative can be arranged. It is John's belief that since he serves just one meal a day it's got to be super.

All of the guest rooms have undergone what John refers to as "major surgery" and now have, along with the normal things, stereo sets with a selection of tapes, hair dryers, trouser presses, clove/orange sachets in the closets, and other amenities, including handmade shoehorns, umbrellas for all the guests, and binoculars strategically placed in the front bedrooms.

Each arriving guest is presented with a small booklet, especially inscribed with his name, which contains a diamond mine of information to enhance a three-day stay (the minimum according to the tariff sheet). It contains a complete description of each of the meals served and a list of the attractions in the Lake District, including cinema, public gardens, art galleries, libraries, all of the outdoor recreational facilities, guided walks, and a generous dollop of interesting Lake District statistics about mountain heights and lake dimensions.

The setting is superb. As I stood on the terrace watching a solitary, silent sailboat beating its way across the lake, I overheard a conversation between two other guests, wherein one guest said, "I'm going to spend the entire day on the balcony of our room. I'm settling down with a chair and a book and just let the lake, the hills, and the sky envelop me. It's no wonder that Wordsworth felt such a lift from this countryside."

MILLER HOWE, Windermere, Cumbria LA23 1EY. Tel.: (09662) 2536. A 13-guestroom country house hotel in the English Lake Country, 1 mi. from Windermere. Modified American plan. Breakfast, tea, dinner served to non-residents. (Dinner by reservation only.) Open early March to Dec. Located within convenient distance of all of the scenic, cultural, and recreational attractions of the English Lake District. Not particularly suitable for children. John Tovey, Resident Owner. (See Index for rates.)

Directions: From the south use Exit 36 from M6. Follow A591 to Windermere, then take A592 to Bowness.

OVER KIRKSTONE PASS

It had been three years since I had taken the Kirkstone Pass road from Ambleside to Ullswater, and once again I was blessed with a fairly clear day. "Fairly clear," in England means that it's not raining at the moment. Once again I had to pause on the upward climb to allow for sheep on the road. With each twist of the road, I could look back down into the valley at the village of Ambleside and its lakes.

On each side the grassy fells changed to bare rock near the top, and every so often I could see the silhouette of an adventuresome sheep along the skyline.

The public house at the crest of the paths was still there. I headed down the steep grade to the north, shifting into second gear and hugging the stone wall on the left side of the road as closely as I could to accommodate the buses on their way up. Soon, I was on the floor of the valley, which was brilliantly lit by sunlight through the pass. It was late May and there were very few other cars on the road, although there was a bank holiday weekend coming up and I was sure that this section would be much traveled. (It is always best to allow for bank holidays, if possible, when planning a vacation in Britain. All Britons love to go "on holiday" then.)

At numerous small parking areas along the road, a few people had left their cars taking to the nearby footpaths over the fells. They wore heavy boots and knickers, carried raingear, and usually wore wool caps. I noted a few vacancies at the B&Bs, but it was still early in the day and the season was not really under way. Even so, these would be filled before noon, as people from the city arrived in the Lake Country for the holidays.

The road continued on through Patterdale and Glenridding, the latter located on the shores of Lake Ullswater. The road was occasionally overhung by precipitous granite cliffs, reminding me of the lake country in northern Italy. Some mergansers and mallards were making tiny ripples in the otherwise glasslike surface of the lake, which faithfully reflected the mountains on each side. Here and there was a beach with coarse sand.

One of the sights that continually amazed me in this country, as well as in the Lancashire Fells, was seeing the stone walls that march right up one side of the mountains and down the other. They are formidable barriers placed, no doubt, to establish boundaries and to keep sheep under control. They are kept in extremely good repair. I understand that it is the custom here, just as it is in rural New England, for people to walk along each side of the walls together, replacing the stones that have been disrupted by frost and weather.

This time, I turned left on the A5901 to the west and went through and over the mountains, once again past several fields of sheep. It's such a wondrous sight to see the care and affection that exists between the mother lamb and her lambkins. Such complete innocent trusting, care, and love.

SHARROW BAY COUNTRY HOUSE HOTEL
Lake Ullswater (near Pooley Bridge), Cumbria

For forty years paeans of praise have been heaped upon Sharrow Bay by travel writers and food critics alike. The first group extolled the lake and mountain scenery. (The view from the main drawing room overlooking the lake and the mountains won an award as being the best in Great Britain a few years ago.)

Food guide writers are expansive in their description of chef Francis Coulson's true gourmet offerings. They have rhapsodized over the roast loin of English lamb Doria cooked on a bed of cucumbers and shallots and served with a red currant and orange sauce; the roast sirloin of Scotch beef served with Yorkshire pudding and horseradish cream sauce; and the choux pastry with a filling of partridge, duck, chicken, and herbs and served with bacon. When it comes to the sweets, even my masters in this field, the food guide writers, are humbled before the white peaches with grated apple, orange juice and cream; the chocolate brandy cake; and the famous sticky-toffee sponge cake served with cream. I would dearly love to introduce my good friend and *chef extraordinaire*, John Ashby Conway of the Farmhouse Restaurant in Port Townsend, Washington, to both Francis Coulson and Brian Sack, and then just sit back and listen to their conversation.

Sharrow Bay is situated on the northeast edge of Lake Ullswater in the English Lake District. It is owned and operated by two men whose interests seem to have blended beautifully. Francis Coulson does all the cooking and his partner, Brian Sack, handles the myriad details that are connected with the rooms and the "front of the house." The real beneficiaries of this partnership are the Sharrow Bay guests.

The main house sits on twelve acres of garden and woodlands, and there's about a half-mile of lakeshore for all the guests to enjoy. In addition to the twelve rooms in the main house, there are other accommodations available, including a converted farmhouse about one mile up the lake, where long-staying guests may enjoy the peace and solitude.

On my most recent visit, both Brian and Francis reminded me that a few years ago I had skipped the main course at lunch and had decided on three "starters" and a dessert. In fact, Francis remembered that I had had the French peasant vegetable soup and the purée of carrots and oranges, the supreme specialty of the house. "I'm sure," he added, "I also served you some chicken livers in a pastry shell."

Talk to anyone who has ever visited Sharrow Bay, and it seems that they inevitably sigh and say, "Ah, yes."

SHARROW BAY COUNTRY HOUSE HOTEL, Lake Ullswater (near Pooley Bridge), Cumbria CA10 2LZ. Tel.: (08536) Pooley Bridge 301. A 30-guestroom (26 with private baths/showers) country house hotel on the edge of Lake Ullswater. Open from early Mar. to early Dec. Breakfast, lunch, tea, dinner served to non-residents (please reserve). Minimum booking for overnight guests includes bed, breakfast, and dinner. All of the scenic, cultural, and recreational attractions of the Lake Country within a short distance. No credit cards. Not suitable for younger children. Francis Coulson, Brian Sack, Proprietors. (See Index for rates.)

Directions: Use Exit 40 from M6 and follow A66 for ½ mi. Go through the roundabout and turn left on A592 to Ullswater. Turn left at the lake, pass through village of Pooley Bridge, then right at small church and signpost, "Howtown and Martindale." After 100 yds., turn right at crossroads signposted, "Howtown and Martindale." Sharrow Bay is 2 mi. along this road.

THE MILL
Mungrisdale, Penrith, Cumbria

I have been trying to think of an inn included in the North American edition of *Country Inns and Back Roads* that would most closely resemble the Mill, which is located at the foot of the mountains in northern Cumbria.

I think the Seven Pines Lodge in Lewis, Wisconsin, the Inverary Inn in Baddeck, Nova Scotia, and the Jordon Hollow Farm in Virginia would be fairly close, but because all of these inns are highly individual, I guess we could only borrow a few features of each of the three mentioned.

Richard and Eleanor Quinlan purchased the Mill from Pam and David Wood in 1985. Both of them had experience in the hospitality field, and they were delighted with the opportunity to have their own place.

As Richard explained it to me, "Eleanor does the cooking. She is most particular about her homemade soups and sweets, and she serves quite a few regional dishes from Cumbria. Tonight, she is doing a curry and she decorates the dish with at least a dozen tidbits. Sometimes people don't know whether to wear them or eat them. We think that dinner is the height of any guest's stay here at the Mill and I think that most of our guests share our enthusiasm."

In the main house there are seven guest rooms, four with private baths. The original "Old Mill" has been converted into a suite of rooms (two doubles, spacious lounge, and a private bathroom). They retain all of the Old World look, with their original heavy oak beams. There is a wonderful view over the river which flows through the grounds.

Mungrisdale is an unspoiled Lakeland village comprising a 16th-century inn and church together with a cluster of farms and shady sycamores against a background of blue-gray crags and soft mountain slopes.

As Richard wrote in the very colorful and useful brochure about the Mill: "From the seclusion of our little-known beauty spot, the whole of the Lake District can be easily explored and many other areas are accessible for day trips, such as the Solway Coast, the Scottish border country, Hadrian's Wall, the Yorkshire Dales, and the Penninnes.

Eleanor was quick to point out that within the immediate vicinity there are a wildlife park and a great many places of historic interest, as well as a wide range of activities available, including fell walking, rock climbing, pony trekking, bird watching, sailing, fishing, hang gliding, and golf.

With quite a few country house hotels in Cumbria, I was delighted to find this snug little guest house, which incidentally is now the possessor of a recommendation from the British Tourist Authority.

Reader Comment: "My husband and I had the pleasure of staying one week at the Mill, which was not long enough. The owners were wonderful attentive hosts. In our experience this was the most hospitable establishment we have ever visited. It was personal and yet afforded privacy. The food was excellent, the rooms were attractive and comfortable with attention to details; it has fresh flowers, tea service and cookies."

THE MILL, Mungrisdale, Penrith, Cumbria CA11 OXR. Tel.: (059 683) Threlkeld 659. A 9-guestroom guest house located about 20 mi. from Carlisle in the English Lake Country. Bed, breakfast, and the evening meal included. Open every day from March 1 to Oct. 31. No credit cards. Richard and Eleanor Quinlan, Proprietors. (See Index for rates.)

Directions: Leave the M6 Motorway at Penrith (Junction 40) and take the A66 road for Keswick. The Mill is 2 mi. north; watch for signpost midway between Penrith and Keswick.

THE PHEASANT INN
Bassenthwaite Lake, Cockermouth, Cumbria

"I think that we are best described as being a residential English country pub." I readily agreed with innkeeper Barrington Wilson's evaluation of the Pheasant Inn.

This welcoming inn is set in the countryside at the head of Bassenthwaite Lake with Thornwaite Forest behind. The 16th-century L-shaped building is white with black trim, and there is a very pleasant lawn and extensive gardens in the rear. When I visited, the poppies were out in great numbers, as well as some of the other early summer flowers.

Over the rather rustic entrance are some mounted birds of the region, including several pheasants. There are several other references to this noble bird, including a handsome painting against a background of lakes and mountains. The snug conviviality of the interior is emphasized by low, beamed ceilings, patterned curtains, and comfortable lounges with chintz-covered furniture, log fires, and fresh flowers.

Over the years, apparently both Mr. and Mrs. Barrington Wilson and previous owners had collected a number of Lake Country memorabilia, including a mounted fish with a notice that it was caught in 1921 by one of the hotel guests. I was also interested in a novel collection of prints of old British inns that were at one time included in cigarette packages.

There are twenty spotless, comfortable guest rooms at the Pheasant, all of which have private bathrooms.

The innkeeper thoughtfully provides his guests with an excellent map of Keswick ("Kezz-ik"), which shows hotels and pubs in the area serving bar lunches and snacks. This is particularly important, because it's possible to motor all over the Lake District, as well as walk on the fells (hills), and it is good to know where there is a friendly pub. A hearty bar lunch usually includes some specialty of the house such as meat pies and salads, and many of these smaller places have a house pâté of which they are very proud.

After a day of motoring and walking in the Lake Country, it is most pleasant to return to the Pheasant and settle down in the lounge where there is a view of the blue mountain peaks and the dark green fir trees. There are many good American and British magazines scattered about.

The dinner menu consists principally of good English cooking, including braised ox tongue, roast turkey with bread sauce, roast capon with bacon and bread, and rhubarb and ginger pie served with cream.

Sailing, boating, fishing, walking, pony trekking, fox hunting (on foot), exhibitions, festivals, visiting the Roman Wall, and touring the Lake Country by car, are just a few of the many things enjoyed by Pheasant Inn guests.

This part of the Lake District is particularly beautiful in spring and autumn when the trees are at their loveliest.

THE PHEASANT INN, Bassenthwaite Lake, Cockermouth, Cumbria. Tel.: (059 681) Bassenthwaite Lake 234. A 20-guestroom traditional residential English country pub (inn) in the English Lake District. Open Jan. to Dec. All Lake Country scenic and recreational attractions nearby. No credit cards. W. E. Barrington Wilson, Proprietor. (See Index for rates.)

Directions: From Keswick, follow A66, 7 mi. on west side of Bassenthwaite Lake.

NORTHERN CUMBRIA

This part of Cumbria closely resembles Scotland with its narrow-passage roads and steep fells, and also Norway, which, in places, has much the same scenery. I decided to go to Scale Hill by way of Keswick and was delighted to find that the road, actually the long way around, was alpine in nature but completely safe. Although it was a Sunday afternoon, the high season had passed and there was a paucity of traffic.

The road winds and twists alongside a lake, continues up over a pass, and drops down into the dales with a descent that is breathtaking. Low gear is the word for both going up and coming down, but it is worth every great inch of it. This is one of those roads where British courtesy is to be commended. Many cars pull off in the lay-bys to let others pass. I only regret I was unaccompanied and there was no one to share this really wonderful adventure.

The clouds put on a remarkable show. The mist at the top of the fells would shift unexpectedly and let in a little ray of sunshine and a patch of blue sky.

Most spectacular were the great profiles created by the mountain skyline. My mind played tricks as I read various shapes into all of them. The valley widened out and I could see several swift-flowing streams tumbling down from the tops of the hills. It reminded me of just such sights while cruising the Norwegian fjords. Now, after a very pleasant journey I could see the unmistakable outline of Scale Hill Hotel in the distance.

SCALE HILL HOTEL
Loweswater, Cumbria

Much to my delight, Scale Hill turned out to be a small hotel quite resembling the Pheasant at Cockermouth, ten miles to the north. It is a two-story white building with impressive views out over the meadows toward the fells. There is a pleasant garden in the rear, with many benches permitting visitors to quietly enjoy the spectacular scenery. The view from the front is a little more threatening, as the fells seem to be much higher and, under a leaden sky on the day of my visit, more ominous.

However, there was nothing ominous about the tempting Saturday afternoon tea being served by a very pert miss to the many people who happened by to enjoy the warm coal fire, the cups of tea, and the enticing scones with whipped cream and jam.

As is the case with most inns of this type, there is a residents' lounge separated from the main lobby. It was occupied by a black cat with white paws, who was curled up contentedly by the fire.

Upstairs, the hallways have many photographs, sporting prints, and the unmistakable air of an old British inn. The guest rooms look clean and comfortable and, once again, enjoy the marvelous view.

There is a tiny bar, which was not open during the time of my visit, but I peeked through the window and could well imagine that it provided a pleasant atmosphere for locals and visitors alike.

Innkeepers Michael and Sheila Thompson provide a hearty menu with four courses. Some of the main dishes include shoulder of lamb, local trout, Solway salmon, roast turkey, and roast duck with applesauce.

A modified American plan that includes dinner is available. Picnic lunches are provided for guests who either walk the fells or motor through the countryside.

Michael Thompson explained that there's been an inn here since 1633. The property was originally a farm, and because it was located at the top of the hill, it became customary for the stage drivers to stop and give the horses a rest and for the farm to provide some hearty bread and cheese for the travelers. This quite naturally led to the establishment of the inn, or to what would be known then as a pub.

SCALE HILL HOTEL, Loweswater, English Lakeland, Cumbria. Tel.: (090085) Lorton 232. A 14-guestroom (mostly private baths) traditional country inn in the northern Lake District. Dinner, bed, and breakfast served to houseguests. Dinners served to non-residents. Advance reservations are accepted for a minimum of 2 nights. Open year-round, although an inquiry would be in order during the deep winter months. Most conveniently located to enjoy all of the English Lake scenery and attractions. Walking, fishing, bird watching, golfing, horseback riding, and many other recreational advantages nearby. Michael, Sheila, Heather, and Hazel Thompson, Resident Proprietors. (See Index for rates.)

Directions: M6 to Penrith, A66 to Keswick to Braithwaite; turn left over Whinlatter Pass to High Lorton and on to Scale Hill.

CROSBY LODGE
Crosby-on-Eden, Carlisle, Cumbria

"This is, indeed, the Border Country," said Patricia Sedgwick, as we were enjoying a cup of tea in the sunny dining room of the Crosby Lodge Hotel. (I realize that this book sounds as if I subsist on tea, but it is the marvelous British way of expressing hospitality and I've enjoyed dozens of cups of tea and cakes with hoteliers and innkeepers from Inverness to Mousehole and from County Galway to Norfolk.)

"Hadrian's Wall, which is just a few miles away, was constructed by the Romans to keep the raiding Scottish tribes from marauding the lands to the south. We are within a day trip of Edinburgh, both the east and west coasts, the Cumberland and Northumberland country, and the Scottish lowlands. The Lake District is a few miles away to the west."

Until 1970, Patricia and her husband, Michael, lived in nearby Carlisle where they operated a restaurant. "Michael is an expert chef," she said proudly, "trained in both London and Switzerland. I was born in Carlisle, and I've never moved away.

"In the years we've had Crosby Lodge we've gradually upgraded it. You'd be surprised how run-down it was when we first saw it in October, 1970. Now we've done all the bedrooms over and added further guest rooms in the stable block. I guess you'd call us a country house hotel and restaurant. Our prices for rooms include a full English breakfast. We have a nice walled garden that is available to our guests. Most of the people who stay here spend the days touring about and return in time for dinner."

It was obvious that the Sedgwicks had done much to improve both the interior and exterior of this country house, built around 1805. The two towers in front are connected by a crenelated battlement that, of course, has never seen any sieges.

Many trees grace the spacious lawn, and meadows are abloom with flowers.

As I made a reluctant departure after a pleasant tour of the house and grounds, Patricia extended a friendly invitation to return in the future.

CROSBY LODGE, Crosby-on-Eden, Carlisle, Cumbria CA6 4QZ. Tel.: (022873) Crosby-on-Eden 618. An 11-guestroom manor house hotel, 4½ mi. east of Carlisle in the lush Cumbria countryside. Open mid-Jan. to Dec. 23. Breakfast, lunch, dinner served to non-residents. Restaurant closed Sun. evenings. Convenient for tours through the English Lake District, the Scottish lowlands. Hadrian's Wall, Carlisle Castle, Rosehill Theatre, and other scenic and cultural attractions nearby. Mrs. and Mrs. G. M. Sedgwick, Resident Owners. (See Index for rates.)

Directions: From M6 use Exit 44. Follow B6264 approx. 2 mi. Turn left at crossroads, still following B6264 sign. Approx. 2 mi. to hotel, just through Crosby village. Crosby Lodge stands on right at the top of the hill.

FARLAM HALL HOTEL
Brampton, Cumbria

"There are other Bramptons in Britain," explained Alan Quinion, "but we're the one near Carlisle. That's why it's necessary to be very careful about fully identifying some of the villages and towns." Alan and I were enjoying a relaxing chat in front of the crackling fire in the residents' lounge in Farlam Hall.

He was telling me the fascinating story about the long search he and his wife and daughter, Helen, and son, Barry, had made, looking for a country house to convert into a hotel. "We had looked for at least two years, and even as tired and run-down as this place was when we saw it, we knew that the location and situation were exactly perfect for us. The house had the right feeling . . . the 'vibes' were right, and we just ached to bring it to life."

And bring it to life is exactly what the Quinion family has done since they moved to Farlam Hall in 1975. The departments of the hotel are divided almost equally, with Barry, the chef, being responsible for the kitchen and the food. "He has worked in some excellent restaurants," said his father, "and is very well trained. We're building our strength on his foundations. If the food and genuine comfort are good enough, people will seek you out."

Daughter Helen and her husband, Alastair, are mainly responsible for the reception and running of the dining room.

"Mrs. Quinion takes the responsibility for the decor, the furnishings, the housekeeping, and generally looks after all of us," he smiled. "And I believe we need some looking after. I handle the accounts, supervise the gardens and outside developing, and run the bar."

At dinner, I had ample opportunity to sample some of Barry's cuisine. The starter was avocado mousse, the main course was beef Wellington served in a very crisp pastry jacket, and the cheese selection was one of the most extensive I'd ever seen.

In a moment of complete madness, I accepted Mrs. Quinion's suggestion that I try both a small helping of the raspberry mousse, which was decorated with whipped cream, and the chocolate gateau. Heavenly.

Farlam Hall started life as a 17th-century farmhouse and was enlarged in stages. It subsequently became the elegant Victorian manor house it is today, set in its own gardens with an ornamental lake and stream.

FARLAM HALL, Brampton, Cumbria CA8 2NG. Tel.: (069-76) Hallbankgate 234. A 13-guestroom (private baths) country house hotel, 11 mi. from Carlisle in the vicinity of the Roman Wall. Open Mar. to Jan. Dinner served to non-residents. Color TV in guest rooms. Ample Lake Country and Northumbria recreation and sightseeing nearby, including the Roman Wall and three golf courses. Quinion Family, Proprietors. (See Index for rates.)

Directions: Leave M6 at Carlisle, Exit 43; follow A69 (Newcastle Rd.) to Brampton. Leaving Brampton, take right fork (A689) to Hallbankgate and Alston. Hotel is 2½ mi. along this road on left.

For room rates and last time for dinner orders, see Index.

In Britain, acceptance of a hotel booking by telephone or in writing is generally regarded as a legally binding contract. If it's necessary to cancel, advise the hotel immediately. If they are unable to re-let the room, the hotel may be entitled to claim compensation—usually two thirds of the agreed price—and any deposit would be included as part of this payment.

NORTHUMBERLAND

There is a marvelous system of very fast roads in the United Kingdom; those running from London, north, can be divided into two basic roads. The M6 goes as far north as Carlisle and then breaks up into a series of good routes to both coasts, as well as to Glasgow or Edinburgh. The M1, when it is not a Motorway, becomes the A1. The A1 continues north through York, Durham, Newcastle-upon-Tyne, and into Edinburgh by way of Berwick-upon-Tweed. Of the two roads, the M1 (A1) is the least used north of Newcastle. In Northumberland it provides one of the most scenic routes in Britain. In this edition I have provided some accommodation suggestions on and just off the A1 that would be ideal for an overnight visit and even longer, as there are literally hundreds of castles, beaches, and nature preserves along the Northumberland coast.

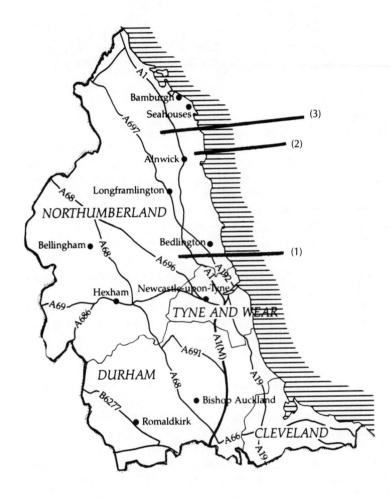

NORTHUMBERLAND

LINDEN HALL HOTEL
Longhorsley, Northumberland

This magnificent country house, set in 300 acres of breathtaking parkland and woods, was originally built in 1812 for Charles William Bigge, a local industrialist and banker. Recently rescued from ignominy, Linden Hall has been converted into a most impressive hotel.

Newly planted linden trees flank some stretches of the almost-mile-long private drive to the hotel.

The drawing room and inner hall have a sweeping staircase, a magnificent dome, huge chandeliers, and gorgeous carpets. The walls are adorned with very large oil paintings. The aura of grandeur is unmistakable. It is proper, but not stuffy; elegant, but not formal.

The various-sized guest rooms have been carefully furnished and each is fully equipped with a private bathroom, color television, a direct-dial telephone—and, of all things, a baby-listening service. All guest rooms have unbroken views of the countryside, the formal gardens, and the extensive woodland walks.

The decor and the furnishings of the restaurant are in keeping with the remainder of the hotel. Floor-to-ceiling windows allow panoramic views over the croquet lawn, as well as the formal gardens and parklands.

There are large vegetable gardens adjacent to the hotel that supply some of the provender. The menu is extensive to say the least.

In contrast to the Georgian opulence, the Linden Pub, converted from the old granary, conveys a complete change of mood and atmosphere. It has exposed beams, an open fire, and a most interesting inner gallery. A collection of enameled advertising signs of a bygone age adorn the walls. The sheltered courtyard has barbecue facilities and such outdoor pub games as quoits, boule, and draughts.

On the day of my visit there was a formal wedding party being held in another part of the hotel, and male members of the wedding party were wearing the famous grey top hat so fashionable at Ascot. This was England at its 20th-century best, with ladies and gentlemen "dressed to the nines." The air was warm, the sky was clear, and the expectations for the marriage were obviously very high. They were certainly off to a great start.

LINDEN HALL HOTEL, Longhorsley, Morpeth, Northumberland. Tel.: (0670) 56611. Telex: 538224. U.S. reservations: 800-223-5581. A 45-guestroom (private baths) luxurious country house hotel in a former 1812 Georgian mansion, set in 300 acres of parkland and woods. Breakfast, lunch, and dinner. Open year-round. Billiards, table tennis, outdoor tennis, and croquet on grounds. Many museums, stately homes, foot paths and backroading nearby. All modern amenities. (See Index for rates.)

Directions: Take A1 north out of Newcastle-upon-Tyne and turn onto A697 just above Morpeth. Linden Hall is just a short distance north of the village of Longhorsley.

MARINE HOUSE PRIVATE HOTEL
Alnmouth, Northumberland

Continuing on the A1, my next stop was Alnmouth, an attractive small seaside village that was once a small seaport not particularly noted for its righteousness. These matters, I am told, have receded into the past and the village is now a very popular resort.

The Marine House Hotel is a large, comfortable stone house, built on the edge of the village golf links, with fine views of Alnmouth Bay. The seaside sands are of a very fine consistency and bathing, boating, sea and river angling, and pony trekking are much favored.

I think the real point about stopping off here is that it is a very natural small hotel that would be quite popular with the British because of its location and because of its relatively reasonable tariffs. It isn't the kind of place that the visitor to England would be likely to find, because it is a little out of the way. It affords an opportunity for an English seaside hotel experience with very friendly and affable proprietors. Four of the guest rooms face the sea and there is a little terrace and a garden, which also share this pleasant view.

Proprietress Sheila Inkster does all of the cooking, and this includes roast beef, Yorkshire pudding, roast turkey, and creamed potatoes.

If the reader stays here, please send me a card with your impressions. It had an appeal for me.

MARINE HOUSE PRIVATE HOTEL, Alnmouth, Northumberland NE66 2RW. Tel.: (0665) 830-349. An 8-guestroom traditional small seaside hotel (some shared baths). Open all year. Breakfast and dinner served daily. Overlooking a 9-hole seaside golf course. Seabathing, yachting, pony trekking nearby. Sheila and Gordon Inkster, Proprietors. (See Index for rates.)

Directions: Alnmouth is on the Northumbrian coast between Berwick and Newcastle, and east of Alnwick, off the A1. Can be reached by London-Edinburgh railway, 1 mi. away.

TUGGAL HALL
Chathill, Northumberland

"Perhaps the most surprising aspect of this part of Northumberland is the numerous superb, sandy beaches all along the unspoiled coastline. The nearest one is just a fifteen-minute walk from us and there is marvelous bird watching and also a seal colony on the Farne Islands."

Naomi Barrett had joined us after dinner in the attractive drawing room—also a guest dining room—of Tuggal Hall, a distinguished country house that traces its origins back to the 13th century. We were all seated around the fireplace, where a coal fire burned brightly.

Naomi poured coffee and continued extolling the virtues of Tuggal Hall as a center for a pleasant holiday. "There are seven golf courses nearby, excellent fishing on several different rivers, as well as sea fishing off the coast, sightseeing on the many islands, marvelous walking in the Cheviot Hills, and more castles and historic sites than could be visited in a week, all within a short drive."

Tuggal Hall is a part of the Wolsey Lodges consortium and, like the others I have visited and have included in this book, it is of first-class quality. There are two very large double bedrooms, and dinner is available by advance request. Naomi pointed out that guests who stay more than one night might prefer to take the evening meal at one of the several good restaurants in the area.

The house faces south, surrounded by trees and gardens overlooking farmland with eastern views to the sea. It is only about seventy miles to Edinburgh by car on the A1. It's possible to make a day trip to that famous Scottish city by taking the train in the morning and returning on the 5:00 p.m. train, arriving in Chathill at 6:30.

TUGGAL HALL (Wolsey Lodges), Chathill, Northumberland NE67 5EW. Tel.: (066 589) Chathill 229. A 2-guestroom (private bath) country house accommodation just a short distance from the seacoast. Open year-round. Breakfast included in room rate; evening meal on request. Ideally situated with miles of sandy beaches for walking and exceptional bird watching; golf courses, fishing, sightseeing, and many castles nearby. Mrs. Naomi Barrett, Proprietress. (See Index for rates.)

Directions: Coming north on A1, exit at the Alnwick Bypass. Turn off at Denwick and follow B1340, watching for a very simple sign on the side of a barn that says Tuggal Hall. It is on the left-hand side of the bend, 10 mi. north Alnwick. If you pass a sign that says Tuggal Grange, you have gone too far.

In Britain, acceptance of a hotel booking by telephone or in writing is generally regarded as a legally binding contract. If it's necessary to cancel, advise the hotel immediately. If they are unable to re-let the room, the hotel may be entitled to claim compensation—usually two thirds of the agreed price—and any deposit would be included as part of this payment.

Rates for a room for two people for one night with breakfast, except where noted, are included in the Index of this book. They are not to be considered firm quotations, but should be used as guidelines only.

Wales

Wales is utterly fascinating and to me quite mind-boggling. The people are friendly and accommodating, the scenery runs the gamut from beaches to great mountain peaks, the numerous castles are all history-laden, and the varied opportunities for a holiday are literally uncountable.

Wales has three impressive national parks, including Snowdonia Park, the haunt of intrepid mountain climbers and holiday seekers. Brecon Beacons Park is perfect for pony trekking and walking.

Llangollen is the home of the world-famous International Musical Eisteddfod in July. "The great little trains" in Wales afford several opportunities for amusement.

Just a word about the Welsh language: Unbelievable. I say that to give encouragement to anyone who has tried to pronounce the "lls," "ffs," and a few of the totally unfamiliar combinations of consonants. Fortunately, the Welsh people have a good sense of humor and are probably adjusted to the mangling of their native tongue. Give it a try, it's part of the fun, and the Welsh give "A" for effort.

List of common Welsh words and some meanings in English:

> *aber — mouth of a river*
> *bryn — hill*
> *plas — mansion*
> *coed — woods*
> *llyn — lake*
> *eglwys — church*
> *caer — fort*
> *newydd — new*
> *bedd — grave*

From the mountains, lakes, and seacoasts of Wales have come such notables as David Lloyd George, Sir Henry Morton Stanley (of Stanley and Livingston fame), Dylan Thomas, Richard Burton, and Merlin, King Arthur's wizard.

Wales is filled with stories of bards, poets, and heroes. No one can possibly understand and fully appreciate Wales in just one visit.

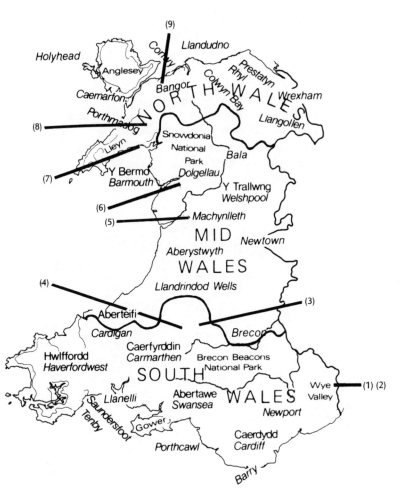

WALES

THE CROWN AT WHITEBROOK
Whitebrook, near Monmouth, Gwent

I was in the Wye River Valley traveling south on A466, the road from Monmouth to Chepstow. On the east bank, it's Gloucestershire, England, and on the west, it's Gwent in Wales.

At the river crossing, there was a signpost clearly marked Whitebrook, the village where the Crown is located. The road doubled back on the west side of the river for a short distance and then became a single passage route. I began to feel somewhat tentative about the expedition when the road passed through some barnyards and twisted its way around huge boulders; however, I pressed on and was rewarded with the sight of the village.

The Crown proved to be a very jolly place, a traditional village inn (as opposed to a country house hotel), which probably dates back to 1680. My hosts were John and David Jackson. John grabbed a fistful of keys and we took a quick tour of most of the twelve guest rooms, all of which have either a bath or shower. (Sometimes inns and guest houses have w.c.'s and baths down the hall.) These rooms have been modernized with intercommunications systems, direct-dial telephones, and built-in radios. The Manor Room has a four-poster bed and a whirlpool bath.

The two brothers have most interesting backgrounds. Until about twelve years ago, they operated a family-owned restaurant in Weston-Supermare. John then went off to Bermuda for about six years after which he returned to London, working in some of the famous restaurants.

On the other hand, David went to Nigeria where he met and married

Collette, a very attractive Irish girl. Now the brothers are united, and view the Crown as a family venture.

The menu at the Crown is predominantly French, including several Continental dishes, for which David is gaining a most commendable reputation. He finished very high in the Chef of the Year competition, recently reaching the regional finals.

On the other hand, John is a Master Sommelier, one of the very few wine waiters to pass the examination run by the Worshipful Company of Vintners in the city of London. Their respective qualifications provide guests with the best possible assurance of quality and professionalism.

I'm happy to say that John was able to join a group of almost one hundred *CIBR* innkeepers from North America, Britain, and Europe at a most enjoyable seminar in the state of Arizona. John's talk on wines and wine service was one of the highlights.

The Crown is situated in the hills next to a brook flowing into the Wye through the steep wooded valley, on the edge of Tintern Forest. It reminds me a great deal of parts of New England and North Carolina. There are many roses, rhododendrons, irises, pansies, and other flowers, as well as oak, ash, and beech trees, which provide homes for nightingales, owls, and magpies.

For many travelers, the Crown may provide an introduction to Wales, and I'm sure the Jackson family will make it a cordial stay.

Reader Comment: "This was our second visit and we'll return every year. Wonderful food! Typical bedrooms—smallish but comfortable."

THE CROWN AT WHITEBROOK (near Monmouth), Gwent NP5 4TX. Tel.: (0600) Monmouth 860254. A 12-guestroom village inn in the true inn tradition, located approx. 4 mi. from Monmouth and about 2½ hrs. from London. Breakfast, lunch, tea, and dinner served every day. Walking in the Tintern Forest, fishing for salmon in the River Wye, and golf on the three local courses provide interesting recreation. The Jackson Family, Innkeepers. (See Index for rates.)

Directions: Traveling west on M4, take the first exit after crossing the Severn Bridge, follow signs for Monmouth (A466) through Tintern and Llandogo. At Bigsweir Bridge, turn left for Whitebrook. The Crown is 2 mi. up a narrow country lane.

THE KING'S HEAD HOTEL
Monmouth, Gwent

The King's Head Hotel is aptly situated in Agincourt Square. It is a historic 17th-century building that has been tastefully and imaginatively modernized to meet the needs of the 20th-century traveler. It owes its name, perhaps, to Henry V, but Charles I often visited the hotel in the early part of his reign, and it is said that the royalist landlord of the period set up a large plaster panel of the king's crowned head and shoulders in what is now the hotel bar. This cozy old-fashioned room has a curious plaster ceiling heavily molded in a design of wreaths of fruit.

All bedrooms have private baths and color TV.

Monmouth is an ideal touring center for the Wye Valley and the Royal Forest of Dean. The surrounding countryside abounds with magnificent viewpoints, picnic places, ancient castles, churches, and abbeys, and offers fishing, sailing, horse riding and walking.

THE KING'S HEAD HOTEL, Monmouth, Gwent. Tel.: (0600) Monmouth 2177. A pleasant in-town hotel open year-round. (See Index for rates.)

Directions: Monmouth is a few miles north of Chepstow, the M4, and the Severn Bridge.

TŶ MAWR COUNTRY HOUSE HOTEL
Brechfa, Dyfed

Except for the distinctive Welsh signposts, I might well have been in Vermont. The road and surroundings—the rushing brook, the boulders, and the fir trees—reminded me of the back way between Wells and Cambridge Springs, Vermont. This area is right on the border of the Cambrian Mountains, some of the most remote upland country in southern Wales. There are large tracts with no roads crossing them.

Now, following the simple directions, I arrived at the village of Brechfa, hidden in the valley and steep rolling hills surrounding the River Cothi. I spotted Tŷ Mawr almost immediately—a restored 16th-century house standing on the banks of the Marlais, a smaller stream.

My feeling of being in Vermont was heightened even more when I stepped inside the front door. Except for the very old building, I might well have been in a Vermont ski lodge. The interior walls were of stone and heavy supporting beams, brightened by a generous use of colorful draperies and wall hangings. It had a modern contemporary look, but at the same time, I sensed a keen appreciation of the past.

Three of the walls in the attractive residents' lounge were done in massive stone, and a fire crackled merrily in the fireplace. The combination of the old and new was highlighted by the contemporary furniture and the colorful prints on the walls. I noted quite a few familiar-looking American and British magazines.

There are five double bedrooms at Tŷ Mawr, one with twin beds, and all with private bathrooms. They are furnished, as is the rest of the house, with an eye toward blending the furniture and draperies with the stone walls and oak beams.

Brechfa is a truly rural Welsh-speaking area, and throughout the year there are always local farming and social events, such as sheep shearing, horse sales, haymaking, pony racing and trotting, village fêtes, and the Eisteddfodau. It is really quite natural.

The sea is within a half-hour's drive, and there are many beaches along the Pembroke and Cardigan coasts which are just a short distance away. There are lots of ancient castles to explore, as well as the Roman gold mines, the woolen mills, and Brecon Beacons National Park. There's lots of good fishing as well as golf courses in the area and horseback riding or pony trekking.

Brechfa is a reasonable drive to Fishguard, the place to catch the ferries to Rosslare and Cork in Ireland.

A bit of Vermont in Wales. This is a sort of reverse exchange, because years ago a great many Welshmen and their families immigrated to Vermont's slate-quarrying hills and valleys near Wells and Poultney. The choirs in Vermont's small country churches are swelled with the rich Welsh voices. There are still strong connections with the rugged Welsh homeland.

Reader Comment: "Spectacular scenery. We had to watch the signposts very carefully. Nice people."

TŶ MAWR COUNTRY HOUSE HOTEL, Brechfa (near Carmarthen), Dyfed. Tel.: (026 789) Brechfa 332. A small 5-guestroom country house hotel and restaurant 12 mi. from Carmarthen and 30 min. from beaches on the Pembroke and Cardigan coasts. Closed last 2 wks. in Feb. Ruined castles, Roman gold mines, woolen mills, picnic areas, Brecon Beacons National Park, and nature reserves nearby. Fishing and horse riding on the grounds. Rough shooting, golf, walking nearby. Flaherty Family, Proprietors. (See Index for rates.)

Directions: Follow A40 from Llandeilo to Carmarthen. Watch for B4310 on the right and follow 6 mi. to Brechfa.

It's not that the distances are very long in the British Isles, it's the many diversions along the way that sometimes make it impossible to estimate traveling and arrival times. Last order times for dinner are included in the Index so that you can see what time you must arrive in order not to find the kitchen door locked. If you are going to arrive later, call ahead—there isn't a hotel/inn listed here that will not make some provision to feed you if they know you can't make it before the kitchen closes.

TRAVELING IN WALES

The roads are all paved, even those that look like little single yellow or blue lines on the map. Even the roads marked in red with three numbers, such as A485, are inclined to be narrow; four-number roads can become single passageways every so often, but not the three-number variety. I found the four-numbered roads basically more fun.

On checking the routes, I discovered that the center of the town was a key point. This is where the signposts are located, and once out in the country there are very few reassuring route numbers until the next crossroads. The villages all have Welsh names and this can be confusing, especially with a two-worded village name where none of the letters are vowels. I gave up trying to pronounce them, because I realized I was trying to associate them with English sounds and not with Welsh sounds.

I found the best way to go from point to point was to stop at the crossroads and check the signposts, even though I might not be able to do anything except look at the name of the village. People of whom I inquired directions were most accommodating, and in some cases I had to go into the pub with the map, rather than trust myself for any pronunciation. My approach was, "Oh pardon me, sir, can you show me where we are on this map?"

Counties are not mentioned as much in Wales as they are in England, but people are very proud to be from North Wales or from Mid-Wales or South Wales.

Just as April is an ideal time to be in the south of England, May is an excellent time for traveling in Wales. School is still in session and there aren't as many travelers on the road, especially in caravans (known as trailers or mobile homes in North America).

Whenever I asked someone in Britain about the length of time it takes to get from point to point, I found that it was a good idea to double the estimate. Britons drive much faster than North Americans, besides which they are used to the narrow-passage roads.

*Quite frequently I found myself on the top of a hill in a brief shower
looking down into the valley or hill beyond, which was bathed in sunshine.
Instead of wearing traditional blue jeans or something similar, Welsh
farmers running tractors in the fields generally wear suit coats, and
sometimes a shirt and a tie. Men wear a variety of hats and caps here. A
deerstalker hat is quite popular with many different men. There are also
wool caps of varied designs. On Sundays, gentlemen are turned out in very
good sport jackets with either grey or fawn-colored trousers and suede
shoes.*

LLWYNDERW HOTEL
Abergwesyn, Powys

The wild highlands of central Wales retained their medieval roads until
a few years ago, when one of Europe's most successful new road systems
was developed. Now this Welsh landscape, with its rare birds and flowers,
lies open before the motorists of today. Thus far these splendid roads
remain almost empty of traffic, skirting huge lakes and climbing craggy
moorland wildernesses, most enticing to the painter, the walker, the
fisherman, the photographer, the bird watcher, the naturalist, and the
tourist.

A small Georgian house built in 1796 on earlier foundations, Llwynderw lies 1,000 feet above sea level, protected by ancient beeches and
oaks, without another house in sight. It has a comprehensive library and is
most conveniently located to enjoy much of the Welsh landscape and
various cultural attractions, including the world-famous Bodnant Gardens, Caernarvon, Conwy, and such castles as Harlech and Pembroke.
Llwynderw is described as enjoying an utter lack of hotel commercializa-
tions. The proprietor likes to cook Welsh mountain mutton, which is a
very rare item these days, and enjoys meeting the great variety of interesting guests who have followed the advice of friends or guidebooks who say
that it is "well worth a detour."

*LLWYNDERW HOTEL (Pride of Britain), Abergwesyn, Llanwrtyd Wells,
Powys LD5 3TW. Tel.: (05913) 238. U.S. reservations: 800-323-3602. A
quiet country house hotel in central Wales. Closed Nov. 1 to mid-March.
Two-night minimum required. (See Index for rates.)*

*Directions: Follow A40 to Llandovery, bear north on A483, and turn off at
Llanwrtyd Wells.*

*Rates for a room for two people for one night with breakfast, except
where noted, are included in the Index of this book. They are not to be
considered firm quotations, but should be used as guidelines only.*

TYN-Y-CORNEL HOTEL
Talyllyn, Towyn, Gwynedd

I was cruising north on the A487 through the gorgeous mountain country in Wales. It reminded me of several similar places in other parts of the world, such as the beautiful valleys in northern New Hampshire and the mountains of northern Italy. One notices small white dots lost among the green mountainside fields, which become on closer inspection the ubiquitous Welsh sheep. The houses in the villages are of stone typical to the area, which runs from greyish-green to black. The corners of the steep roofs are decorated with little ornamental figures.

The road to the village of Towyn turned off to the left of A487, and the Tyn-y-Cornel Hotel was located in the smaller village of Talyllyn, en route to Towyn. (Signposts in Britain usually indicate the farthest village from the turnoff point.) The road dropped down through evergreen forests and alongside a lake, tucked in between two steep mountains. The scene was idyllic to say the least. Fortunately, the sun had come out and the clouds had broken, and everything was bathed in golden light. I could see the hotel at some distance down the lake with the mountains behind it.

Subsequently, I met Clive and Shirley Thompson, the directors of the hotel, and learned that the lake was owned entirely by the hotel and was noted for trout fishing, reserved for residents staying in the house. "We only allow fly fishing and we have a strict nine-inch limit," explained Shirley.

"And flies and casts are kept in stock at all times," added Clive. "The best fishing months are April, May, June, and September."

"Our guests are always delighted with the unusual number of birds we have," said Shirley. "We have swans, cormorants, wild ducks, and great crested grebes on the lake. Our garden is a meeting place for all the wild birds in the vicinity, as well."

I remarked on the similarity of the scenery to the fjords in Norway, and both of them said that many of their guests had already noted the resemblance. "It is because the sides of the mountains are so steep next to the lake."

The hotel, besides having such a marvelous view of the lake and the mountains, proved to be a most comfortable and pleasant place. There are bedrooms in the main house and also some newer bedrooms in converted farm outbuildings. The latter all have a very beautiful view of the lake, along with central heating, radios, color TV, and direct-dial telephone. "Each room is provided with a hot water bottle," said Shirley. "Sometimes they are most welcome, indeed."

"We have some excellent walking and driving here in the Welsh mountains." Clive remarked. "It's a very pleasant place to stay for touring the Cambrian Coast and the Snowdonia National Forest. We can arrange pony riding on the slopes nearby and it's quite surprising how many of our guests enjoy it, even though it may be their first time astride a horse."

One of the other interesting attractions in this part of Wales is the Talyllyn narrow-gauge railway, which runs down the valley to the coast. There are several of these small Welsh railroads. I understand that this one is the most picturesque and unusual. There are also three golf courses within a short drive of the hotel.

All in all, it sounds like a wonderful place to stop for two or three days just to take in the marvelous Welsh scenery.

TYN-Y-CORNEL HOTEL, Talyllyn, Towyn, Gwynedd LL36 9AJ. Tel.: (065477) Abergynolwyn 282. A 16-guestroom lakeside hotel in the beautiful mountains of western Wales approx. 60 mi. from Chester and Shrewsbury and 10 mi. west of Dolgellau. Open Easter to Nov. Breakfast, bar, lunch, and dinner served to non-residents. Heated outdoor swimming pool, sauna, solarium, and fishing on grounds. Riding and pony trekking, golf, swimming, walking, and watersports on lake in season nearby. Clive and Shirley Thompson, Directors. (See Index for rates.)

Directions: Locate Shrewsbury on a map of Wales and follow Route A458 almost due west to its junction at A470. Follow A470 to a point near Dolgellau and then south on A487 just a few miles, with an eye out for the road to Towyn, off to the right. Follow this road to Talyllyn.

BONTDDU HALL HOTEL
Bontddu (near Dolgellau), Gwynedd

I was enjoying what the British call a "good tea" in the Green Room at the Bontddu (pronounced "bont-thee" in Welsh) Hotel on an afternoon whose mood was alternately sunny and stormy. The magnificent view of the Mawddach Estuary and Cader Idris range of mountains are alternately spectacular and clear or quickly obscured by fog or a hailstorm. This view, which is above all else the distinguishing feature of the hotel, is an unforgettable blend of water, mountain, and wood—one of the most splendid in the highlands of Wales.

All of the drawing rooms and the dining room are situated on the view side of the hotel, as are most of the guest rooms.

The Bontddu Hall was the only three-star hotel that I visited in Wales, and it had all of the unmistakable accouterments of a luxury resort. There was a very impressive entrance hall, much wood paneling, and the high-ceilinged public rooms had rich-looking furniture and draperies. The cloistered entrance was decorated with a most unusual collection of shining cavalry helmets, resplendent with horsehair plumes.

There are twenty-six guest rooms, all with private bathrooms, and these include a newer section of a more modern design.

Although I could not stay for dinner, there was an obvious emphasis on food, since the dining room is called the Gourmet Room. This might be because *Gourmet Magazine* gave a most favorable review of the hotel's menu a number of years ago, making particular mention of the North Wales lamb, lobster, salmon, smoked trout, and pheasant.

This is really a most impressive area of Wales, quite convenient for a holiday of longer duration. Guests may play golf at several famous courses nearby, and there is fishing, walking, or swimming on the sandy beaches.

Incidentally, Bontddu has won the "Prettiest Village in Wales" title three times.

Reader Comment: "If you're in the mood for a big hotel, this is a good experience."

BONTDDU HALL HOTEL, Bontddu (near Dolgellau), Gwynedd. Tel.: (034149) Bontddu 661. A 26-guestroom luxury hotel 5 mi. from Dolgellau. The hotel has an inspiring view of the famous Mawddach Estuary and the Cader Idris range of mountains near some outstanding golf courses. Open from Easter to Christmas. Breakfast, lunch, tea, and dinner served to non-residents. May be reserved from U.S. by travel agents through Dial Britain. Tel.: 800-424-9822. (See Index for rates.)

Directions: Use Exit 12 from M6 and go left on A5 towards Shrewsbury. From Shrewsbury take A458 to Dinas Mawddwy, then follow A470 to Dolgellau and A496 toward Barmouth.

BWLCH-Y-FEDWEN COUNTRY HOUSE HOTEL
Penmorfa, Porthmadog, Gwynedd

I leaned against the door watching Gwyneth Bridge prepare my breakfast, cooking the eggs exactly as I ordered.

"This is a coaching inn dating back to 1664," she said, deftly sliding two sunnyside-up eggs onto a warm plate and then adding a rasher of bacon and a few small sausages. "Arthur and I have been here for ten years and I think we have finally gotten things in order." This selfsame Arthur Bridges, he of the ready smile and fierce beard, joined us in the kitchen at that precise moment.

"Good morning," he boomed. "I hope you slept well. I see that you were out early this morning on a walk and I am glad that we had some of our usual beautiful weather for you." His eyes twinkled as he picked up the waiting breakfast plates and disappeared into the dining room.

"Arthur is really awfully good with the guests," said Gwyneth, as she bustled about preparing still more breakfasts. "He's very well informed about Wales and has some of the greatest stories."

Bwlch-y-Fedwen is situated in the middle of Penmorfa village, two miles from Porthmadog, and one mile from Tremadog.

The hotel has now been fully modernized in a warm and homey manner, which, at the same time, retains its original character. Antique furniture, oak beams, stone walls, and huge open fireplaces and candlelight in the dining room and bar create a very friendly and warming atmosphere.

During a lull in the kitchen activities I asked Gwyneth about the evening meal. "Well, our local lamb is really our specialty." she replied. "And of course we have local salmon in season. Our guests all seem to enjoy my sweets, including the 'Queen of Puddings,' another of our specialties. I also enjoy making meringues."

My bedroom was most comfortably furnished, with a view of a little garden in the rear and then down across the valley to some of the North Wales mountains.

I must add a word about the spic-and-span appearance of the Bwlch-y-Fedwen. Cleanliness is one of the virtues highly prized by Britons everywhere, but this particular hotel has to get the lifetime "Mr. Clean Certificate" for neatness. Not only were the bedrooms and public rooms most tastefully decorated, but nothing, and I mean *nothing,* was out of place.

Gwyneth and Arthur . . . you're terrific!

BWLCH-Y-FEDWEN COUNTRY HOUSE HOTEL, Penmorfa, Porthmadog, Gwynedd LL49 9RY. Tel.: (0766) Porthmadog 2975. A 6-guestroom hotel, approx. 70 mi. from Chester in North Wales. Open from Apr. to Oct. Meals are served to residents only. Within a short distance of the mountains of Snowdonia National Park, and within an easy drive of the many castles, railways, and other attractions of North Wales. Walking, climbing, fishing, golf courses, and sailing available nearby. No credit cards. Mrs. Gwyneth Bridge, Proprietor. (See Index for rates.)

Directions: From Chester follow A55 to Mold, then Ruthin. Here, use A494 to Cerrigydrudion. Take A5 to Betsy-Y-Coed and Capel Curig. Turn left on A4086 and then A498 for Beddgelert to Tremadog. Follow A487 to Penmorfa. This road leads through some of the most spectacular mountain scenery in Wales. I also realize that these are most confusing directions. May I suggest that having a map of Wales in advance and tracing the road under more leisurely circumstances would be an excellent idea.

SYGUN FAWR COUNTRY HOUSE HOTEL
Beddgelert, Gwynedd

I well remember the day. I was absolutely exhilarated. I had spent the previous night at the Bwlch-y-Fedwen, at Penmorfa, and as a result of hearing about the beauty of the Mount Snowdon area had decided to drive into this section of Gwynedd in Northern Wales, although it was not on my original itinerary. The way led upward through some beautiful mountains to the village of Beddgelert. The morning was beautiful with the sunlight sparkling on the river. Reaching the village center, I followed the A498 up the valley toward the pass of Llanberis.

On my way out of Beddgelert I saw the sign that pointed over the river and said, "Sygun Fawr Country House Hotel." I just couldn't resist it. And what a happy impulse that was. For one thing, it directed me to this very attractive 17th-century Welsh manor house with beautiful views of the Gwynant Valley and the Snowdon Range. It also introduced me to two very warm and hospitable proprietors, Norman and Peggy Wilson.

Norman is from Lancashire, and after all, anybody with the name Norman is bound to find a receptive audience in me. As we were touring the house, he explained that *sygun fawr* means "high bog"—literally, a high peat bog.

The rooms were very clean and comfortable with mountain views. Downstairs, in a little back bar, which is used mostly by diners and friends, Peggy came out of the kitchen and we all had a cup of lovely morning tea.

"We found a wonderful new way of life up here," Peggy said. "We aren't Welsh, but the people of the village have taken us in most heartily. I've learned how to cook many of the traditional Welsh dishes, as well as those from England. We have visitors from all over the world, but I must say that in spite of all of our efforts, we simply can't get Americans to walk!"

We all had a good laugh at this and I hope this book encourages Americans to try, rather than hurrying through Britain and attempting to see Wales in three days, to settle down and find a place like Sygun Fawr and stay for three or four days to "get the feel" of the land.

As we stepped outside in the morning sunshine, I remarked to Peggy and Norman that this part of Wales reminded me a great deal of Norway, and they said that many other guests had also made that observation, although it was not the Norway of the fjords. "It's the mountains and flowers, I think," said Norman. "You're headed toward Mount Snowdon now, and you'll see what I mean."

Yes, I, too, like the other Americans (not so much the Canadians), had to hurry on to get over the next hill and follow the river to the seaside and beyond. Someday, I'm going back to see Norman and Peggy and spend a week.

Reader Comment: "We were well taken care of. The Wilsons made us feel right at home."

SYGUN FAWR COUNTRY HOUSE HOTEL, Beddgelert, Gwynedd LL55 4NE. Tel.: (076-686) Beddgelert 258. A 7-guestroom (private baths) somewhat secluded country house hotel. Approx. 3 hrs. from Chester. Open all year. Dinner served to non-residents. Within an easy drive of all scenic points in North and Mid-Wales. Located in the scenic Snowdon area. No credit cards. Norman and Peggy Wilson, Owners. (See Index for rates.)

Directions: The A483 runs north and south along the imaginary boundary between Wales and England. There are several roads going west, including the A5, which can be followed west to Capel Curig, where 4086 goes southwest into A498 at Pen-y-Gwryd. The Snowdon area and Beddgelert are slightly to the south on A498. The hotel is just a few minutes from the center of Beddgelert over the brook on A498. Coming from farther south in England, after locating Beddgelert, using the above directions, work out your own way; it's really not difficult.

RHIWIAU RIDING CENTRE
Llanfairfechan, Gwynedd

I quickly learned that the main interest at Rhiwiau Riding Centre was, of course, horses and pony trekking. However, as Ruth Hill, who is a qualified member of the BHSAI (British Horse Society) and the proprietress, explained, "Our guests don't spend every waking hour on the back of a horse. We are situated most conveniently for exploring Snowdonia and the Isle of Anglesey, as well as Llandudno, Conway, and Colwyn Bay. In fact, there's a good number of guests who prefer our secluded, somewhat natural atmosphere and do a minimum of riding."

The accommodations are somewhat similar to those of an American motel. There are six rooms that will accommodate two people at a time and all have a shared shower; some have conventional beds and others have bunk beds.

The menu includes chicken and mushroom pie, vegetables from the garden, and all home-cooked and prepared dishes that satisfy the outdoor appetite.

Since the emphasis is on riding, Ruth suggested that jeans or jodhpurs be packed as well as a warm jersey, riding boots, or sensible shoes.

It may well be that the Rhiwiau Riding Centre is not for all of the readers of this book, and I suggest that anyone who is intrigued by my remarks would do well to write to the centre for a more complete brochure. It is a totally natural, informal place where visitors can enjoy riding instruction, and some really excellent supervised trail rides into the mountains.

Reader Comment: "We were ambivalent about this place. If one is into horseback riding, it's just the ticket. The scenery is spectacular. The accommodations were as you described. The food was not to our taste, but others devoured it with gusto."

RHIWIAU RIDING CENTRE, Llanfairfechan, Gwynedd LL33 0EH. Tel.: (0248) 680094. A 6-guestroom (shared bath), somewhat informal guest ranch facility located about 5 mi. from Conway. Rates are available for both adults and children which include full board and riding. Bed and breakfast or MAP available; as well as weekend and 7-day rates. Most suitable for children. Open every day in the year. Dinners to non-residents by reservation. No credit cards. Located on the northern coast of Wales, with horseback riding as the principal recreation. Hill walking, tennis, golf, fishing, mountaineering, and rock climbing are nearby. Ruth Hill, Proprietress. (See Index for rates.)

Directions: From London, take the M1 to Birmingham; M6 to Chester; A55 to Llanfairfechan. Turn left at the traffic lights and right at the top of the hill. After 1 mi. turn left and point upward (well signposted, if I remember correctly).

Scotland

Welcome to Scotland, or, as it is expressed in Gaelic, Ceud mile fáilte. *Translation: "a hundred thousand welcomes." (Try pronouncing it "cute mela falsha.")*

Scotland has some of the most beautiful and rugged scenery in the world—mountains, firths, glens, lochs, and islands. Scotland is tartans, haggis, oat cakes, pipes, kilts, trews, grouse on the wing, Highland games, hundreds of ruined castles and abbeys, golf, monsters, sheep on narrow roads, hidden fishing villages, and rich farmland.

Scotland is also history, a history intertwined with heroes and villains. One of the best ways to prepare for a trip to Scotland is to read the history and identify with some of the personalities: Robert the Bruce, Mary Queen of Scots, Rob Roy MacGregor, Flora Macdonald, and Bonnie Prince Charlie. Read about the Campbells, Macdonalds and Bloody Glencoe, the Glorious Revolution, Bannockburn, and Culloden.

Return to Sir Walter Scott's poems and novels. He perhaps unknowingly became Scotland's best press agent.

To further enrich a Scottish experience, dip into the poetry of Robert Burns, the novels of Robert Louis Stevenson, and the famous trip to Scotland by Doctor Samuel Johnson, described by his biographer, James Boswell, himself a canny Scot.

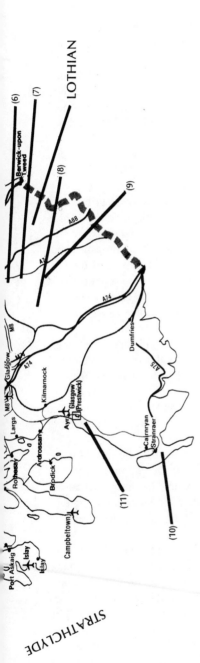

SCOTLAND

GEORGE HOTEL
Edinburgh

Graeme Mackenzie, innkeeper of the Sandpiper Inn in Carmel, California, put me on to the George. So, I thought I'd pop in for a look while I was in Edinburgh.

I liked the feel of the lobby right away. There were a few people having tea in a raised, carpeted, and balustraded section that was lined with high arched windows. Comfortable upholstered chairs were grouped around small tables, and the windows were draped in a lovely fabric that echoed the cream and blue decor.

It was a rather imposing foyer, with its marble floor and Grecian pillars. Chris Jarvis, who took me in tow, explained that the building had housed the Caledonian Insurance Company from 1881 to 1935.

The Carver's Table Restaurant, just beyond the foyer, had been the tellers' hall, and it, too, is a very impressive room with an extremely high domed ceiling and skylight, tall pillars, and arched windows.

Chris, who is sales manager for the hotel, was very enthusiastic about the Carver's Table, which specializes in traditional roasts, grilled steak, and Scottish salmon at quite reasonable prices. I liked the way the tables were arranged with low-backed banquettes, and the color scheme of mauve, gray, and beige was very pleasing. Le Chambertin is another, more intimate restaurant, which features French cuisine.

Chris showed me a few of the guest rooms, and they were nicely furnished in a traditional style, with pleasant floral draperies and matching bedspreads. All of the rooms have private bathrooms, and they are completely equipped with direct-dial telephones, color television, hair dryers, trouser presses, and other amenities, as well as 24-hour room service. Most rooms have a view either of the Firth of Forth or of Edinburgh Castle.

I thought the staff at the reception desk seemed friendly and alert, and I'd noticed when I walked in that the boys at the entrance were very helpful with bags and such, when guests drove up. They have valet service and private parking. Chris told me that they are happy to assist their guests with arrangements for sightseeing, mapping out day trips, and obtaining tickets for the theater.

The George has a classic Georgian exterior, with the staid, conservative appearance one would expect of a solid insurance company or bank, and in that respect it doesn't look much different from the other buildings in this financial district—except for its next-door neighbor, the early-19th-century St. George's Church, with a marvelous soaring spire.

For all its sober demeanor, the George seems to be a warm and hospitable place. Chris was telling me about their nightly entertainment, called A Scottish Evening, which features a Scottish dinner and singing, dancing, pipers, musicians, and, as Chris says, "kilts, bagpipes, and all sorts of Scottish things." It sounds like a lot of fun.

GEORGE HOTEL, George St., Edinburgh EH2 2PB. Tel.: 031-225-1251. Telex: 72570. A 195-guestroom superior in-town hotel within 5-min. walk of the center of Edinburgh. Hotel restaurants serve breakfast, lunch, and dinner daily. Reservations suggested. Open year-round. Valet parking. Help with arrangements for sightseeing and various events. John Acton, General Manager. (See Index for rates.)

Directions: West of St. Andrews Square, between David and Hanover Streets.

THE HOWARD HOTEL
Edinburgh

Edinburgh has many great and luxurious hotels; however, I was looking for a good, small, conservative, well-run, personal hotel where I thought our readers would be able to feel at home after a long drive north. Imagine my delight on learning that Arthur Neil of the Open Arms in Dirleton had acquired just such a hotel. I was happy to follow his fairly simple directions to see it for myself.

The Howard Hotel attracted me immediately in that it is situated in a former townhouse on a quiet street and, in that respect, resembles Number Sixteen in London.

By coincidence I arrived at lunchtime, and so went down to the first floor to have a good bar lunch, along with the other business people of the city. The selection was extremely broad, including various types of salads, vegetables, fruits, eggs, and cheeses.

The hotel also has a more formal dining room with quite an extensive menu, and dinner here could be quite relaxing after a day of seeing the sights of the city or the Firth of Forth countryside.

The Howard is located in the Georgian New Town of Edinburgh, close to the George and Princes Streets shopping district. One of its advantages is that it has its own car park.

The Edinburgh Festival is generally the last two weeks in August and the first week in September, and if you are planning to stay at the Howard during that time, you should reserve at least six months in advance.

Reader Comment: "We liked the hotel; it's simple and yet very clean, friendly, and charming. . . ."

THE HOWARD HOTEL, 32 Great King Street, Edinburgh EH3 6QH. Tel.: (031 557) 3500. Telex: 727887. A 25-guestroom hotel (private baths) in a quiet section of Edinburgh, ideally situated to enjoy the many attractions of the town. Private car park. Breakfast, lunch, and dinner. Open all year. Reservations may also be made for the Open Arms at Dirleton and vice versa. Arthur Neil, Proprietor. (See Index for rates.)

Directions: From George St. in the center of Edinburgh turn down the hill at Hanover St.; Great King St. is the 5th street down; turn right and the Howard is on the left. Park in front of the hotel to check in.

THE ALBANY HOTEL
Edinburgh

A very discreet brass plate on the front of the building identifies the Albany Hotel, which is actually a series of three 1812 Georgian townhouses. Albany Street is typical of Edinburgh's business and financial district, with the imposing facades of 19th-century townhouses lining both sides of the very wide New Town boulevards.

Pauline Maridor took over the hotel in 1982, and she is almost always there to welcome her guests. This is a modest, unassuming small hotel, just around the corner from the shopping district. With BBC-TV, Scottish-TV, and the Playhouse Theatre close by, Pauline often has guests from the media and entertainment fields. In fact, she told me that members of the Black Ballet Jazz Company and the French Ballet of Nancy had just been there for the Edinburgh Festival.

Since the hotel is a listed historic building, there are limitations on the amount of renovation that can be done. For instance, Pauline is not allowed to put in a lift (elevator), which means that you can get your exercise going up and down the beautiful Adams spiral staircases. There are three of them with lovely Adams cupolas over the third floor.

The guest rooms are simply furnished in a contemporary style, with those on the back looking out over a very pretty little walled hillside garden with green lawns, flowers, a rowan tree, and ivy and various plantings. This little garden area is also used for outside dining when weather permits.

The guest rooms are equipped with color TV, radio, telephone, and makings for coffee or tea, and they all have private bathrooms. If you like, a continental breakfast can be served in your room.

P.M.'s Restaurant in the basement is open for breakfast, lunch, and dinner, and offers an extensive menu, featuring traditional Scottish dishes.

This is an informal and quiet little hotel, and if you're planning to attend the Edinburgh Festival in late August be sure to make your reservations months in advance.

THE ALBANY HOTEL, 39 Albany St., Edinburgh EHI 3QY. Tel.: 031-556 0397 or 0398. Telex: 727079. A 21-guestroom small in-town hotel, a few minutes' walk from the center of town. Restaurant is open for breakfast, lunch, and dinner; reservations necessary. Closed Christmas and New Year's. Convenient to buses and the downtown shopping district. Pauline Maridor, Proprietor. (See Index for rates.)

Directions: From Princes St., enter St. Andrews Sq. and turn right onto Queen St., then left on Dublin St. Take first right on Albany St. There is parking on the street or in a nearby car park.

For room rates and last time for dinner orders, see Index.

THE OPEN ARMS HOTEL
Dirleton, East Lothian

"Our guests find that the Open Arms is perfectly suited to the visitor who wants to be near Edinburgh, but prefers to stay in the country."

Arthur Neil, the managing director of this village hotel, was explaining some of the interesting sights and activities of this corner of Scotland, which borders on both the North Sea and the Firth of Forth.

"We have eight golf courses within easy driving distance," he commented. "The sandy local soil enables the golfer to play in almost any weather, summer and winter. There are also many beaches and numerous beauty spots nearby."

We were enjoying a chat in the drawing room and he noticed that my attention was drawn to the ruins of the famous Dirleton Castle, just across the quiet village street.

"Our guests love to roam inside of those walls," he said. "It's one of the most famous ancient monuments in the British Isles. Time has dealt most graciously with the old 11th-century castle—it has taken on a great mellowness of age."

I had seen quite a few of the carefully kept guest rooms, each with its own private bath. Mr. Neil made a point of mentioning that service is available in the rooms at no extra cost.

We did have a moment or two to talk about some of the items on the menu, including a mussel and onion stew, something which I must confess I had never heard of until visiting the Open Arms.

Mr. Neil spoke at some length of his interest in encouraging the young people of Scotland to become involved in the hotel business; he has set up some standards for industry practice and training programs that I found most admirable.

Arthur Neil is also the proprietor of the Howard Hotel, located in a very pleasant residential area of Edinburgh. When telephoning either one or the other hotel, arrangements can be made for either place.

Incidentally, the symbol on the stationery and brochures for the Open Arms is a stylized version of a young lady in a colorful costume with long hair curling over her shoulders holding her arms out with such bountiful offerings as oranges, apples, pears, grapes, and other fruits and vegetables. The motto of the house is, "Where welcome ever smiles and farewell goes out sighing."

THE OPEN ARMS HOTEL, Dirleton, East Lothian. Tel.: (0620 85) Dirleton 241. U.S. reservations: 800-243-1806. A 7-guestroom village hotel, 20 mi. east of Edinburgh. Open every day in the year for breakfast, lunch, tea, and dinner. Within a short drive of many historic and scenic attractions and adjacent to active sports such as tennis, golf, fishing, walking, and riding. Arthur Neil, Managing Director. (See Index for rates.)

Directions: From Edinburgh: follow A1 to Berwick, using Musselburgh Bypass and watch for roundabout indicating A198 to No. Berwick on the left. The road passes through Gullane to Dirleton.

GREYWALLS
Gullane, East Lothian

Greywalls is the Americans' "golf club away from home." It's a mashie-niblick shot from the fairways and greens of the world-famous Muirfield golf links. The great and near-great of golfdom have played Muirfield, and the hotel guestbook includes such names as Palmer and Nicklaus.

To avoid any misunderstanding, the proprietor of Greywalls, Giles Weaver, points out that being in residence at the hotel does not automatically provide an introduction to Muirfield. "To play, one has to make one's own arrangements with the Secretary." So come prepared with letters from your home club and other documents—they take such things seriously at Muirfield. Not everyone can be accommodated.

So much for golf. I can assure any golfers that even if they cannot play Muirfield, the ten other courses in East Lothian contain some surprises and challenges.

As suggested earlier, Greywalls has a definite clublike atmosphere. Several of the drawing rooms are lined from floor to ceiling with books and have cheery fireplaces. The furniture is deep and comfortable, inviting conversation with new acquaintances.

The rather opulent guest rooms overlook the fairways and greens of Muirfield and the Firth of Forth beyond. On the opposite side of the hotel there are some gorgeous gardens with many roses and beautiful delicate purple irises, which were in bloom during my visit.

Greywalls is a luxurious, highly reputable country house hotel. Guests are made to feel as if they are in a private home, and there is a casual and natural atmosphere.

The amenities are numerous, including fresh fruit and good books in the rooms, as well as telephones and TV's. There is a call button in both bedrooms and bathrooms to summon the bellman, if needed. Everything has been done, as the saying goes, "to the nines."

GREYWALLS (Pride of Britain), Duncur Rd., Gullane, East Lothian EH31 2EG. Tel.: (0620) 842 144. U.S. reservations: 800-323-7308. A 23-guestroom elegant country house hotel, immediately adjacent to the famous Muirfield golf links on the Firth of Forth and 19 mi. from Edinburgh. Breakfast, lunch, dinner served to non-residents. Open every day in the week. Closed during the winter. It is wise to check in advance for accommodations at any time. In the historically rich and beautiful natural area of scenic beauty in East Lothian. Golf and many other sports available nearby. Giles Weaver, Proprietor. (See Index for rates.)

Directions: From Edinburgh take the A1 through Musselburgh and then watch carefully on the left for A198, which leads eastward to Gullane. Turn left at the end of Gullane Village at the signpost; Greywalls is 300 yds. further on.

DALHOUSIE CASTLE HOTEL
Bonnyrigg, Lothian

Although Dalhousie Castle has dungeons and foundation walls dating back to the 13th century, as well as a main structure built in 1450, only twenty years later than Borthwick Castle, the differences between the two castles are very great.

Dalhousie Castle has seen many additions and modifications over the years, as evidenced by the different styles of architecture. When I walked through the low, unassuming door into the entrance hall, I was really surprised at the rather baroque grandeur of the reception area. A curving double staircase leads up to a reception room with a high vaulted ceiling and a cupola decorated in pale blue and gilt. The room has an almost chapel-like feeling.

My favorite rooms in the castle are the library and the dining room. The library is paneled in a beautiful blond wood and lined with shelves filled with books. The stone mullioned windows look out on a peaceful field, and the leather chairs and sofas are deep and comfortable. A grouping around the black marble fireplace has a huge, low table with a lovely arrangement of dried flowers on it. The manager, a most accommodating young man, told me that they serve hors d'oeuvres and before-dinner refreshments, as well as after-dinner coffee in this room. There is a hidden panel in one wall that I challenge you to find.

The dining room is an adventure in itself. You walk down curving stone steps into the dungeon. It is a real dungeon with blackened stone walls and great iron-barred doors. There is a suit of armor standing in a large niche and great medieval weapons on the walls. Individual cells contain four or five tables each. Thick carpeting, pink tablecloths, tapestry-covered chairs, candlelight, and the lilting strains of a lute make it an intriguing and romantic experience.

The menu offers a wide selection, including grilled Tay salmon, River Tweed trout with lemon and thyme stuffing, roast local lamb, pot-roasted chicken in a claret sauce, breast of Aylesbury duckling in a port wine sauce with black currants and rosemary, and several choices of Angus beef prepared in various ways. The appetizers and sweets offerings are quite diverse.

This castle was built by the Ramsays, Earls of Dalhousie, and has remained in their hands for eight centuries. Its early history is rife with battles. It is the last castle in Scotland to have been besieged in person by an English king—Henry IV in 1400. The Ramsays hold an illustrious place in Scotland's history. They no longer reside in the castle, having leased it out to various tenants since the turn of the century.

Some of the guest rooms I saw were quite sumptuous, with tall windows draped in heavy velvet, handsome wallpaper, carved wood bedsteads, little medieval writing desks, tapestries, and oil paintings. There are some fireplace rooms, and they all have private bathrooms, TV, and telephones.

DALHOUSIE CASTLE HOTEL, Bonnyrigg, Lothian EH19 3JB. Tel.: Gorebridge (0875) 20153. U.S. reservations: 800-221-1074. A 24-guest-room castle hotel on the River Esk in a rural area, 9 mi. south of Edinburgh. Breakfast included in tariff. Lunch and dinner served to the public, reservations preferable. Open year-round. Games room, darts, arrangements for fishing, riding, clay pigeon and grouse shooting on premises. Historic houses and castles, wool mills, glass works, fishing villages, and all the attractions of Edinburgh nearby. Chris Brennan, General Manager. (See Index for rates.)

Directions: From Edinburgh, take the A7 for 7 mi. to Eskbank, continuing at roundabout on A7 for 1 mi. Turn right under bridge towards Carrington, then left at first crossroads by the church. After 200 yds. turn left at hotel sign and immediately right.

BORTHWICK CASTLE
North Middleton by Gorebridge, Midlothian

If you have a taste for a bit of adventure and for the experience of a medieval castle, then spending a night at Borthwick Castle would be just your cup of tea. I mention adventure because stepping out of your bedroom door right onto the narrow, spiraling stone steps that thread the two great towers can be somewhat challenging.

This is truly a historic structure, built in 1430 by Sir William Borthwick with the express purpose of establishing an impregnable fortress. On a promontory once surrounded by water on all sides, originally with a portcullis and drawbridge (no longer in evidence), the castle has two massive, square, 110-foot-high towers with 10-foot-thick stone walls.

Mary, Queen of Scots, and her third husband, the Earl of Bothwell, lived here in 1567 during their final days of freedom. In 1650, under attack by Cromwell, the master of the castle refused to surrender, causing Cromwell to send him the message, "If you necessitate me to bend my cannon against you, you must expect that I doubt you will not be pleased with." The partial destruction of the wall caused by Cromwell's cannon can still be seen today.

Stepping through the low door of the entrance, you walk into the impressive Great Hall, with a forty-foot-high vaulted ceiling and an absolutely mammoth stone fireplace. There are leather couches and easy chairs grouped around the fireplace, which is decorated with suits of armor on either side. Antlers, deer and ram heads, large tapestries, and oil portraits decorate the walls. The atmosphere is actually quite homey, with the lighting and comfortable seating. The day I was there a very long, highly polished table was set for dinner with sparkling crystal and china and gleaming silver. The tall-backed dining chairs are upholstered in a deep maroon and the floor is carpeted from wall to wall.

The guest rooms, as I mentioned, are entered right from the spiral stairwell. They are simply furnished, with whitewashed stone walls. Private bathrooms have been carved out of the ten-foot-thick walls and tend to be small and simple. The room where Mary Stuart slept has a beautiful fireplace and a regal mahogany four-poster with deep red draperies. There are two alcoves with paneled walls and benches, where it is thought her ladies-in-waiting may have sat.

The cuisine is traditional Scottish, and the menus look quite tempting, with a choice of two entrées and appetizers, a soup, a sorbet between courses, and some interesting desserts. The menus I saw featured salmon steak with fresh herbs, tournedos of lamb with ginger sauce, roast Angus sirloin, and veal escalope with Madeira. Some of the desserts were strawberry kiwi Pavlova, raspberry and chocolate gateaux, gingernut log, and American chocolate pie. Manager Patricia Hills translated their Scottish dinner menu for me. Cock-a-leekie soup is made with chicken, rice, potatoes, and onion; haggis wi' neeps an' tatties is sausage with turnips and potatoes. I forgot to ask her what cranachan wi' brambles might be.

There are surrounding woodlands and a trout stream. This is an ideal place to soak up the atmosphere and a sense of Scotland's embattled history.

BORTHWICK CASTLE, North Middleton by Gorebridge, Midlothian EH23 4QY. Tel.: Gorebridge (0875) 20514 or 21747. A 10-guestroom (private baths) 1430 medieval castle in a little agricultural valley, 12 mi. south of Edinburgh. Breakfast included in tariff. Dinner served to the public by reservation only. Badminton and bicycles on grounds; arrangements for salmon and trout fishing, shooting, riding, and golf. Historic sites, country walks, and all the attractions of Edinburgh nearby. George and Patricia Hills, Managers. (See Index for rates.)

Directions: From Edinburgh, take the A7 south towards Galashiels. In North Middleton turn left on a country road. Pass the school and Borthwick Church. The castle is ¾ mi. from the turn.

CRINGLETIE HOUSE HOTEL
Peebles, Borders

It's not often that someone has lunch at a country house hotel while on vacation and then returns the next year and buys the hotel. But that is just what Aileen and Stanley Maguire did in 1971. He and his wife were so taken with Cringletie House and the surrounding countryside, as well as that kind of life, that they became instant hoteliers and have never looked back.

Mr. Maguire manages the hotel and his wife is head chef. I have the impression that he is a man who runs a tight ship. As he showed me around the hotel, he had an eagle eye out for every detail, making sure that doors shut properly, straightening a curtain here, picking a bit of lint off a carpet there. And I doubt if we missed a single room in our tour as we trotted around corners, down zigzag hallways, and up winding stairs, looking in on guest rooms large and small, twin-bedded and double-bedded, and all cheerful, pleasant, nicely decorated, well kept, and immaculate.

I looked out turret windows, tall bay windows, dormer windows under the eaves, nursery windows with bars across them—and each and every one of them has a lovely view. The views are of rolling hills, green fields, grazing sheep, and beautiful 200-year-old copper beech, lime, and silver birch trees. The grounds are immaculately kept, with lawns, gardens, and a curving drive up to the house that is lined with masses of daffodils in the spring. One very lovely view is down over the town of Peebles and off to rolling hills in the distance.

Mr. Maguire's staff was busily readying the two dining rooms for dinner when we looked in. The tables were set with white cloths, linen napery, and silver. There were tall windows with carved moldings overlooking the tennis court, and one table was set in the turret section with curved windows looking out on the winding drive. Both dining rooms had a fireplace and were decorated with oil paintings and fresh flowers.

The residents' lounge is a lovely big room with paneled walls and comfortable chairs upholstered in a soft rose flocked velvet. The domed ceiling has a rococo painting with flying cherubs and clouds, and the walls are decorated with 17th- and 18th-century portraits and landscapes.

Mr. Maguire and I sat in the downstairs lounge for a cup of tea and some background history on the house. He told me that the very large impressive portrait in the residents' lounge was of Sir Alexander Murray, the high sheriff of Peebleshire in 1646 and a supporter of Charles I. His son built the original house in 1666, of which only a little dovecote remains. The present house, which looks very much like a Scottish castle, with its corner turrets and gables, was built in 1861. (Mr. Maguire said it isn't big enough to be a castle.) It remained in the hands of the Murray family and, by marriage, the Sutherland family for over 100 years, until 1963.

Aileen Maguire, who did all of the interior decoration of the house, runs the kitchen, and her husband calls the cuisine "imaginative home cooking." He says she "reads cookbooks like some people read novels."

Cringletie House has been listed in the *Good Food Guide* for fifteen years, he tells me. When I pressed him for some of their more popular dishes, he mentioned fruit-stuffed supreme of chicken with cinnamon sauce, roast duckling with morello cherry sauce, and baked chicken Parmesan with tomato and basil sauce. In looking over their menus, I noted also kidneys in whisky and cream, loin of pork with apricot and sage dressing, and a fillet of sole with orange, chive, and caper sauce. There were a number of appetizers and a sweets trolley with all sorts of goodies, including Mr. Maguire's particular favorites: hazelnut meringue and praline Vacherin.

Within a half-hour's drive of Edinburgh with all of its attractions, Cringletie offers a very pleasant escape to peace and tranquility after a busy day in the city. By the way, Peebles, only a few minutes down the road, is a sweet little town with some very nice shops, and one in particular has beautiful original designs in hand-woven wool sweaters. It's called Wool Gathering.

CRINGLETIE HOUSE HOTEL, Peebles, Borders EH45 8PL. Tel.: (07213) 233. A 16-guestroom (some shared baths) distinguished mansion house in the Eddleston valley between the Moorfoot and Meldon hills, 20 mi. south of Edinburgh. Full breakfast is included in the tariff. Lunch and dinner served to the public by reservation. Closed Jan. and Feb. Croquet lawn, putting green, tennis court, and walks on 28-acre grounds. Golf, trout and salmon fishing, swimming, horse riding, parkland walks, many historic sites and stately homes, as well as Edinburgh and its attractions nearby. Stanley and Aileen Maguire, Proprietors. (See Index for rates.)

Directions: From the North British Hotel in Edinburgh, take the A7 toward Penicuik (do not go towards Galashiels) to the A703. Continue 2 mi. past Eddleston. Road is signposted for Cringletie.

THE PHILIPBURN HOUSE HOTEL
Selkirk

It is possible to drive from London to Edinburgh in one day, but please don't do it. A much more enjoyable, maybe even a more *civilized,* way is to take it in easy stages and spend two nights at each stop along the way. This book is based on that premise.

After an enjoyable trip through the lovely Scottish Lowlands (I'm sure you will agree they have been misnamed), one of the stops might well be the Philipburn House in Selkirk, south of Edinburgh in the Borders.

This country house hotel is set in the heart of Sir Walter Scott country in the Dale of Ettrick and Yarrow. The original house was built in 1751 and the exterior has that wonderful feeling of Scottish austerity that at times can be most attractive.

The interior has obviously been well designed and coordinated, and the lounges, poolside restaurant (oh yes! I said poolside), and public rooms all have a wonderful glow about them, partially provided by some extremely attractive pine woodwork.

I was seated at one of the tables in the poolside restaurant, talking with Anne Hill, who with her husband, Jim, is the owner of Philipburn House, about what Americans would find entertaining and diverting while on a holiday in Scotland.

"Just imagine that it's morning now," Anne began, "and the sun is already warm—slanting over the nearby Border hills, and the scents of pine, heather, and peat are in the air. Your American friends can spend a day in the hills with Davy Fordyce, our resident guide, who is a sort of craggy person with a warm and friendly personality and a grand sense of humor. A walk with Davy provides a rich insight into the history and romance of the Borderland, the hills, the forests, the rivers, the lochs, the ancient towers, the poetry, the legends, the songs, and the rich wildlife that abounds in our territory. How's that for starters?"

I had to admit that I was already convinced. Other activities that provide a holiday atmosphere include horseback riding in all seasons (because there is an indoor riding school nearby), 200 miles of trout and salmon fishing, which can be arranged, garden and woodland walks, golf, swimming in the pool, quite a rarity for Scotland.

Each accommodation is different, including spacious country house bedrooms, family suites, poolside suites, and cottages. All of these look over the lawns and woodlands to the hills beyond. All have private bathrooms and color television.

Anne continued, "We believe that dinner here is the highlight of the day and, perhaps after a last dip in the pool, I meet all the guests and help them with the difficult task of trying to choose from the menu items. We have such traditional dishes as freshly caught fish, as well as pheasant stuffed with raspberries and wrapped in bacon, roast pork stuffed with apple, fillet of sole, mallard duck, and venison served with poached pears, cherry port, and cranberry sauce."

During my stay I saw no other Americans, but lots of British families with children, and since my idea of travel is not only to look at the scenery but to meet the people, here's a wonderful opportunity to meet our British cousins as they enjoy a good holiday. By the way, there is much entertainment and diversion for children with provisions for serving them at teatime, giving their parents an opportunity to relax for a few moments. The Hills have three children of their own and believe that people need a holiday as much as, if not more than, the children, so they provide as many things as possible to entertain the younger generation.

THE PHILIPBURN HOUSE HOTEL, Selkirk TD7 5LS. Tel.: 0750 20747/21690. A 16-guestroom (private baths) country house hotel about an hour from Edinburgh. Breakfast, lunch, tea, and dinner served daily. Open year-round. Swimming pool on grounds. Ample facilities to amuse young people. Golf, fishing, shooting, and hill walking. Jim and Anne Hill, Proprietors. (See Index for rates.)

Directions: Locate Selkirk, south of Edinburgh. Coming from the south on A7, ignore the right turn in the middle of Selkirk and continue on over the river towards A708. A sign for Philipburn House is at a T-junction.

KNOCKINAAM LODGE HOTEL
Portpatrick, Wigtownshire

Even now I can close my eyes and experience once again the sunset at Knockinaam. The setting is breathtaking, for the lodge sits in its own little naturally created row of rugged cliffs, and the broad expanse of lawns invites a walk toward the sea among the box hedges and the wild flowers and roses.

I was reminded of the coast of northern California—Carmel, Monterey, and even farther north. The entire experience of the sea, sky, and the rugged cliffs impressed itself upon me forever.

The owners of Knockinaam are two very attractive people, Connie and Marcel Frichot. They've done a perfectly splendid job of infusing the entire hotel and the staff with their enthusiasm.

Marcel puts it this way: "Most people come to Knockinaam for the peace and relaxation, but the guests who feel so inclined can walk, fish, play golf, visit the gardens at Logan and Castle Kennedy, or simply explore one of the few areas of Scotland as yet largely undiscovered."

Connie joins in, "Yes, I should say quite undiscovered, particularly by North Americans. There are many larger, smarter hotels offering more

facilities, but what we have is unique and we think that our guests enjoy the homey feeling, as well as the really serious attention given to our food. Furthermore, in these difficult times when everything is very expensive, you can still rely on a friendly smile and a good word. When guests arrive, we do our best to make them feel welcome. Their spirits are lifted when they catch the first glimpse of Knockinaam and its beautiful setting. Once inside, they need to relax, so we offer them something refreshing, explain to them how the telephone works, and carry their luggage upstairs."

I would hope that many of the readers of this book will break away from the standard practice of many first-time visitors to Scotland and make a real effort to visit this southwest corner. It is actually less than two hours' drive from Prestwick, and passengers on the night flight from North America can be here at Knockinaam between 10 and 11 a.m., allowing them an almost two-day stay, even though they may remain for only one night. The car ferry to Ireland is just a few moments away and not likely to be as crowded as some of the better-known terminals.

Knockinaam Lodge is a little out of the way, but it is a rewarding, relaxing experience and travelers should plan to spend a minimum of two nights.

KNOCKINAAM LODGE HOTEL (Pride of Britain), Portpatrick, Wigtownshire DG9 9AD. Tel.: 077-681-471. USA: 800-323-3602. A 10-guestroom (private baths) seaside country house hotel on the extreme western end of the Scottish Lowlands. Breakfast, lunch, and dinner served. Open Easter to Jan. Excellent walking, fishing, golfing, swimming, and driving nearby. Convenient for a first overnight stop after landing at Prestwick. Connie and Marcel Frichot, Proprietors. (See Index for rates.)

Directions: Portpatrick is 119 mi. from Carlisle (A75) and 101 mi. from Glasgow (A77). From Stranraer, travel south on the A77 toward Portpatrick and 3 mi. after the village of Lochans, turn left at the main hotel sign.

MARINE HOTEL
Troon, Ayrshire

If you are flying in or out of Prestwick Airport, the Marine Hotel can provide sensible accommodations either the night before your departure or the day of your arrival.

Actually, the building is rather impressive for its size alone. It's a big, multistoried, red sandstone building that provides holiday accommodations for Britons and their Continental neighbors who enjoy the game of golf. It stands between the Royal Troon and the Portland golf courses and I saw many golfing holiday-makers arriving and departing, complete with their golf bags.

There are two restaurants—the Fairways Restaurant, overlooking the bay and golf courses, and Crosbie's Brasserie, a lively restaurant/bar offering imaginative and inexpensive meals from morning until the "wee small hours." There is also an impressive sports and leisure club, available free of charge to guests staying in the hotel.

Bedrooms are comfortable and all have private bathrooms and the other British hotel amenities.

MARINE HOTEL, Troon, Ayrshire KA10 6HE. Tel.: (0292) 31-4444. A large, conventional hotel (private baths) a few minutes from Prestwick Airport. Open year-round. Breakfast, lunch, and dinner served daily. Quite convenient to many nearby golf courses. Located in Robert Burns country; his cottage at Alloway and other Burns memorabilia nearby. (See Index for rates.)

Directions: Troon is to the west of M6. Follow any of the roads to the middle of town and make inquiries.

DRIVING IN THE SCOTTISH HIGHLANDS

Motoring in the Highlands is marvelous. It is also very different. Fortunately, by the time I had reached this incredibly beautiful country I had quite a few days of driving on the left side of the road so that my reactions were good.

The entire experience from the broad expanse of the extraordinary scenery to the minutiae of the individual plants, flowers, trees, houses, rocks, animals, and clouds make it sensational backroading.

Like the fjord country of Norway, the White Mountains of New Hampshire, the Grand Canyon of Arizona, and the Himalayas of Tibet, the Scottish Highlands have a wildness completely their own. One of the qualities I like is that, with all of the ruggedness, there is a certain gentleness, because almost everything is covered with green grass and heather. It is only the mountain crags that are without vegetation.

Sheep and cattle in the road are a way of life. The roads in the Highlands are so curvy and twisty that when I took a moment to look at a loch or a glen I frequently found myself confronted by a cow in the road. Much of the time I was traveling on roads only wide enough to accommodate one car. However, they were all paved and in good shape. There are turnouts every 50 or 100 yards, and the courtesy of the road determines which car going in the opposite direction should pull over and wait for the other car. The question naturally comes as to what happens when two cars meet in the middle between two turn-off places? My experience was that everyone was quite considerate and very frequently there would be two cars backing up, each expecting to allow the other car to continue. Cars traveling at a leisurely pace also pull over to the side, allowing those who are traveling faster to pass. Ninety per cent of the time great courtesy is shown by all concerned and everyone acknowledges with a friendly wave of the hand.

Quite a few Scottish innkeepers will hold a telephone reservation only until five o'clock in the afternoon. Some of the popular American credit cards are only good in the more luxurious hotels, although traveler's checks are accepted. I carried British traveler's checks and had no problems. I was never able to buy gasoline (petrol) with anything except cash.

Watch out for bank holidays; change money or traveler's checks the Friday before; I got caught on a few Mondays with no pounds sterling.

There is a lot of sunshine and also a lot of "Scottish mist." I was glad to have a lightweight nylon jacket with a hood.

THE CREGGANS INN
Strachur, Argyll

I believe that one of the biggest thrills in my life was being mistaken for Sir Fitzroy Maclean. It happened on my last visit to Creggans Inn, where some American ladies were taking a very special tour of Scottish gardens. With a big smile, one of them spoke to me.

"Oh, Sir Fitzroy," she exclaimed, "we're all so thrilled that you happened to be here at Creggans Inn during our visit!" Then all of the ladies clapped their hands. Can I tell you that for about three seconds I stood there basking in my false glory, wondering how I was going to get out of this situation, when the *real* Sir Fitzroy Maclean appeared. Somewhat sputteringly I explained that *he* was the man to whom they were referring. Well, there was lots of general laughter and then he was kind enough to introduce me.

I couldn't have chosen a lovelier day for my second visit to the Creggans Inn, and the panorama of mountains, sky, and loch was absolutely glorious. My first visit had been in considerable contrast—a showery afternoon with great rolling clouds occasionally allowing a shaft of golden sunlight to brilliantly light Loch Fyne and the village of Strachur.

This time, coming from the north, I had driven from Oban and stopped at the village of Inveraray, just across Loch Fyne from Strachur. Oddly enough, Creggans Inn was plainly visible across this narrow stretch of water, but in order to reach it, I had to drive up to the far end and down the other side, following a hairpin-curved course. There's a famous castle at Inveraray where, among other things, a cannon from the Spanish Armada ship *Florida* is on display. The ship itself is supposedly still under the sands and silt in the harbor of Tobermory on the Isle of Mull.

Sir Fitzroy traces his family well back into both Scottish and American history. During World War II, he was Winston Churchill's personal liaison with Marshall Tito of Yugoslavia. Later, he served in Churchill's cabinet and was a member of Parliament. In America, he is well known as an author, with three books on the Balkans to his credit.

Lady Veronica Maclean is also an author in her own right and is particularly well known as a travel journalist and writer of cookbooks.

Creggans is an old West Highland inn with a tradition of homey comfort and individual attention to the visitor. It is ideally situated amidst magnificent scenery for walks and excursions by land and water. It serves the needs of local people as well as the tourist.

Mrs. Laura Huggins, the innkeeper, and I had time for a nice chat in the reception area of the inn, where there are numerous brochures, folders, and booklets about all of the historic and natural attractions within a short drive of Strachur. Some of them, including *Castles and Gardens of Argyll* and *Woodland Walk, Strachur,* are by Lady Maclean.

"We've had very many faithful visitors, who have come from your book *Country Inns and Back Roads, Britain and Ireland*," said Mrs. Huggins. "Some of them have come back a second time. We're beautifully located for people to stay a few days and enjoy trips to Inveraray, Benmore, the Isle of Bute, Eckford, Easdale, Loch Lomond, and Glencoe. We can arrange deer stalking, fishing, and boating. Swimming, wild-life watching, and pony trekking are available. We have our own private woodland walk as well."

I thought the menu was quite extensive for what Sir Fitzroy insisted was a "humble Highlands inn." It included rainbow trout, honey-baked ham, various kinds of beef and lamb, mackerel, and duckling Montmorency. Their seafood menu includes native oysters, langoustinos, and smoked salmon. "Lady Maclean completely supervises the menu," he remarked. "It's a sort of interesting combination of English, Scottish, American, French, and northern Italian cooking."

A permanent marker outside, just a few paces from the dining room of the inn (which has a gorgeous view of the loch), commemorates the visit of Mary, Queen of Scots, who landed here 400 years ago on her way through the Highlands. I tried to imagine that perhaps the incredible beauty of the loch brought a few moments of joy to that ill-fated lady.

THE CREGGANS INN, Strachur, Argyll PA27 8BX. Tel.: (036986) Strachur 279. U.S. reservations: 800-243-1806. Telex: 778425 INN-CREG. A 22-guestroom (all private baths) lochside country hotel, 50 mi. from Glasgow in the Scottish Highlands. Open all year. Breakfast, lunch, tea, and dinner served to non-residents. Very convenient for tours into the Highlands as well as visits to innumerable Scottish castles and gardens. Sea and loch fishing, boating, bathing, woodland walks, birding, stately homes, archeological and garden tours, pony trekking nearby. Just across the loch from the town of Inveraray and its castle. Sir Fitzroy, Lady Veronica Maclean, Charles E. Maclean, Partners; Laura Huggins, Manageress. (See Index for rates.)

Directions: From Glasgow, follow road to Loch Lomondside, Arrochar, the "Rest and be Thankful," the A83 and A815. Also by Gourock, take the car-ferry across the Clyde to Dunoon and follow the A815.

Rates for a room for two people for one night with breakfast, except where noted, are included in the Index of this book. They are not to be considered firm quotations, but should be used as guidelines only.

THE ISLE OF COLONSAY

Anyone looking for a truly "different" travel experience, where there is practically no commercial intrusion and where it's possible to feel the thrill of being alone and secluded, will enjoy the Isle of Colonsay.

Although visitors are very much encouraged to come to Colonsay and to enjoy its special attractions, it does not offer any synthetic entertainments. There are no tourist traps, no amusement arcades, or fun fairs. Nor are there day-trippers, because the ferry only runs twice a week. Caravans (camping vehicles) are not allowed, and only educational and scientific organizations are given permission to camp in tents.

There is one general store, used by all of the islanders. The arrival of the ferry is an Event, and guests of the Isle of Colonsay Hotel invariably hurry down to the dock to watch the unloading.

However, for anyone who is content with a holiday built around the natural amenities and social life of a small Scottish island, Colonsay has plenty to offer. In the summer, there are several beaches for bathing and picnicking. The walking is superlative along the beaches, roads, and paths, and among the rocks and cliffs and several caves, which were probably inhabited as long as six thousand years ago. There is much of interest to the archeologist and antiquarian, including various standing stones and ancient ruins.

Colonsay is the larger of two islands in the Outer Hebrides, joined at low tide by a narrow sandy beach called the Strand. The second is Oronsay Island, which lays claim to a most important event in history—it is said to have been where St. Columba landed on his way to Iona from Ireland in the middle of the 6th century.

ISLE OF COLONSAY HOTEL
Isle of Colonsay, Argyll

This story began in Ireland a few years ago when I first met Kevin and Christa Byrne, who are now the hoteliers at the Isle of Colonsay Hotel. At that time, these two attractive young people, graduates of Trinity College in Dublin, had enthusiastically embarked on a career of hotelkeeping.

A short time later I received a letter from Kevin, who is a tall red-bearded man with a fascinating gift of conversation, to the effect that they were moving to the Isle of Colonsay to take over the hotel.

So I found myself on the ferry from Oban, arriving at the wharf, where the selfsame Kevin was waiting in a former London taxicab to drive me to his small hotel, in sight of the ferry dock.

Kevin immediately enveloped me with his enthusiasm. "I'm glad you're coming here now," he said. "We've put things in beautiful

shipshape order, but it's been a lot of work. Christa has really been magnificent, being both mother and hotelier. Ah, here we are." He pulled into the small parking lot, scattering some of the ubiquitous sheep.

Kevin was right, the additions were shipshape and the accommodations were clean, comfortable, and, without a doubt, cordial. Furthermore, he had a very good chef, and the menu included Colonsay oysters and other local seafood, as well as hearty and tasty native lamb.

Guests become involved with each other almost immediately, exchanging experiences at the end of the first day and joining forces on subsequent days. There's ample opportunity to meet the islanders, because the hotel has the only pub on the island.

I spent almost a whole day on a walking excursion of one portion of the island with two American women. We climbed over fences (legally) and followed rocky roads over cliffs and moorland, sandy beaches, and lily-filled lochs, rhododendron woods, cultivated lands, farms, and hills. It was a day to be remembered.

During one of my long conversations with Kevin, I remarked that someone ought to write a book about Colonsay.

"Somebody already has," he replied with great glee, whereupon he presented me with a copy of a book entitled, *The Crofter and the Laird,* by John McPhee (Farrar, Straus and Giroux, New York). Author McPhee visited the island in the late 1960s because he, like so many other McPhees, McAfees, and other permutations of the name, have ever been drawn back to the land of their ancestors. The people he wrote about still live on the island, including the schoolmistress with whom I visited on the very last day of school.

A recent letter from Kevin told a tale of the extensive improvements he and Christa have accomplished since my last visit. All the double guest rooms now have private bath/showers, and there are three new self-catering chalets that will be suitable for families. Along with a number of other amenities they have added to make their guests more comfortable, they have also developed some services and facilities for visiting yachtsmen.

Because the railroad station in Oban is right next to the ferry dock, it's possible to reach Colonsay using public transportation from any point in England and Scotland. A chartered boat ride around the islands is also a singular experience. Automobiles are not necessary, and the hotel has bicycles.

Please check all sailing schedules and other important details with Kevin Byrne when making bookings.

I believe I've presented Colonsay as it really is. Incidentally, the hotel is the only such accommodation on the island. If it's "your kind of place," you'll love it.

ISLE OF COLONSAY HOTEL, Colonsay Island, Argyll PA61 7YP. Tel.: (095 12) 316. An 11-guestroom (mostly private bath/showers) village inn located on an island 37 mi. from Oban. Full central heating. Open every day in the year. Breakfast, lunch, tea, and dinner served. Exceptional hill and muir walks. Bicycles and boats available. Primitive and challenging golf course; fishing. Kevin and Christa Byrne, Resident Proprietors. (See Index for rates.)

Directions: Colonsay is, with the aid of the railroad and the ferry, available to all parts of Britain. The train station is a few steps from the ferry dock. All sailings are from Oban (Railway Pier). Check with hotel for days and hours of sailing (2½ hrs.); meal service provided on board. Cars may be left on mainland; really not needed on island.

ARDANAISEIG
Kilchrenan, Argyll

Ardanaiseig is in Argyll, in the heart of the mountainous region, over which the Clan Campbell held undisputed sway for centuries. This gracious mansion, built in 1834, was until recently a family home.

The first owner was so inspired by the setting of his new house on the shore of Loch Awe that he began planting a great garden. A number of conifers and other rare trees still stand. The grounds are replete with rhododendrons and azaleas.

The guest rooms have big, chintzy chairs, polished tables, and fresh flowers, and the entire atmosphere is warm and relaxed. Each bedroom has its own bathroom.

The hotel has its own private pier on the loch and boats from which to fish or explore and picnic on the many islands not too far away. There is a fishing beat on the River Awe and various hill lochs for the serious fisherman.

Ardanaiseig is a most pleasurable experience.

ARDANAISEIG (Pride of Britain), Kilchrenan, by Taynuilt, Argyll. Tel.: (08663) 333. U.S. reservations: 800-323-3602. An impressive Scottish country house hotel, just a short distance from Oban. Breakfast, lunch, and dinner served daily. Two-night minimum stay. Closed mid-Oct. to Easter. Woodland trails, croquet, tennis court, and clay pigeon trap. Michael and Frieda Yeo, Resident Directors. (See Index for rates.)

Directions: Take A85 east from Oban and watch for hotel sign.

TAYCHREGGAN HOTEL
Kilchrenan, by Taynuilt, Argyll

Even if you will never visit Taychreggan Hotel, please write the proprietors, John and Tove Taylor, and tell them I suggested you ask for the brochure of the hotel. With many excellent full-color photographs and an engaging personal description, it is one of the best I've seen anywhere. As I was on my way from Connel across A85 toward a luncheon at Creggans Inn, I saw a sign for Taychreggan Hotel leading down a country road. It was just on a whim that I decided to see what was at the end of the road.

What I found was the little village of Kilchrenan, a cluster of houses and a post office, and a little farther on, the Taychreggan Hotel.

It is situated on the shore of Loch Awe, which, at twenty-four miles, is the longest fresh-water loch in Scotland.

The older part of the building was originally a drovers' inn. In subsequent years, substantial additions were made to the old stone house and further imaginative construction has created a three-sided cobbled courtyard. The fourth side of this very sunny environment is a glassed-in passageway connecting the old house with the new.

I was quite disappointed that Mr. and Mrs. Taylor were not in residence during my brief visit, but I was much impressed with the cordiality of the staff.

There are traditional bedrooms, as well as some that have been more recently created. The decor is plain and simple; good straight colors and pine. The overall effect is one of light and warmth.

One of the great advantages of staying at the Taychreggan is the opportunity to meet and perhaps engage the services of the local ghillie for a fishing guide. Of course he knows all of the waters and islands of Loch Awe and is ready for serious fishing with a generous dollop of humorous anecdotes.

I was not there for dinner, but the menu included Scottish as well as Continental main courses. My whim to visit Taychreggan turned out to be a good one and I would recommend that travelers plan on spending two nights, not only to enjoy the hotel, but also the many outdoor diversions within a few miles, at most, of the hotel.

A departing young American couple were enraptured with Taychreggan and full of regret that they had engaged a room for only one night.

Reader Comment: "Thank you so much for leading us to this delightful spot. Our room was charming, with matching wallpaper and curtains—there were even matching padded coat hangers. Plants and flowers were everywhere."

TAYCHREGGAN HOTEL, Kilchrenan, by Taynuilt, Argyll PA35 1HQ. Tel.: (08663) Kilchrenan 211. U.S. reservations: 800-243-1806. A 17-guestroom (14 with private bathrooms) lochside hotel in the western Highlands. Open from Easter to mid-Oct. Rates include dinner. Breakfast, lunch, tea, and dinner served. Riding, sailing, fishing, shooting, walking, gardens, and historic places, as well as many day trips. John and Tove Taylor, Proprietors. (See Index for rates.)

Directions: From A85 turn off at Taynuilt onto B845 for Kilchrenan. Follow B845 to the village; the hotel is just beyond.

ISLE OF ERISKA HOTEL
Ledaig, Connel, Argyll

Robin Buchanan-Smith leaned back in his chair and raised his eyes to heaven. Because he is the Reverend Buchanan-Smith, it occurred to me that this particular attitude was not unusual for him at all. However, this time he was pondering a question I had put to him about his innkeeping philosophy.

He returned for the moment to more terrestrial environments. "I believe that it's 'taking care of people.' Looking after people means personal attention, and I drill this into our small, youngish staff at every opportunity.

"My wife, Sheena, and I keep an eye on everything, and fortunately, the staff is quite dedicated. It's really like a house party. Eriska combines the two oft-forgotten ideals of the modern world—Romanticism and Realism."

He paused for a moment to add a dollop of cream to my cup of tea and continued, "One of our guests stayed here and then went back to California, saying that he had seen everything. He was referring to the fact that there was a British prime minister seated in our parlor, smoking a nine-inch cigar and reading Jane Austen. The prime minister was Harold Macmillan."

Eriska's setting on the shores of the Firth of Lorne is superb. It is on a small island one mile by half a mile, and is reached by a private bridge—this little bridge is important, because it does create a marvelous feeling of being set apart.

On this sylvan island, the hotel stands in the middle of a lovely green lawn dotted with maple and copper beech trees, and accented with rhododendron, wild orchids, sea pinks, and irises.

The building is Scottish Victorian baronial, and true to its tradition, has turrets and battlements from which there are additional and revealing views of the mountains and firths. I was intrigued to learn that there were trekking ponies available from stables right on the hotel grounds, as well as tennis and fishing. There is also water skiing and wind surfing on the firth. The English-style croquet, played with great politeness, was for blood. The feeling of being on a Highland estate is heightened by the presence of roe deer, badgers, heron, and even, on occasion, golden eagles. The milk and cream are from a herd of Jersey cows and there are well-tended vegetable gardens.

The interior is characterized by log fires, wood-paneled walls, and elegantly decorated plaster ceilings. The drawing room where the P.M. smoked his cigar, enjoys a view of the lawn and firth. The guest rooms all have their own private bathrooms.

At tea that afternoon, I joined four other Americans who had just returned from an excursion to the islands of Mull and Iona.

Oddly enough, it was Jim Mellow from St. Louis who first recommended that I visit the Isle of Eriska. He particularly made note of the roast pheasant and the breakfasts that would have pleased Pangloss.

Later, as I was walking on the shore of the firth, I caught a snatch of conversation from a young hand-holding couple . . . "This is the most romantic place I could ever imagine. It far exceeds my greatest expectations."

Reader Comment: "When we first arrived it was a rainy, damp day, and we had tea and scones by the fire. It was delightful."

ISLE OF ERISKA HOTEL, Ledaig, Connel, Argyll PA37 1SD. Tel.: (063 172) Ledaig 205. A 16-guestroom elegant country house hotel on an island in Scotland's western Highlands, 100 mi. from Glasgow. Open early April to end of Nov. Lunch, dinner served to non-residents. Fishing, riding, croquet, tennis, water-skiing, wind-surfing, beach walking on grounds. Speed boat excursions around the island. Sailing, golf nearby. Stunning views of Loch Linnhe and the Atlantic Ocean. Many castles and places of historic and natural interest nearby. Robin and Sheena Buchanan-Smith, Resident Owners. (See Index for rates.)

Directions: From Glasgow, take A82 past Loch Lomond to Tyndrum, then A85 to Oban, turning left onto Fort William Rd. at Connel on A828. Cross Connel Bridge, proceed 3 mi. to Benderloch and look for hotel signs.

ARDSHEAL HOUSE
Kentallen of Appin, Argyll

"That is Loch Linnhe, and beyond are the hills of Morvern. Strontian Pass leads out to a point that is about as far west as you can get on the British mainland."

Bob Taylor, resplendent in kilts, and I were standing in the window of the billiard room of Ardsheal House looking down across the broad meadow to the loch and the mountains beyond. We were enjoying the

absolutely magnificent show being put on by nature, presumably for our special benefit. Overhead, the deeply stratified clouds were parting and closing, allowing unexpected bars of brilliant sunshine to spotlight the hills and the loch, a sight truly beyond words.

He continued my geography and history lesson: "This is an area known for bloody battles and feuds among the Highland clans," he said. "There are many tales of Bonnie Prince Charlie. In fact, this house, built in 1545 by the Stewarts of Appin, was totally sacked by the Duke of Cumberland during the uprisings of 1745. What is here was rebuilt on the old foundations in 1760. Later sections were built in 1814, and this wing with the billiard room, in 1850.

"Ardsheal plays an important part in Robert Louis Stevenson's *Kidnapped*. It was only a mile or so from here where the infamous murder of Appin took place, providing Stevenson with a great deal of material for his book."

It comes as a surprise to many of the guests at Ardsheal House that Bob, a Princeton graduate, and his wife, Jane, and their sons, Brigham and Jason, are from the United States. Previously they had been pursuing successful careers in banking and advertising, but decided that they wanted to try something as a family that provided them with a greater opportunity for expression—a broader challenge.

To make a long story short, on a trip to Scotland they discovered this historic house, and the family decision was made to convert it to a country house hotel. They are at Ardsheal from April to November. In the winter, they return to their home in New Paltz, New York.

The reception hall is paneled in oak and there's usually a cheery fire blazing on the old stone hearth. A glassed-in porch on the lochside is made for watching sunsets and seals (or monsters) or for enjoying the peace and beauty of the Scottish Highlands. The dining room faces the garden and another glassed-in extension brings the flowers and sky even closer.

All of the spacious guest rooms have private baths, and all the beds are provided with electric blankets.

"Because we are Americans, we can appreciate the fact that our overseas guests frequently enjoy lots of activity. We have our own tennis court, and there's fishing, sailing, and boating, as well as horseback riding nearby. We try to persuade Americans to enjoy the British sport of hill walking and I think we've got some of the best starting right at our doorstep."

At dinner that evening, which included Loch Linnhe salmon, I made the acquaintance of Ray and Mary Rendall from Northumberland, and we discovered that Ray and I had both been in India at the same time and had a few "old soldier" stories to exchange. They had been there for a three- or four-day holiday, and Mary was particularly complimentary about the menu, which has received a glowing review by Craig Claiborne in the *New York Times.*

Ardsheal House is just off A82, the principal road from Oban to Inverness, a few miles south of Fort William. Due west is Mallaig and the Isle of Skye.

There's a postscript to my pleasant stay at Ardsheal House, which took place the following winter, when Bob and Jane drove from New Paltz and I drove from the Berkshires, all meeting at the Redcoat's Return Inn in Tannersville, New York. It was a most enjoyable reunion and another chance to talk about Ardsheal House. It would be just another month when the Taylors would be heading back to their beloved Kentallen of Appin, enthusiastically looking forward to another season. The Scottish adventure would continue.

ARDSHEAL HOUSE, Kentallen of Appin, Argyll PA38 4BX. Tel.: 063-174-227. A 13-guestroom country house lochside hotel overlooking the spectacular view of the western Scottish Highlands. Approx. 17 mi. south of Fort William. Breakfast, lunch, tea, and dinner served every day in the year from Easter through Oct. Minimum stay of 2 nights with advance booking. Tennis on the grounds. Hill walking, beach walking, sailing, riding, pony trekking, fishing, and golf nearby. No credit cards. Jane and Bob Taylor, Proprietors. (See Index for rates.)

Directions: From Glasgow take the A82 to Crianlarich. Continue on A82 to roundabout at Ballachulish Bridge; then follow A828 toward Connel and Oban. Ardsheal is about 4 mi. on the right. Well signposted.

INVERLOCHY CASTLE
Fort William, Inverness-shire

In Scotland, the word "castle" means a great many different things. Sometimes it means a fortress that may have withstood many attacks. However, Inverlochy Castle is a totally benign place, built by the first Lord Abinger in 1863 near the site of a 13th-century fortress. Turrets and battlements aside, it resembles a sumptuous Italian villa or an elegant French chateau.

The two-story-high great hall has lavishly frescoed ceilings, large oil paintings, and opulent furnishings; all dominated by a crystal chandelier that seems suspended in space. Inverlochy played host to Queen Victoria in 1873, and in her diary she wrote, "I never saw a lovelier or more romantic spot."

The dining room and other drawing rooms, as well as the unusually large guest rooms, are all beautifully decorated and fitted with fine, elaborately fashioned furniture.

Such a castle should have a princess to preside over it, and indeed there is one: Mrs. Grete Hobbs. This attractive, sophisticated woman is the owner, and is originally from Copenhagen. We talked about what is involved in providing hotel accommodations in a castle.

"I've been fortunate enough to travel to a great many different countries in the world. And this house has many things I found most attractive while traveling."

The house and grounds of Inverlochy Castle are entirely private, and are not open to non-residents for viewing.

INVERLOCHY CASTLE (Relais et Chateaux de Campagne), Fort William, Inverness-shire PH33 6SN. Tel.: (0397) 2177. Telex: 776229. A luxurious 13-guestroom private castle hotel, about 3 mi. north of Fort William. Dinner provisions for non-residents are limited. The western Highlands scenery and other impressive centers of natural beauty are within a pleasant drive. Tennis and fishing are available at the castle; golf, riding, and walking are available nearby. Open from March to Nov. Mrs. Grete Hobbs, Proprietor. (See Index for rates.)

Directions: Inverlochy Castle is 3 mi. from the center of Fort William on the A82, and approx. 6 mi. from Spean Bridge. The entrance is set back from the road, but is well signposted.

LOCH NESS HOUSE HOTEL
Inverness

It's hard for me to picture Alistair MacPherson without his kilt, whether it be on the streets of Stockbridge, Massachusetts, or on the grounds of the Loch Ness House Hotel.

I was introduced to Alistair by his sister, Morag, who is one of my neighbors in the Berkshires. I was delighted to learn that he was the keeper of a most reputable hotel in Inverness, Scotland, and we enjoyed a very congenial lunch at the Red Lion Inn.

Since that time I've learned a great deal about the Loch Ness Hotel and have seen Alistair on several occasions.

As he explains it, "The hotel, originally built as a private house around 1882, has been altered by way of the addition of private bathrooms and one bedroom extension, and now has twenty-three guest bedrooms. Since Marjorie and I took over the hotel we have fully refurbished the dining room and reception area, and done extensive redecoration. We have also created two four-poster bedrooms, which have been fully redecorated with a bathroom *en suite.*

"Our Copper Kettle lounge hums with animated talk in front of a cozy log fire and sometimes there are Highland concerts of music and dancing."

When I asked him to describe the menu, Alistair replied that fresh Scottish salmon and scampi, as well as venison and scallops, are just a few of the special tastes of Scotland that are included. "Scottish recipes call for local produce, such as fruit and vegetables, as well as game and fish and local cheeses, and all of these are available in our Highlands."

The Loch Ness House is ideally placed for touring or relaxing in the Highlands. It's only a fifteen-minute walk from the center of Inverness, and there is a picturesque view of the Torvean Golf Course and the Caledonian Canal.

I promised myself that next time I see Alistair MacPherson I'll be wearing *my* kilt.

LOCH NESS HOUSE HOTEL, Glenurquhart Rd., Inverness IV3 6JL. Tel.: (0463) 231248. A 23-guestroom (most have private bath) hotel located at the gateway to the western and northern Highlands of Scotland. Modified American plan available. Lunch and dinner served to non-residents. Open every day. Fishing, golf, skating, curling, castles, and wonderful car travel and walking just outside the door. Alistair and Marjorie MacPherson, Owner-Innkeepers. (See Index for rates.)

Directions: Inverness is at the apex of several important highways from the south of Scotland.

It's not that the distances are very long in the British Isles, it's the many diversions along the way that sometimes make it impossible to estimate traveling and arrival times. Last order times for dinner are included in the Index so that you can see what time you must arrive in order not to find the kitchen door locked. If you are going to arrive later, call ahead—there isn't a hotel/inn listed here that will not make some provision to feed you if they know you can't make it before the kitchen closes.

INVERNESS AND LOCH NESS

When I asked Alistair MacPherson of the Loch Ness House Hotel about the famous Loch Ness monster, a beatific smile crossed his handsome Scottish face.

"Most people know two things about Inverness. It's where the best English is spoken and where the Loch Ness monster is a neighbor. I've never seen the monster myself, but it's often been described as the world's greatest mystery. It was first recorded by the 7th-century monk Adamnan. He related how it attacked one of Saint Columba's party, only to be deterred by an invocation from Columba himself. From that day the monster has never harmed another human being. Of course, it's the subject of serious scientific study by expeditions all over the world. Everything from space-age technology to yellow submarines have been used to track down this creature. Much of the equipment and many of the results can be seen at the Loch Ness Centre in nearby Drumnadrochit."

For centuries Inverness has stood at the crossroads of the Highlands, the historical starting point and goal of travelers in the North. Now improved roads and new bridges bring much of the Highlands within a few hours' drive.

Inverness is a good center for traveling in all four directions and visiting the many castles and historic spots. For example, a monument at nearby Culloden marks the site of the last pitched battle on British soil. It was fought in 1746 between the Duke of Cumberland's forces and the Jacobites, marking the end of Bonnie Prince Charlie's struggle for the throne. There's also Cawdor Castle, which has strong associations with Macbeth *and Shakespeare.*

The wild Highlands to the north and west have always held a strong attraction for visitors to Scotland.

THE CLIFTON HOTEL
Nairn, Nairnshire

J. Gordon Macintyre, the hotelier at the Clifton Hotel in Nairn, is a man of many gifts. Among them is the mastery of the simple declarative sentence. With this in mind I'm going to use his prose to describe this hotel. Let me say that Mr. Macintyre himself is a very elegant gentleman, and on the occasion of my meeting him he was wearing an absolutely smashing beige suit with champagne-colored shoes. As we toured all of the guest rooms and public rooms I realized that the decorations, furnishings, and ambience were really an expression of his individuality. But enough of that. Let's hear what he has to say.

"The Clifton Hotel, with only grass and trees between it and the sea, overlooks the whole stretch of the Moray Firth and commands an unrivalled view of the Ross-shire and Sutherland hills. The beach, tennis courts, and swimming baths are only two minutes' walk away, and the hotel is equidistant to both golf courses. We can obtain fishing, shooting, and riding by arrangement, given advance notice.

"Many things go towards the unique atmosphere of this small, charming, and very personal hotel—a Victorian house, most decoratively revived and carefully restored, abounding with flowers, paintings, colour, and an interesting collection of objets d'art. A sense of the theatrical, backed up by cleanliness, really good food, and masses of hot water, make this an ideal establishment in which to relax and unwind from the stresses of modern living.

"The hotel has only sixteen guest rooms on two floors. Each room is individually designed and decorated and all have private baths. We have several rooms with really *enormous* beds. The public rooms include a writing room, a television room, a bar, and the drawing room, where a log fire is always burning, except in the very warmest weather. The restaurant is the cornerstone of our cardinal reputation. Also, for the last three years we have served lunch in the small but exquisite Green Room, with a menu that features fish and seafood along with other dishes.

"During the winter months, from October to May, a number of plays, concerts, and recitals are staged in the hotel.

"The evening meal includes six to eight main courses. The dining room also serves as a theatre and recital hall during the winter months."

Believe me, the Clifton Hotel in Nairn is one of the most singular experiences in the British Isles.

THE CLIFTON HOTEL, Viewfield Street, Nairn. Tel.: (0667) Nairn 53119. A 16-guestroom (mostly private baths) elegant hotel in a resort town on the shores of the Moray Firth. Lunch and dinner served daily. Open from late Feb. to early Nov. Conveniently located to enjoy day trips to the northern and western Highlands, as well as golf and recreation nearby. J. Gordon Macintyre, Proprietor. (See Index for rates.)

Directions: Nairn is on the A93, which runs east and west between Inverness and Banff. The best procedure is to make inquiries in the center of town for the Clifton Hotel.

TULCHAN LODGE
Advie, Grantown-on-Spey, Morayshire

King Edward VII used to visit Tulchan to shoot and fish. Now the lodge is open from April to mid-October, not only for sportsmen, but also for travelers to enjoy the atmosphere of a bygone age. The beautiful scenery of the sparkling mountain rivers, pine forests, and open moorland provide a wonderful setting.

The lodge has an impressive collection of paintings and sporting firearms, and the splendid paneled hall and library, elegant drawing room, and billiards room hark back to the age of opulence.

Each of the eleven guest rooms has an *en-suite* bathroom with shower.

The Spey River is one of the premier salmon streams in the world. There are four beats, all fully equipped, and ghillies provide expert guiding. The season is from February 11 to September 30.

The purple heather hills provide exciting grouse shooting between August 12 and the end of September.

Home cooking features Scottish and international menus, with an emphasis on Scottish beef and lamb, and game from the estate, as well as fresh local seafoods, lobsters, and vegetables from the garden.

TULCHAN LODGE (Pride of Britain), Advie, Grantown-on-Spey, Morayshire PH26 3PW. Tel.: (08075) 200 & 261. U.S. reservations: 800-323-3602. An 11-guestroom fishing and shooting lodge converted into a most comfortable country house hotel. Open from April to mid-Oct. Two-night minimum stay. Conveniently located to visit all of Northeast Scotland with its many historic sites and golf courses. (See Index for rates.)

Directions: Follow B9102 from Grantown to the lodge.

THE NORTHEAST CORNER OF SCOTLAND

Scotland isn't really very large, but there is so much to see! For instance, the entire Grampian region and in particular the northeast corner is tucked away from the busy through routes. Looking toward the sea, it's virtually undiscovered by visitors. It's a land of fishermen and farmers, with fishing villages nestling under the cliffs along the coast and small farm villages and market towns dotting its rolling interior. There are miles of peaceful main roads and quiet little side roads for excursions and picnics.

Robert Bruce was here and it was the home of many a character in fact and fiction. There are many castles, great and small houses, gardens, and countryside areas, many maintained by the National Trust for Scotland.

I visited this area in late June, which is supposed to be the threshold of the "high season." I found it uncrowded, very comfortable, and largely undiscovered by the overseas visitor to Britain.

ROTHES GLEN HOTEL
Rothes, Morayshire

I had cut across the Morayshire countryside, deserting the coast for the back roads that would eventually lead me to Craigellachie and then north to the village of Rothes. The late June day was providing a perfect ambience for this lovely section of Scotland, which is peaceful farming country and from the look quite prosperous.

After passing through the village of Rothes, I could see the silhouette of the Rothes Glen Hotel on the left side of the road, its Victorian turrets, towers, and crenelated battlements overlooking a group of Highland cattle with their long curved horns and russet shaggy coats.

Once inside, I was struck by the similarity in design to other castlelike hotels scattered throughout Scotland. The imposing main entrance hall had a skylight and a winding staircase to two floors. The carpeting was rich and walls were hung with many oil paintings of Scottish scenes. There was an abundance of Victorian tables and chairs and other ornamentation. The ceilings of the dining and drawing rooms were ornamented.

From Donald and Elaine Carmichael, proprietors, I learned that they have almost fully modernized this old building, designed by the architect who built Balmoral Castle. All the bedrooms are equipped with electric blankets, shaver sockets, radios, intercoms, a child-listening service, direct-dial telephones, trouser presses, and tea and coffee makers.

The menu features the best Scottish beef and freshly caught shellfish and fish from the Moray Firth.

Golf and salmon fishing are the principal pursuits of Rothes Glen guests, with eleven golf courses within twenty miles. These courses offer a reasonable weekly rate on greens fees.

Guests who wish to see the surrounding countryside, in less than an hour can be in Inverness, the gateway to the scenery and lochs of the Highlands. Winter sports areas are also nearby.

Mrs. Carmichael pointed out that Rothes Glen was "quiet and low key" and there were no "night porters or any activities that would keep people up late in the evening." It impressed me as being comfortable, well kept, conservative, and neat—all in the tradition of Scottish country house hotels.

ROTHES GLEN HOTEL, Rothes, Morayshire IV33 7AH. Tel.: (03403) Rothes 254. A 19-guestroom country house hotel in the beautiful glen of Rothes, 63 mi. west of Aberdeen. Open from Mar. through Dec. Breakfast, lunch, tea, dinner served to non-residents. Putting green on grounds. Many golf courses and salmon fishing nearby. Donald and Elaine Carmichael, Owners. (See Index for rates.)

Directions: Turn off the main Aberdeen/Inverness highway at Elgin onto A941. Rothes is just south. Hotel is clearly signposted.

PITTODRIE HOUSE HOTEL
Pitcaple, Grampian, Aberdeenshire

I hope that everybody who visits Scotland will take a few extra days to spend in Aberdeenshire. This area to the north of Aberdeen and south of the Firth of Moray has the largest group of ancient castles and historic houses in Scotland, and the rolling countryside with its busy farms, sweeping horizons, vast meadows and woodlands is a joyful experience. Along the coastline are old fishing villages where hearty Scotsmen still ply their ancient endeavors.

The Pittodrie House Hotel is wonderfully located to visit all of Aberdeenshire. It sits in an estate of 3,000 acres of mixed arable, forest, and hill land, with the peak of Bennachie providing a dramatic backdrop.

In June, the private road leading through the parkland to the hotel was lined with Queen Anne's lace and the rhododendrons were in glorious profusion. I emerged from the forest, following the sweeping curve to the left, and there sat Pittodrie House, dominated by a three-and-a-half-story, vine-covered tower with additions on both sides.

The entrance is through a massive door and into a reception area that features an almost overpowering staircase. "Perfect," I thought, "for a descending bride or a nude."

My host, owner Theo Smith, told me that his grandfather had pur-

chased the property in 1900, and he had opened it in 1977 for the first time as a hotel. "The family paintings and antique furniture have remained in the reception rooms and guest rooms, and I hope we have kept the atmosphere of a family home rather than a hotel."

As one might expect of a castle in Scotland dating to 1480, Pittodrie House has some interesting history. The original building was burned down by the Marquis of Montrose; he was eventually executed in 1650. The main building was a Z-plan castle and this was rebuilt in 1675; the traces of this early history lend an air of antiquity to the place.

The lounges have very high ceilings and many oil paintings that date back two or three hundred years—there is even one of His Royal Majesty, George III. There are gorgeous tapestries, many sporting prints, highly decorated mirrors, rugs that seem almost priceless, and furniture I would expect to find in either a castle or a museum.

Many of the guest rooms have four-poster beds, and enjoy views of the meadows, forests, and parkland. It is really quite romantic. All guest rooms have color TV, radios, and private baths.

Pittodrie House seems to run off in all directions because there have been many new sections added over the years. Theo grew up in this house and he said it was a great place to play "hide and seek."

One of the bathrooms contains a Victorian shower that I'm certain must have been a marvelous feat of engineering in its time, and is still in use today. The water spray comes not only from overhead, but from three sides as well.

Theo excused himself to attend to a wedding party and suggested that I might be interested in seeing the walled garden. In typically British fashion, he said, "It's really quite nice, actually." This was the understatement of the day.

The walled garden is one of the most extraordinary I've ever seen. It covers three acres divided into a series of small gardens, each about the size of two tennis courts. There were gardeners wearing rubber boots working among garden pools, rose gardens, and a lavish display of flowers of every type and description. Part of the garden was devoted to vegetables served at the hotel.

At Pittodrie House, in addition to the incredible setting, the extensive acres, the Billiard Room, the fantastic gardens, and that incredible bathtub . . . they also make their own ice cream!

PITTODRIE HOUSE HOTEL, Pitcaple (by Inverurie), Grampian, Aberdeenshire AB5 9HS. Tel.: (046 76) Pitcaple 202. U.S. reservations: 800-243-1806. A 12-guestroom (private baths) country house hotel in a restored 15th-century castle, 20 mi. from Aberdeen. Open every day of the year except Christmas Day and Boxing Day. Lunch and dinner served to non-residents. Tennis, squash, snooker, and croquet available on grounds. Fishing and hill walking nearby. Pittodrie House is convenient to all of the National Trust properties and other great houses and castles in Aberdeenshire. Theo Smith, Owner. (See Index for rates.)

Directions: From Aberdeen take the A96 toward Inverness to Inverurie. Continue on, taking the first turning to the left (1½ mi.) signposted to Chapel of Garioch. At the village take the first right fork at the shop and follow signs for hotel.

ROSE VILLA
Fortingall, Aberfeldy, Highland Perthshire

My good friends Michael and Maureen Turner, formerly of the Fortingall Hotel, have embarked on a new venture that bids fair to be of great interest to the readers of this book.

Fortingall, as can be seen by looking at the map, is almost in the dead center of the Scottish Highlands. This convenient location makes it the hub for a series of wonderful trips in all directions.

As Michael says, "We are ideally located for people who would like to have a true Highlands experience with the convenience of returning to the same warm, snug home every night."

They have converted their lovely home in Fortingall into just such an experience. A part of the house was the original village schoolhouse, dating back to 1720. There are three guest bedrooms, all named after choice roses. There is electric central heating and also open log fires when the weather is cold.

Rates at Rose Villa include dinner, bed, and a full Scottish breakfast, and the dinners include many international dishes and Scottish specialties served on a table d'hote basis.

Perhaps the most unusual feature is the chauffeur-driven Scottish tours that Michael refers to as his "Dram" ("Daily Roundabout and Meander"). They begin when you're collected from a nearby airport or railroad station and driven back to settle in at Rose Villa. From then on daily tours can be arranged, some long and some short, to suit the guests' needs.

"We are convinced that our central situation, allied to our local knowledge, will give those guests who opt for our 'Dram' a truly unique holiday," Michael observed. "I think if your readers would get in touch with us by telephone I can explain it most adequately.

"Antiquers will find much to interest them around the house. We can often help and advise on the acquisition of antiques in Scotland."

I'm looking forward to visiting Michael and Maureen in the near future. It sounds very much to me as if Michael's "Dram" might be an excellent solution for getting the most out of a visit to the Scottish Highlands.

ROSE VILLA, Fortingall, Aberfeldy, Highland Perthshire PH15 2LL. Tel.: 088 73 335. (International: 4488 73 335). A 3-guestroom private home, originally a 1720 village school house, in the Scottish Highlands. Rates include dinner and a full Scottish breakfast. Open all year. Please telephone for full details. Convenient to golf, salmon and trout fishing, stalking and shooting, pony trekking, walking, climbing, and nature. Chauffeur-driven tours available. No credit cards. Michael and Maureen Turner, Proprietors. (See Index for rates.)

Directions: Take A9 north (Inverness Rd.) 23 mi. to Ballinluig. Turn left onto A827 to Aberfeldy. Turn right just beyond square onto B846 (Tummel Bridge Rd.) to Coshieville (5 mi.). Turn left on road marked Fortingall, 3 mi. to thatched village and Rose Villa. Pickup from airport or rail station available.

THE KENMORE HOTEL
Kenmore, by Aberfeldy, Tayside, Perthshire

On November 2, 1572, Sir Colin Campbell gave the first lease of the Kenmore Hotel to his servants, Hew Hay and spouse, thereby establishing what is said to be the oldest hotel in Scotland.

All of this information, including a translation from the original language of the lease, is included in a most interesting book, *Four Hundred Years Around Kenmore,* written by Duncan Fraser, and presented to me by the innkeeper of the Kenmore Hotel, Ian MacKenzie.

Despite the fact that numbering among its visitors over the past four hundred years have been royalty, foreign dignitaries, and possibly the most revered guest of all, Robert Burns, the Kenmore Hotel does not put on any airs! It's a jolly place where the local farmers and countrymen stop in at the pub and, no doubt, raise many a toast to Bobbie Burns, who spent the night of Wednesday, the 29th of August, 1787. He wrote a tribute to Kenmore on the wall that can still be seen, now under a protective sheet of glass. This room has been named the "Poet's Parlour."

Ian MacKenzie pointed out that the Fifteenth of January Festival, celebrating the opening of salmon season, is "verra important." Almost every Scot enjoys fishing and the River Tay is one of the most famous fishing streams in Scotland.

"The River Tay actually starts right here in Loch Tay," he explained, "and a great many of us gather on the banks of the river here at the hotel and then we march down to the river shore, where a bottle of Scotch whiskey is broken over one of the boats and everybody toasts the season. It's really a most convivial idea and then we come back here and continue the festivities. As you can imagine, there's very little fishing done that day, and there's a big party that night."

Today, the Kenmore consists of the original building and two more adjacent structures. There are thirty-nine rooms at this ancient inn, all with private baths and showers. Rooms look out either over the village or the River Tay to the rear.

"I believe it could truthfully be said that we are in the very heart of Scotland," he declared. "We're very convenient for trips to Edinburgh, Aberdeen, Inverness, Oban, and Glasgow. We're open all year and there's skiing on Ben Lawers, or on the slopes of Aviemore, Glencoe, or Glenshee. Our walking is some of the best in the Highlands."

As might be expected in this part of Scotland, the menu includes Tay salmon and Aberdeen Angus beef dishes.

Ian advised me that June would be a good month to come to Kenmore, because the weather is very pleasant and it is in advance of the more popular months of July and August. Fishing months are April, May, and early June, and then September and October.

THE KENMORE HOTEL, Kenmore, by Aberfeldy, Perthshire PH15 2NU. Tel.: (08873) Kenmore 205. U.S. reservations: 800-243-1806. A 39-guestroom (private baths/showers) traditional village inn in the beautiful lake area of Scotland's Highlands. Open all year. Breakfast, lunch, tea, dinner served to non-residents. Hill walking, fishing, skiing, golf, riding, and pony trekking available. Pitlochry Festival Theatre and many museums and art galleries within a short drive. Ian H. MacKenzie, Manager. (See Index for rates.)

Directions: From Perth take A9 (Inverness Rd.) to Ballinluig (23 mi.). Turn left for Aberfeldy on A827 (10 mi.). Continue to Kenmore on A827 (6 mi.). Kenmore Hotel is in village square.

PORT-AN-EILEAN HOTEL
Strathtummel, Tayside, Perthshire

The leading sailboat had reached the buoy marking the far end of the course and was now coming about, ready to sail a broad reach on the final leg of the course. "Sometimes," said Gordon Hallewell, "they set their spinnakers."

Gordon and I were seated in the lounge of the Port-an-Eilean country house hotel, the bow window providing us with an excellent view of Loch Tummel and the almost daily sailboat race. The hotel, standing in twenty acres of natural woodland and formal gardens with magnificent views of lochs and mountains, was once the Duke of Athol's shooting lodge. It is at the start of the legendary "Road to the Isles" and at the geographic center of scenic Scotland.

"We are open from mid-April to mid-October," he said. "Many of our guests find that a holiday in early spring or autumn finds the countryside most beautiful. The roads are less crowded and log fires are most welcome in the evening after a good dinner."

From the very moment I had stepped through the front door I was impressed with the unusual number of contemporary oil paintings. Gordon explained that he and his wife, Evelyn, are collectors; I believe they have successfully blended some landscapes by modern painters among the more traditional works of earlier periods.

The general architecture and design of the building can be characterized as Scottish Victorian baronial, and the high-ceilinged drawing rooms and dining rooms are very elegant, with handsome wallpapers and many framed prints and originals providing a rich complement to the rugs and furniture.

` "We're quite well situated for the guests who would enjoy a few days of rest and relaxation," he remarked. "It's possible to tour both the west and east coasts within a day or to take a short drive to Edinburgh, Inverness, or Aberdeen. We have facilities available for shooting and fishing. There are several beautiful walks that start right here at the hotel."

Gordon then suggested that we take a tour of the guest rooms and perhaps even look at the kitchen. As we wound our way up the handsomely paneled open staircase, Gordon told me that there are ten guest rooms, all with their own private baths. Many of them have a magnificent view of the loch. "The Duke wanted to provide his sporting guests with the best of accommodations," he said. The Hallewells have taken great pains to furnish the rooms in an appropriately Victorian style.

Returning to the first floor, Gordon handed me the menu for the evening, saying, "We always have trout and salmon from the loch, and venison and Scottish lamb in many different variations. Our approach to cuisine concentrates on the good cooking of a limited menu. Besides offering breakfast, tea, and dinner to non-residents, we can also supply hearty packed lunches for our houseguests who want to spend a day out-of-doors."

As we strolled on the lawn next to the loch, Gordon noted that the sailing dinghies were all at the far end of the loch and told me the view was so admired by Queen Victoria that it has since been called "The Queen's View."

PORT-AN-EILEAN HOTEL, Strathtummel (near Pitlochry), Perthshire. Tel.: (088 24) Tummel Bridge 233. A 10-guestroom (private baths) lochside country house hotel, almost in the geographical center of the Scottish Highlands, 10 mi. from Pitlochry. Open from mid-April to mid-Oct. Breakfast, tea, and dinner served daily to non-residents. Fishing and boating available at the hotel; 5 golf courses and hill walking nearby. All of the delights of Scottish Highlands are within an easy driving distance. No credit cards. Mr. and Mrs. Gordon Hallewell, Resident Proprietors. (See Index for rates.)

Directions: Follow A9 north of Pitlochry, then turn west from bypass on B8019 to Kinloch Rannoch. Hotel is 9 mi. along this road on left.

HILLHEAD OF DUNKELD
Dunkeld, Perthshire

Mists hovered over the lowering peaks, and it was easy to imagine witches lurking in nearby Birnam Wood, as I drove into *Macbeth* country.

The spectacular landscape of the Scottish Highlands commences here in central Scotland, and the A9 winds north between wooded hills, past old stone walls and fields and the peaked slate roofs of little villages.

I was bound for Dunkeld on the River Tay, and as I passed through the town of Birnam and turned off the A9, I could see Hillhead on the slope above Dunkeld. Crossing the river on the Sir Thomas Telford Bridge, I drove into this interesting little town, where the beautiful old cathedral contains ruins dating back to the 9th century. I turned right almost immediately on Brae Street and followed the narrow, winding road to the top of the hill. There, across a flat expanse of green lawn, framed by huge, beautiful trees, stood the handsome many-gabled and chimneyed mansion called Hillhead of Dunkeld. Jess Miller decided to keep the name when he bought it in 1986.

For many years Mr. Miller and his family had owned Dunkeld House, which I wrote about in earlier editions of this book. Now, with many of his original staff, including his chef of fifteen years, Donald McClementes, he has established this small, elegant country house hotel. Jess showed me around the grounds and we walked to the edge of the lawn. Situated as it is at the head of the hill, overlooking the slate roofs of the town, the sparkling River Tay, and a panorama that stretches out past the valley to the distant mountains, Hillhead offers one of the finer views in Scotland. "Our sunsets are glorious," he said. "Guests will often sit here and watch them."

Inside, he introduced me to the very affable and accommodating Peggy Macaulay, who manages the hotel and sees to all the details. As Jess and I sat together over a delightful tea of feather-light scones and butter and jam, looking out of the tall bay window across the lawn to a gorgeous copper beech, he told me how he'd been able to renovate this 1840s house

in a matter of months. Glancing around at the soft grays, blues, roses, and mauves of the drawing room and lounge, with fireplaces, damask draperies, oil paintings, books, and fresh flowers, I complimented him on creating a most inviting atmosphere.

The guest rooms, freshly painted in pale pastels with floral chintz draperies and dust ruffles, are individually decorated and have modern tiled bathrooms with towel warmers. They are also equipped with color TV, radios, and the makings for tea or coffee. They all have views of either the town and River Tay or lawn, trees, and gardens. From my corner room, on one side I looked out over the terraced sunken garden, encircled by a carved balustrade, and on the other the famous view over the town.

The information packet on the writing desk had suggestions for all sorts of interesting diversion, including a long list of books available in the hotel's library and a fascinating history of Scottish pearls, which have been fished from Scotland's rivers for centuries.

There were some Scottish burrs and a German accent or two in the buzz of conversation in the dining room that evening. Peggy Macaulay told me they have local patrons for both lunch and dinner, as well as many guests from Europe and America. I enjoyed the beautifully done River Tay salmon and noted that the table d'hote dinner menu offered a nice range of beef, pork, chicken, and a vegetarian dish. There is also an extensive à la carte menu. The chef had told me the menu is changed daily, with emphasis on local meats, game, and produce. In fact, their smoked salmon comes from the smokehouse at the bottom of the hill.

The next morning I emerged from under a warm and cozy duvet to discover a world of gray rain and mists, and after a hearty breakfast of ham and eggs, fluffy scones with butter and jam, and lots of hot coffee, I retreated to the warmth and comfort of the cheery fire in the drawing room. Others of better character than I had donned their macs and Wellies for a tramp through the woods, armed with maps of the many trails and places of interest. It was not long, however, before the sun was shining brightly and the sky was a lovely blue, and it was time for me to take my leave.

HILLHEAD OF DUNKELD, Brae St., Dunkeld, Perthshire PH8 OBA. Tel.: (03502) 8851 and 8852. A 5-guestroom (private baths) country house hotel overlooking the famed salmon river Tay and the town of Dunkeld, 12 mi. north of Perth. Breakfast, lunch, and dinner served to the public by reservation. Open year-round. Wheelchair access. Hard-surface tennis court, croquet lawn on grounds. Arts, drama, and music festivals in summer, historic sites, championship golf courses, salmon and trout fishing, walking and hiking trails, Birnam Wood, historic castles nearby. Peggy Macaulay, General Manager; Jess Miller, Owner. (See Index for rates.)

Directions: From the A9 (Perth-Inverness Rd.), turn right after first Birnam sign to Dunkeld. Cross the Telford Bridge over the River Tay. In Dunkeld, turn right at Brae St., and continue to the top of the hill through gateway to the hotel.

THE CAIRN LODGE
Auchterarder, Tayside

"Well, Bruce," said one gentleman to the other, "have you got your golf clubs in the boot?" The two of them were looking out the bay window of the drawing room at the velvety putting green. (It's impossible to reproduce the Scottish burr on the printed page.) The atmosphere was informal and the conversation lively in this very pleasant room, with its tall windows framed by draperies in shades of apricot and avocado. There were two or three groups of guests enjoying light lunches, with their chairs drawn up to coffee tables. I had stopped in for a spot of lunch, on the recommendation of Jess Miller at Hillhead of Dunkeld, and was relishing my smoked salmon sandwich.

The lady sitting nearest to me, who was originally from Brazil, had just told me that Scottish rolls were called "babs," and that her mushroom soup was wonderful and the babs were lovely, light, and soft.

On my arrival, lunch was going full tilt, with guests being shown to their tables in the lovely, very gracious dining room, where a more formal and extensive lunch was being served.

I would have to call Cairn Lodge a real "find." It has a warm, informal quality that made me feel immediately at home. The rooms are light and airy, and the furnishings and decorations are both comfortable and rather elegant, with many fresh flowers and plantings. There are lots of books, magazines, and newspapers in evidence. In addition to the pleasant drawing room, where light lunches and afternoon refreshments may be enjoyed, there is a most attractive little lounge, which looks out on a pretty garden. Just off this room is an enclosed sun room with easy chairs, also looking out on the garden, where there are masses of roses, along with lots of other flowers and an expanse of green lawn. A little outside patio with white garden furniture is another area where refreshments are served.

The five guest rooms (plans are afoot for an additional five or ten rooms) are all beautifully and individually furnished and immaculately kept. They all have color TV, the makings for tea and coffee, and plates of fresh fruit.

The menus look enticing, with such dishes as langoustine tails with orange cream sauce, veal cutlets with raspberry vinegar, and venison with wild mushrooms. The main course is served with fresh vegetables and there is a nice selection of interesting appetizers. I saw the sweets trolley and everything looked absolutely scrumptious.

Golfers come to this area for the great courses—the famous Gleneagles is a mile away. The Auchterarder course is across the street, and there are several other well-known courses nearby.

The Cairn Lodge is in a residential neighborhood, and is named for the tall mound of stones, called a cairn, at its side entrance, which was constructed by a local man, John Campbell, in commemoration of Queen Victoria's Diamond Jubilee in 1897. It provides a convenient landmark for guiding you to a most pleasant sojourn at an extremely friendly and delightful place.

THE CAIRN LODGE, Orchil Rd., Auchterarder, Tayside PH3 1LX. Tel.: (07646) 2634. A 5-guestroom (private baths) attractive country house hotel in a residential section of Auchterarder, in the Strathearn Valley between Stirling and Perth. Breakfast included in tariff. Breakfast, lunch, and dinner served to the public by reservation. Closed Christmas and New Year's week. Putting green on grounds. Gleneagles, St. Andrews, Muirfield golf courses nearby. Fishing on the Earn and Tay rivers, shooting, hill walking, pony trekking, swimming, wool shops, antiques, and Auchterarder Heritage Center with displays and exhibitions of Scotland's last working textile steam engine. No pets. Gilberto Chiodetto, Managing Director. (See Index for rates.)

Directions: Coming north on the A9, Auchterarder is well signposted. In Auchterarder take the first left onto Orchil Rd., continue 200 yds. to the lodge on the right.

Ireland

Ireland is a land of old stone walls that are grown over with honeysuckle and roses, a land of fields, farmhouses, and small villages. In Ireland it is possible to find an old gate standing abandoned because the great house that it once served no longer exists.

It is a conservative land, bordering on the austere. The houses are very much alike and individuality is expressed by different-colored trims.

Essentially, the countryside charm lies in the fact that Ireland is still an agricultural country, and everywhere I traveled there were fields with either crops or cattle. The villages on the back roads have very few restaurants, although there are restaurants located on main highways.

There aren't many of the intrusions of modern life in Ireland. Television and radio are found everywhere, but only in a few of the accommodations that I visited did I find them in the guest rooms.

Public telephones can usually be found, one to a village, near the post office.

Frequently, the road passes by some of Ireland's stately homes with their decorated ceilings, tapestries, picture galleries, fine fireplaces, and furniture. These are found in all of the counties of Ireland. There are also many gardens that are open to the public.

There are over one hundred 18-hole golf courses in Ireland, including Portnarnock, near Dublin, described by Arnold Palmer as "the finest in the world."

There are very many interesting connections between Ireland and America. For example, there were several Irish-born signatories to the Declaration of Independence. During the American Civil War nearly 150,000 natives of Ireland served in the Union forces. The first recorded celebration of St. Patrick's Day was in 1762 in New York City. In 1779, the first St. Patrick's Day Parade was held in New York City. Apparently, the Irish have always been fond of coming to America; one legend says that the first Celtic arrival in North America was St. Brendan, the Navigator, around A.D. 550.

Irish-Americans have also had significant influence on literature and drama in the United States. The Nobel Prize went to playwright Eugene O'Neill in 1936, and novelists with an Irish heritage include F. Scott Fitzgerald, James T. Farrell, and John O'Hara.

Special Note

Some comments on several of these accommodations in Ireland are largely the result of recent travel by Marilyn and Charlie Schubert, who are dear friends and formerly owned the Barrows House in Dorset,

Vermont. They were kind enough to share some of their impressions about Ireland and the hotels and farmhouses there.

GETTING TO IRELAND FROM BRITAIN

You can fly from London, Manchester, or other points, landing at Dublin or Shannon airports. You can take the train or drive on the A40 to Fishguard, boarding the car ferry for Rosslare or Cork. I would recommend driving, since cleanliness and convenience aboard the ferry are not the best. Also, there is no help with the luggage.

ACCOMMODATIONS AND FOOD IN IRELAND

Basically, I visited two kinds of accommodations in Ireland. The first type is converted country houses, mansions and castles similar to those I saw in England and Scotland. The menus are frequently both English- and French-oriented.

These somewhat luxurious country mansions and castles are really resort-inns. Most of them have rooms with private baths and serve an elaborate meal. In most cases, I found them owner-operated and comfortably informal. There are usually quite a number of recreational facilities on the grounds, and since they are located in resort areas, there are plenty of additional sports and recreational activities nearby.

The second type of accommodation that I have listed is the farmhouse. Those that I saw had five or six bedrooms and resembled the American farmhouse with the individuality and creativeness of the owners expressed in terms of bright curtains, multicolored sheets, flowered wallpaper, and very comfortable living rooms where the guests and family gather to watch TV or talk. In all cases cleanliness is very important. I understand that the Irish Tourist Board checks the farmhouses to make certain that high standards are being maintained.

The food was generally right off the farm at all farm accommodations that I visited, and this is one of the main points of pride. Meals are very informal, and all the guests sit around a big table, very often with the family.

Incidentally, all of these offer bed and breakfast. Partial or full board is also obtainable for a longer period of time.

TRAVELING IN IRELAND

Sooner or later anyone traveling in the Irish countryside has to get directions from one village to another. Irish signposts are in two languages. *Most of the time one of them is English. The main problem is that the signs only direct the traveler from one village to the next and very seldom to villages beyond. I found that when the village I was looking for was not on my map I had to stop and ask directions. These directions were given in a wonderfully charming, polite, melodious manner and always ended up with the assurance that "you can't miss it." Well, "miss it" I did—quite a few times, in spite of some of the most intricate detail that accompanied each direction.*

The most frequent direction was "straight on." One of the problems was that "straight on" usually led to another four-way crossroads and it was necessary to go through the whole process again.

As in Scotland and England, driving is on the left side of the road. I found very few traffic tie-ups even in the larger cities.

RESERVATION SERVICES

For bookings in hotels, guesthouses, farmhouses, and cottages, contact your nearest travel agent or contact the Central Reservation Service, Bord Fáilte, 14 Upper O'Connell St., Dublin 1, Ireland. Tel.: (01) 735209. Telex: 32462. Here you can book all types of accommodations, including cabin cruisers and horse-drawn caravans.

Throughout Ireland you will see a sign displayed by farmhouses and houses in town and country offering accommodations that have been inspected and approved by the Irish Tourist Board.

Rock of Cashel

IRELAND

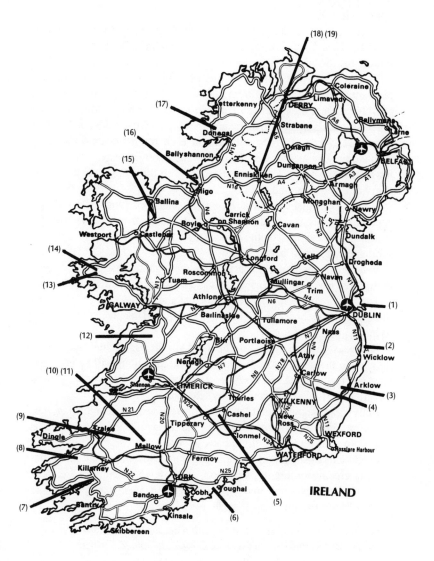

IRELAND

EGAN'S HOUSE
Glasnevin, Dublin

Johnny Egan was fullback captain of the Irish Gaelic football team that played in New York, Boston, and Philadelphia in 1970. In fact, he made three trips to America as a footballer.

This is one of the interesting bits of information I learned during a pleasant evening at Egan's House, a guest house in a very quiet section of downtown Dublin called Iona Park. In a city that has many impressive hotels, Egan's is modest in demeanor, but big on friendliness and service. There are twenty-six rooms in all and each room has its own private bath—quite unusual for a small hotel. The hotel consists of two Dublin townhouses that have been connected, and so there are several different stairways to the second floor.

Dinner is available with a variety of selections, and as Betty Egan explained, "We only serve fresh vegetables and fresh meats. We also offer continental breakfasts or the American-type breakfast with things like scrambled eggs and bacon."

Betty mentioned another service for their guests that I think is quite thoughtful: it's possible to use Egan's as a forwarding address to hold mail.

The whole atmosphere is very informal and homey, and I noticed that there were many experienced travelers who found the place much to their liking.

Overseas guests arriving at Shannon Airport can phone Egan's when they get to the outskirts of Dublin and good directions will be provided. Guests arriving at the Dublin Airport can take either a cab or bus—those directions will also be provided by telephone.

Betty Egan, knowing that I was leaving very early in the morning, gave me a tray with a big bowl of cornflakes and some milk and a flask of coffee to sustain me for the long flight back to New York. She has a little store with all kinds of small items people might have lost or run out of, such as shaving cream, toothpaste, shampoo, and a few souvenirs of Ireland.

Egan's Hotel is small and unassuming, and a great way to get acquainted with the informal friendliness of Ireland.

Note: Not everyone agreed with my enthusiastic observations about how homey and friendly Egan's is. One gentleman named Sullivan felt that it was "too casual with not enough attention paid to important details." I will, with your permission, fall back on an old English saying which I think describes Egan's at this time: "Good value for the money."

EGAN'S HOUSE, 7 Iona Park, Glasnevin, Dublin 9. Tel.: (01) Dublin 303611 or 305283. A 26-guestroom in-town guest house in the middle of Dublin, 15 mi. from the airport. Breakfast and dinner served daily.

Convenient to all of the Dublin shops, museums, and other attractions. Mr. and Mrs. John Egan, Proprietors. (See Index for rates.)

Directions: If you are arriving at Dublin Airport, I'd suggest a taxi to Egan's Hotel. From there, arrangements can be made to pick up a rental car in Dublin city. If arriving by car, have a Dublin city center map available to note directions, and telephone the hotel for specific directions from outside of Dublin.

HUNTER'S HOTEL
Rathnew, County Wicklow

"This hotel has been in my family for four generations; it's a way of life for us." Mrs. Maureen Gelletlie, the owner of Hunter's Hotel, and I were having a midmorning cup of tea in the gardens. It was a dewy morning and the weather promised to be beautiful for the remainder of the day.

The garden, dear to the hearts of Irish people, has sloping lawns, pebbled walks, rustic seats, and flowering shrubs alongside a small river, the Vartry, that flows through one end. A strange phenomenon was the presence of tropical palm trees here and there.

"The hotel has been here for over 200 years. It used to be what is called a coaching inn, the first stop after a good run from Dublin, and horses were changed and coach riders stayed overnight. Today, by car, it is less than an hour.

"I guess we have always been known for our good food," Mrs. Gelletlie continued. "Many people come just for our salmon and sea trout. We have vegetables and fruits from our own gardens. Many people come for afternoon tea, for which we make our own cakes and scones; we really are

famous for our strawberry jam. The garden always has quite a few people in the late afternoon."

Earlier at breakfast, I had talked to a couple from Northern Ireland about their holiday in Wicklow and they told me that this hotel is especially nice for people with children. There were, so they told me, many things for people with families to enjoy in the vicinity. Their plans included touring and walking in the Wicklow Mountains and a visit to the beaches, located a short distance away.

Guest rooms at Hunter's Hotel are quite similar to those of many country inns I have visited in the United States. Two that come to mind are Colby Hill Inn in Henniker, New Hampshire, and the Barrows House in Dorset, Vermont. I found comfortable vintage furniture with gay touches in each of the rooms. Five rooms have their own w.c.'s; others share one on the corridor.

A visitor to Hunter's Hotel in 1815 wrote in the visitor's book, "This superior family hotel has long been celebrated for the beauty of its situation and the excellence of its internal arrangement." Another more recent visitor wrote, "Pleasantly furnished with plenty of bathrooms, hot water, and smiling Irish faces that provide good service."

It looks as if Hunter's Hotel has successfully spanned the centuries.

HUNTER'S HOTEL, Rathnew, Co. Wicklow. Tel.: (0404) Wicklow 4106. A 17-guestroom (5 rooms with private bath/shower) country inn situated 1 hr. south of Dublin. Open all year. Breakfast, lunch, afternoon tea, and dinner served to non-residents. Touring, hiking, golf, tennis, fishing, horse riding, beaches nearby. Mrs. Maureen Gelletlie, Resident Owner. (See Index for rates.)

Directions: From Dublin, take the Wexford road, and at Ashford Village there's a sign on the left that says Hunter's Hotel.

MARLFIELD HOUSE HOTEL
Gorey, County Wexford

Mrs. Mary Bowe and I were in the sumptuous, but comfortable, drawing room of the Marlfield House, discussing the problems of keeping a country house hotel in Ireland in general, and the dinner menu for the previous evening, Friday, the 12th of October, in particular.

"I usually have twelve or fourteen starters and nine or ten main courses," she said. "It's a bit limited tonight."

I glanced down the list of offerings and it seemed more than sufficient to me. The starters included Kilmore crab salad, butter-fried sea trout, and soused herring. There was a choice of three soups, and among the main dishes were roast ribs of beef in a Béarnaise sauce, grilled turbot, seafood pancakes, scallops in cream, and pork chops Normandy. The vegetables were from the garden. Mrs. Bowe told me that they make their own ice cream and butterscotch sauce.

While we were discussing the dinner menu, houseguests and other people from the nearby area had begun dropping in for the Saturday bar lunch. Mrs. Bowe excused herself several times to greet her guests, and this gave me an opportunity to observe the scene.

The drawing room takes up one end of this beautiful old country house, set on thirty-five acres of woodland about one mile from the town of Gorey on the Courtown Road. Marlfield House was the former residence of the Earls of Courtown. My attention was caught by the beautiful flower arrangements on the tables and on the baby grand piano in one corner, and also by the several tastefully chosen country prints. The room had very high ceilings with decorated moldings and there was a handsome marble fireplace.

Mary Bowe rejoined me and suggested that we had better take a tour of the bedrooms before guests began to check in. I followed her up the very impressive winding staircase that curves around a sparkling crystal chandelier hanging from the two-and-a-half-story ceiling. There were fourteen double guest rooms, all with baths, and all furnished most appropriately. Those on the top floor have a panoramic view of the fields and the low hills of county Wexford.

We took just a moment or two to look at some of the beautiful and frequently rare trees on the grounds, including a flowering ash tree, many oaks and evergreens, beeches, and pink and white flowering chestnut trees. She called my attention to a very sturdy California redwood. "We have quite a lot of birds here and about thirty wild ducks. Our two peacocks always amuse our guests."

Marlfield House, situated midway between Dublin and Wexford, is within a short drive of beaches, rugged mountains, and richly timbered valleys, and is in what is known as the "Garden of Ireland."

Reader Comment: "This is a delightful place," writes Marilyn Schubert. "We think that it is one of the best decorated and furnished country houses in Ireland. The Conservatory is most unusual, and Charlie and I both thought that Mary Bowe is a lady of considerable grace, style, and talent."

MARLFIELD HOUSE, Gorey, Co. Wexford. Tel.: (055) 21124. A 14-guestroom country house hotel on Ireland's southeast coast, 57 mi. from Dublin. Closed Dec. 10 to Feb. 14. Lunch, tea, dinner served to non-residents. County Wicklow with beautiful beaches and mountains is nearby; Mount Usher Gardens, Russborough House, and other celebrated beauty spots within easy driving distance. Grass tennis court, croquet on grounds. Golfing, sea bathing, hunting, and fishing nearby. Children over 6 allowed under strict supervision. Mrs. Mary Bowe, Proprietress. (See Index for rates.)

Directions: Gorey is on the Dublin-Wexford Rd.; just before Gorey, turn left before the road goes under the railroad bridge and proceed on the Courtown Rd. Hotel entrance is on right.

LORUM OLD RECTORY
Bagenalstown, County Carlow

I liked Lorum Old Rectory and Betty Young immediately. She was a most accommodating and entertaining person and, like many of my Irish friends, a great conversationalist. She explained that she and her daughter run this 130-year-old, cut-stone farmhouse, while her son-in-law runs the farm.

All of the rooms in the Old Rectory are pleasant and homey—they are not luxurious, but clean and comfortable. One of the first things that attracted me was all of the books that are to be found on shelves throughout the house.

Guests all gather around the table in the evening and enjoy a real Irish farm meal that includes many homemade preserves, breads, pâtés, and the like. Salmon and trout have been freshly caught from nearby streams.

"We've had quite a few visitors from your book," she wrote in one of her recent letters. "Americans who are looking for the 'real Ireland' come for a night and decide to spend two or three, because we are located quite conveniently for many of the attractions of the south of Ireland. In the evening after dinner we spend a lot of time sitting and visiting. That's one

of the nicest things about keeping a guest house, sooner or later all of the world comes to us.

"I am only here for six months of the year now, but my daughter, Bobbie, is running things beautifully. I do hope you will stop on your next visit to Ireland."

LORUM OLD RECTORY, Bagenalstown, Co. Carlow. Tel.: (0503) 75282. A 5-guestroom rural guest house in the southeast of Ireland, 64 mi. from Dublin. Breakfast and dinner served to houseguests only. Open year-round except Christmas. Tennis, golf, river fishing, riding nearby. Within convenient distance of the sea. Beautiful mountain scenery nearby. Betty Young and Bobbie Smith, Proprietors. (See Index for rates.)

Directions: Bagenalstown is south of Carlow, just off the road to Kilkenny. From Carlow, go to Leighlinbridge and then turn sharp left for Muine Bheag. At Muine Bheag take the Borris Rd. Lorum Old Rectory is 4 mi. out on the left side. (All of these are on map.)

KNOCK-SAINT-LOUR HOUSE
Cashel, County Tipperary

I was sitting in Mrs. O'Brien's kitchen enjoying a cup of tea and watching her prepare the evening meal. "Tonight it is ham and chicken," she said, "and we'll have roast pork tomorrow night."

Mrs. O'Brien loves flowers. The house is surrounded on three sides by a truly intricate rock garden of myriad colors. "My mother tends the flowers outside," she said, "and I do the arranging on the inside. It keeps both of us very busy, but we love it."

Color is found throughout the house. Each bedroom is pastel-hued with harmonizing sheets and pillowcases and curtains.

Knock-Saint-Lour House is a farmhouse and almost everything served is homegrown. "I do a lot of freezing in the summer and early fall," she explained, "so that we have our own produce through most of the year."

I noticed a donkey grazing in a nearby field. "Oh, that's for the children. They love it."

She pointed out that there was a good view of the famous Rock of Cashel through one of the kitchen windows. "Everyone wants to visit there."

KNOCK-SAINT-LOUR HOUSE, Cashel, Co. Tipperary. Tel.: (062) 61172. An 8-guestroom (private and shared baths) farmhouse serving dinner and breakfast. Just 1½ mi. from the town of Cashel, where the famous Rock of Cashel is located. Open all year except Christmas.

Golfing, tennis, horse riding and pony trekking available nearby. Mrs. Eileen O'Brien, Proprietress. (See Index for rates.)

Directions: Knock-Saint-Lour is on the Dublin-Cork Rd. (N8), just south of Cashel.

BALLYMALOE HOUSE
Shanagarry, County Cork

The Ballymaloe House is one of Ireland's manor house accommodations. The house is part of an old Geraldine Castle, rebuilt and modernized through the centuries, one portion dating back to the 14th century. It is in the middle of a 400-acre farm on the Cork–Ballycotton road about two miles from the coast of southern Ireland.

Fifteen of the thirty guest rooms are in the main house and there are other lodging facilities in a 16th-century gatehouse and other farm outbuildings.

My room was located on the front, overlooking a very pleasant terrace and some beautiful fields and meadows that stretched out to some low hills a few miles away. I understand that this particular part of Ireland is not developed as a tourist area as yet. The coastal area is just a few minutes away.

After leaving Mrs. Young's in Bagenalstown, I followed the main road south through Thomastown and into Waterford, which is the home of the famous Irish Waterford crystal. From there, the main road heads southwestward with frequent glimpses of the Irish coast, passing through Dungarvan and Youghal. At Ladysbridge, I began another "cat and mouse" game of directions to try to find Shanagarry, the town closest to Ballymaloe. It is quite beyond my limited description to explain how I arrived, but it took at least four stops.

I arrived in the late afternoon and had time enough for a good long soak in the tub and few moments' rest before coming down for dinner.

Shortly before dinner I met some other houseguests in one of the living rooms who were on holiday from Dublin. I realized then that there were a great many children in residence and discovered that it was a long weekend. My new acquaintances had two children and explained that they had been in Ballymaloe several times because the golf, tennis, and swimming is free during July and August.

Dinner was very informal, served by waitresses in attractive costumes who were efficient and answered questions in a very pleasant manner. The menu offerings were basically English and Irish, rather than Continental.

After dinner I took a short walk in the gathering darkness, strolling on the country lanes between the fields of ripening wheat. The lights of Ballymaloe gleamed softly and occasionally I could hear the delighted

cries of some young people who were being allowed to stay up a little longer because it was a special occasion.

After many centuries of existence, I felt that Ballymaloe had really come into its own.

Reader Comment: Marilyn said that this was the place where Charlie was proud he was an Irishman. "Norman, we had a wonderful time here and I was amazed to find out how much of the family is involved. We met another couple at dinner from Belfast and then went on to visit a monastery with them. It was very special." (Ballymaloe apparently made a big hit with both Charlie and Marilyn.)

BALLYMALOE HOUSE, Shanagarry, Co. Cork. Tel.: (021) 652531. A 25-guestroom country house hotel, 3 mi. from the sea on Ireland's southern coast. Lunch and dinner served to non-residents. Closed Dec. 23 to 27. Tennis, golf, swimming pool, fishing, in July and Aug. on grounds. Allen Family, Proprietors. (See Index for rates.)

Directions: From Cork Road: On Midleton Bypass, take Cloyne-Ballycotton Rd. toward Shanagarry. Ballymaloe House is on L-35, 2 mi. beyond Cloyne.

PARK HOTEL KENMARE
Kenmare, County Kerry

The Park Hotel Kenmare, one of Ireland's premier luxury hotels, is a Victorian mansion set on the famous "Ring of Kerry" Drive, directly overlooking Kenmare estuary. In talking with Charlie and Marilyn Schubert it occurred to me that perhaps their impressions of this hotel might prove to be most refreshing.

CHARLIE: I will never forget that day. We were running late and I kept telling Marilyn, who was riding shotgun and co-pilot, that we had taken the wrong turn. She kept insisting that we were on the right road and it was only my exceptional good humor that kept us from having a Donnybrook in Kerry.

MARILYN: Well, I'll not grace that statement by replying to it. I will say that within a few moments we came upon a signpost for the hotel and Charlie breezed into the car park and we went in to get a bite of lunch.

CHARLIE: This is where Kenmare made a big hit with me right off the bat. Although we were too late for lunch they were courteous enough to send us something most delicious, and we sat in the drawing room with the large windows overlooking the lake gardens.

MARILYN: The place had a wonderful air of hospitality. A young newly married couple down from Dublin had also arrived a little late, so we chatted with them and learned that he had formerly worked at the Park Kenmare and had always wanted to return on his honeymoon. It was very sweet.

CHARLIE: We decided right then and there to stay at least one extra night. I inquired about golf courses and learned that there was one of the "Big Six" in Ireland just a short distance away.

MARILYN: That suited me fine because while Charlie would be out chasing the little white ball, I would get a chance to laze about in the sunshine and then take a walk down to the village and do some of the shops.

CHARLIE: I was quite surprised to learn that they have fifty guest rooms, because they create a mood of warmth and hospitality from the very start. There is definitely a small-inn atmosphere.

MARILYN: You have never seen such beautiful interior decorations and furniture. Several of the guest rooms have four-poster beds. There was generous use of chintz with a pleasing coordination between fabrics and the wallpaper, and many handsome mahogany pieces.

CHARLIE: We walked through the gardens that afternoon and relaxed on the patio, awaiting eagerly the arrival of dinnertime. We had heard that this is one of the finest restaurants in Ireland.

MARILYN: Dinner was formal, but, again, very friendly. Outstanding in the dining room were the magnificent fluted glass chandelier and wall sconces. The serving staff was about as deft as any I have ever seen and the Rosenthal china found a fitting background in the heavy Irish linen tableclothes and napkins.

CHARLIE: I had the Irish salmon that evening with wild-mint sauce and, as I recall, Marilyn had the Kerry lamb served with local oysters and a special sauce.

MARILYN: We stayed on not only for one night but for two additional nights, and I had some enjoyable walks down into the village and Charlie burned up the golf courses. One afternoon we both visited the Killarney National Park, which was nearby.

Thank you, Marilyn and Charlie. I would certainly concur with everything that you mentioned and would add to it only that some of the guidebooks of the British Isles have given very high marks to Park Hotel Kenmare.

I will also add that a jacket and tie for gentlemen is the required dress at dinner. This is also one of the few hotels that have children's portions.

I am told that from time to time a harpist also makes an appearance in the lounge.

PARK HOTEL KENMARE, Kenmare, Co. Kerry. Tel.: (064) 41200. U.S. reservations: 800-223-6764. Telex: 73905. A 50-guestroom luxurious grand hotel with outstanding service in a beautiful setting overlooking Kenmare Bay. Breakfast, lunch, dinner served daily. Open from March 28 to Dec. 31. Wheelchair access. TV, games room, tennis, and croquet on grounds. Golf, swimming, salmon fishing, horse riding, and historical sites nearby. No pets. Francis Brennan, Proprietor. (See Index for rates.)

Directions: Kenmare is 60 mi. southwest of Cork on the N22.

CARAGH LODGE
Caragh Lake, County Kerry

"The Ring of Kerry"—doesn't that have the most wonderful, melodious sound? Among the beautiful nature spots that are either on or near the Ring of Kerry, which is really an automobile road for our purposes, are Tralee Bay, Dingle Bay, Bantry Bay, and Healy Pass. In southwest Ireland within a few hours' drive of Dublin and an even shorter distance from Shannon Airport, the Ring has a great appeal for many people.

Charlie and Marilyn Schubert, former owners of the Barrows House in Dorset, Vermont, stopped at nearby Caragh Lodge on their trip to Ireland, and they were telling me about it.

"Marilyn and I have always wanted to see the Ring of Kerry and this was one of the stops that we had planned for many months ahead. It exceeded all of our expectations.

"Now here's the funny part. We found Caragh Lodge, although not without some most amusing roadside conversation and instruction from a young man with a donkey cart. It is on a small rise overlooking Caragh Lake and is back from the road so that the atmosphere is quiet. As we pulled into the courtyard, the innkeepers came to the door to greet us, and Marilyn grabbed my arm and said, 'We know these people; I'm sure they have been to the Barrows House.' They had indeed been our guests, and now we were theirs. We were all surprised and delighted at this happy coincidence."

Surrounded by nine acres of parkland, with lovely gardens and spectacular scenery, the lodge has a really magic setting, with the greenness of the countryside, the blue skies, and the lake combining to lift one into another world. It's particularly attractive when the gorse is in bloom.

With all of the possibilities for recreation, one could spend several days there. There's swimming, fishing, and boating on the lake and horse riding nearby, along with all of the interesting auto touring. The lodge has an all-weather tennis court, bicycles for hire, and a sauna chalet.

Charlie was particularly interested in the fact that there were seven 18-hole golf courses all within a reasonable driving distance.

There are three extra-sized rooms in the main building that have been furnished in excellent taste with private baths. There are additional rooms in other buildings also.

The à la carte menu features sirloin steak, lamb chops, and chicken Cordon Bleu, and some of the house specialties include fresh warm smoked salmon and poached trout with butter sauce. Of course, everything is as local as possible. Dinner reservations are necessary.

Marilyn summed things up for me. "You know, I'm an early riser so I was up while the dew was still on the grass, and there was a wonderful thin cloud over the lake. I walked into the woods and could almost see the 'little people' scampering out of the way. I'd say that Caragh Lodge, with its lovely warm innkeepers, spectacular scenery, and magic setting, is really a jewel."

And I would agree as well.

CARAGH LODGE, Caragh Lake, Co. Kerry. Tel. 066-69115. A 10-guestroom secluded lodge in the Ring of Kerry holiday area. Breakfast is included in the room rate and dinner is served every night, reservations necessary. Open from spring to October. Lake swimming, all-weather tennis court, table tennis, sauna, boating, bicycling, and fishing on grounds. Many golf courses and riding stables nearby. No pets. Michael and Ines Braasch, Proprietors. (See Index for rates.)

Directions: Caragh Lake is 1 mi. off N70 between Killorglin and Glenbeigh.

ASSOLAS COUNTRY HOUSE
Kanturk, County Cork

As I approached Assolas Country House I had a faint will-o'-the-wisp feeling that I had been there before. Like the proprietors of many other country houses in Britain and Ireland, the Bourkes had permitted the vines to find their way up the rough stone walls, and the contrast of the green leaves against the gray stone created a most fetching effect.

I crossed the stone bridge, pausing for a moment to watch the swans on the water and admire what I am sure are some of the finest gardens in all of Ireland. Plantings of tulips around the trees were a lovely touch. The size and beauty of the trees were quite overwhelming.

Assolas is a 17th-century manor house with low, round turrets on either end. It has been the home of the Bourke family for over seventy years. The setting is nothing if not sylvan, with a delightful river coursing through the grounds.

I stepped inside the house and, typical of me, I had entered the wrong door at the back, walking into an immaculate country kitchen. I was greeted by Hugh Bourke and his son, Joe, who was already at work doing the early preparation for the evening meal. I learned subsequently that he

does all the cooking. He clattered about the place with his pots and pans while his father and I chatted a bit. Then Hugh led me into the drawing room, where there was a jolly fire in the fireplace, comfortable sofas and chairs, a huge mirror, and many paintings. We were joined by his wife, Eleanor, who has a very pleasant, natural quality, and we sat and talked about Americans in Ireland, inns in North America, and the joys and problems of being the owner of a 300-year-old country house.

"We had a gentleman who left unexpectedly this morning, rather unhappy," Eleanor said. "He was terribly upset when he discovered that there was no telephone or TV in his room. We bade him farewell and good luck with his accommodations in the future."

Hugh showed me to my unusually large guest room. I admired the lovely view of the gentle Irish landscape and he assured me that all of the views are almost equally enticing. He also mentioned that a few of the rooms boast whirlpool baths.

We started talking about the menu at Assolas and he explained that "we have what we call progressive Irish cooking, and whenever possible we use fresh local produce and home-grown fruit and vegetables. Joe has proved to be a magician in our kitchen. He's got a bit of a reputation for both leg of lamb and leg of pork."

Hugh and I sauntered down to the drawing room and out into the sunny Irish countryside. In answer to my inquiry about guest activities, he said, "Our guests can enjoy lawn tennis and boating. Salmon fishing is available on the Black Water River.

"If you are into golf," he remarked, "we have several golf links, including some international championship courses within easy reach."

Later that evening, Hugh pulled me aside and said, "I've been thinking about your feeling that you've been here before, and I believe this is the answer." He handed me a large, handsome fashion catalog of Etienne Aigner clothing that had been photographed at Assolas. The models, two young women and a young man, were posed in various settings around the estate—against wonderful old stone walls, on a bundle of hay in the barn, in front of beautiful old trees, beside the river. Assolas provided a wonderful setting.

Of course, this was where I'd seen Assolas before. Hugh remarked that often their guests have that same feeling of déjà vu.

ASSOLAS COUNTRY HOUSE, Kanturk, Co. Cork. Tel.: (029) 50015. A 10-guestroom (private baths) comfortable country house in the southwest touring region of Cork and Kerry. Breakfast and dinner served to residents and travelers. Reservations necessary. Light lunch available. Open most of the year. Tennis, croquet, boating, trout and coarse fishing as well as salmon fishing. Challenging golf courses within a short distance. Conven-

*ient to Killarney, the Ring of Kerry, the Dingle Peninsula, Bantry Bay,
Blarney Castle, and historic Limerick. Children under 12. No pets. The
Bourke Family, Proprietors. (See Index for rates.)*

*Directions: From Cork, take N20 north to Mallow, then take N72 west to
R576. Look for signs to hotel.*

LONGUEVILLE HOUSE
Mallow, County Cork

It was at Longueville House that I had my most intriguing contact with
Irish history. Michael O'Callaghan, the resident owner of this handsome
Georgian manor house, and his wife, Jane, entertained me royally with a
high tea that included some simply fabulous homemade ginger cookies. (I
unashamedly pocketed two of them as I was leaving.) Jane, as a Cordon
Bleu–trained chef, has won several awards for her cuisine and supervises
all the cooking.

The house overlooks one of the most beautiful river valleys in Ireland,
the Blackwater Valley. The central portion was built about 1720 on a 500-
acre wooded estate, then the property of an ancestor of Michael O'Callaghan. As Michael said, "Since then, Longueville has had a checkered
history." Now, it has been considerably enlarged and is an excellent
country house hotel surrounded by an area particularly rich in scenery.

The size of the building took my breath away. The entrance is through a
stately arch, and the first thing I noticed approaching the front entrance
was a tremendous brass lock on the door. The center hallway and recep-

tion area are most elegant, as are the library, living room, smaller parlors, and dining rooms. The impressive main staircase rises to the full height of the house on both sides and repeats from the second to the third floor. One of the most unusual areas is a glass conservatory, left over from Victorian days, that contains many tropical plants, tree, and flowers. All the guest rooms that I saw were comfortable, large, and very tastefully furnished.

Over tea I asked Michael about the outdoor sports and recreation in the area. He replied, "Well, athletic salmon abound, as do trout, in the river that runs across the southern boundary of our estate. We are just a few miles from the south coast where there is good sea fishing and shore angling. There are eighteen golf courses in the county, including one at Mallow, which is free to our guests. We have horses and ponies available for trekking nearby.

"Many of our guests spend a great deal of time on the back roads here in County Cork, and driving out to the coast to some of the places of great natural beauty such as Glengarriff, Blarney, and Limerick. Killarney is one hour away.

"There are many castles in this section of Ireland that are open to the public, and quite a lot of history was made in this vicinity. For example, the oak trees that you see out the window were planted in the formation of the English and the French battle lines at Waterloo," he said.

"What about the history that took place nearby?" I asked.

"Well, this part of Ireland was known as Rebel Country," Michael said. "The O'Callaghans had owned this land for 100 years, including the remains of a castle which you can see from our front windows. It is one of my fondest wishes to completely restore this monument and make it available once again. When Cromwell's army invaded Ireland this was one of the few places that was not burned. Cromwell's son-in-law, who was in charge of the army, stayed nearby."

I could see that Michael was beginning to warm to his subject, and I settled back comfortably in the luxurious chair to get a good lesson in Irish history.

LONGUEVILLE HOUSE, Mallow, Co. Cork. Tel.: (022) 27156 or 27176. A 20-guestroom country house hotel situated west of Mallow on the Killarney Rd., 54 mi. from Shannon Airport. Open from Easter to Oct. 20. Dinner served to non-residents by telephone booking. Fishing on grounds; horse riding, complimentary golf nearby. Michael and Jane O'Callaghan, Resident Owners. (See Index for rates.)

Directions: From Shannon: take the road to Limerick, then the Cork Rd. into Mallow. Take the Killarney Rd. for 2 mi. west. From Dublin; take the Cork Rd. to Mitchell's Town and then on to Mallow. Continue on, following above directions on the Killarney Rd.

BEECHMOUNT FARM
Mallow, County Cork

I followed Mrs. Moira Fitzpatrick up the stairs of the 17th-century stone farmhouse to the second floor where I found five guest rooms all furnished in bright colors and all very neat and clean. The second-floor view included the fields and the meadows, and I was happy to see many books and a reading lamp with each bed. The countryside also offers a splendid view of the Boggerogh mountains.

This was a working farm with special dairy cows. Mrs. Fitzpatrick is most conscientious and obviously makes an effort to make her guests feel as comfortable as possible.

According to several letters from Mrs. Fitzpatrick, nothing has changed since my visit except that she has had many of our American readers visit her in the last few years.

Moira's letters are lively, to say the least, and I hope anyone who visits will thank her again for the invitation she sent me to spend New Year's Eve with the family.

BEECHMOUNT FARM, Mallow, Co. Cork. Tel.: (022) 21764. A 5-guest-room 17th-century farmhouse on 187 acres. Fishing, golfing, horse riding, all within 2 mi. Ideal touring center for Cork and Kerry. Open May to Sept. Fitzpatrick Family, Proprietors. (See Index for rates.)

Directions: Beechmount Farm is located just west of the center of Mallow on the road to Killarney (N72). Leaving Mallow, watch for Beechmount sign on right side, pointing uphill.

THE BURREN

Ireland is certainly a land of surprises, and one of the most paradoxical and contradictory surprises is the Burren, a 100-square-mile region in county Clare that provides endless browsing and opportunities for discovery.

Eerie and yet fascinating, the landscape of the Burren appears bleak, yet is far from barren. There are very few trees or shrubs and apart from one small stream there is no trace of a river. Yet the Burren supports a selection of flowers and plants that are found elsewhere as far north as the Arctic regions and in climes far south of Ireland.

Rock and stone predominate, and in their own way support the lux-urious growth of rare flowers. Because the area has been inhabited for 4,000 years, the region is dotted with monuments representing almost every century of man's habitation.

There are forts, ruined castles, caves, tombs, limestone pavements, cairns, abandoned churches, turloughs (dry lakes), and most of all, rare Burren plants that are a delight to the botanist.

Just outside the Burren at the village of Kilfenora there is an interpretive center that gives visual and sound explanations of the geology, botany, and history of the area.

Be prepared to be amazed by the Burren. Information is available on the area at Gregans Castle Hotel.

GREGANS CASTLE HOTEL
Ballyvaughan, County Clare

So entranced was I watching the sunset from the cliffs of Moher that before I realized it a full darkness had fallen. I started driving across county Clare and entered the desolate-appearing section known as the Burren. The lights of the occasional farmhouses along the road reassured me that even if I didn't see any of the inhabitants, I knew there must be someone nearby.

I inquired of a passing motorcyclist as to the road to Ballyvaughan and he assured me that it was "straight ahead." I came upon a reassuring signpost for Gregans Hotel, pointing in the same direction for Corkscrew Hill. Reaching the brow of the hill, I looked down into the deep valley and saw a cluster of lights; I knew that this must be Gregans and following the road (quite aptly named "Corkscrew"), I dropped into the valley and turned into the driveway, flanked by beautiful copper beech trees.

While I was fascinated by the Burren and its strange lunarlike land-scape, I must say I was completely surprised and unprepared for the casual luxury at Gregans Castle. It stands at the head of the valley with dramatic views of the countryside. The owners are Peter and Moira Haden, who arrived here just a few years ago and have created a most comfortable, tasteful, and stylish country hotel. It's an old family house from the mid-17th century and has now been restored and converted with every modern comfort, including private bathroom facilities for most guest rooms. Previous to their venture into county Clare, Peter and Moira had been professional hoteliers. All the cooking is done under Peter's supervision, and Moira is in charge of the dining room service.

The menu on the night of my stay had six starters, including Galway Bay oysters and a seafood quiche. Following the soup, there were stuffed and baked mussels from Ballyvaughan harbor, estouffade of beef in the style of Provence, grilled lobster from the nearby Atlantic, and a cold baked Burren lamb salad.

On the evening of my stay, all of the hotel guests, plus many local patrons, enjoyed a recital of Irish songs by Deirdre O'Brien-Vaughn, a titian-haired songstress who accompanied herself on the Irish harp. Deirdre's explanations of the meanings of the words and stories of the songs, most of which were sung in Gaelic, heightened everyone's pleasure.

Moira and I talked about the Burren. "I believe that it's the flora, rather than the history, for which the Burren is famous," she said. "In the late spring and early summer, the orchids, mountain avens, rock roses, maidenhair fern, and blue gentian are in bloom, and the magnificent colors of the flowers turn the grey landscape into a natural rock garden. You don't really have to know much about botany to appreciate its beauty."

Gregans Castle is fortunately located near the coastal road around the western side of Ireland. It is only fifteen miles from the cliffs of Moher,

and the Hadens can arrange one-day outings to the Aran Isles. Peter also mentioned there is excellent golfing seventeen miles away at Lahinch.

When Marilyn and Charlie Schubert visited there, they were captivated by Gregans Castle. They spoke of Moira and Peter as being "absolutely perfect." "Moira looked beautiful in a lovely silk blouse and linen skirt," Marilyn said. "We hit it off with them immediately, as I gather most of the guests do. Moira said to remind you that each of the rooms has a wonderful, personal feeling about it."

"The rooms are as pretty as any I have ever seen," said Charlie. "The Hadens have a handsome 21-year-old son going to a hotel school in England who will be coming into the business, also a very attractive 18-year-old daughter."

GREGANS CASTLE HOTEL, Ballyvaughan, Co. Clare. Tel.: 065-77005. Telex: 70130. A 17-guestroom country hotel located in the Burren area on Ireland's west side, 36 mi. from Shannon Airport. Closed late Oct. to mid-Mar. Breakfast, lunch, afternoon tea, dinner served to non-residents. Besides walking and touring the Burren, there are beaches, fishing, caves, castles, and monuments nearby. The cliffs of Moher are 15 mi. distant. Moira and Peter Haden, Resident Owners. (See Index for rates.)

Directions: The hotel is on N67 between Lisdoonvarna and Ballyvaughan. This is the most attractive route to use driving from Co. Kerry to Connemara, using the Shannon Estuary (Tarbert/Killimer) ferry. It also affords an opportunity to visit the 600-ft. spectacular Cliffs of Moher.

CASHEL HOUSE HOTEL
Cashel, Connemara, County Galway

Here's a bit of Relais et Chateaux de Campagne luxury in one of Ireland's beauty spots.

The setting is typical of Connemara. Surrounded on three sides by rugged mountains, Cashel House Hotel stands at the head of Cashel Bay in a fifty-acre award-winning garden of flowering shrubs and woodland walks. During my late October visit, there were literally thousands of yellow flowers in bloom, whose gay colors were shown to great advantage against the rather austere white lines of a Georgian-style house. I could hear songbirds who evidently found the exotic flowering shrubs, including rhododendrons, azaleas, camellias, and magnolias, much to their liking.

In contrast to the exterior, the interior furnishings with antiques and 19th-century paintings have many bright colors interspersed with gentle pastels. There were a number of paintings throughout all of the public rooms and dining rooms.

I arrived during the Sunday lunch, and among the local well-dressed

Galway patrons was a table of beaming clergymen, who were also enjoying the noontide comestibles.

The resident owners are Dermot and Kay McEvilly. They passed me back and forth between the two of them because Sunday lunchtime is one of the busiest of the week.

From Kay I learned that Dermot is in charge of the kitchen and the menus. "He places a great deal of emphasis on seafood because we're so close to the water," she said. "We have fresh turbot, sea trout, and salmon, as well as scallops from Cashel Bay. Lamb and beef are plentiful. We serve them in many varieties of sauces. The vegetables come from our own garden whenever possible.

"I think the main emphasis here is on a restful holiday," she said. "Our guests can use our hard tennis court or swim from our little private beach, golf at Ballyconneely, or fish in any of the lakes and rivers. A lot of them go in for mountain climbing, bird watching, horse riding, or just driving around on a picnic. We have two good day trips from Cashel House, which are shaped like a figure 8. I believe that guests using these excursions can see most of Connemara."

This was another place that Marilyn and Charlie Schubert liked very much. They spoke of its "wonderful, warm feeling" and of the numerous small cozy sitting rooms with fireplaces and beautiful gardens.

"Kay McEvilly gave us a delightful table by the window overlooking the gardens. We had a wonderful dinner that night of Irish salmon and lobster Newburg. We talked with Dermot and Kay, and as one-time fellow-innkeepers we had much to talk of."

The beauties of Connemara provide a splendid backdrop for the under-stated elegance of the Cashel House Hotel.

CASHEL HOUSE HOTEL (Relais et Chateaux), Cashel, Connemara, Co. Galway. Tel.: (095) 31001. U.S. reservations: 800-223-6764. Telex: 50812. A 32-guestroom country house hotel located in the Connemara area of county Galway, 174 mi. from Dublin. Open from March to Nov. 1. Golf, fishing, boating nearby. McEvilly Family, Proprietors. (See Index for rates.)

Directions: From Galway, Cashel can be reached via the N59 Oughterard–Clifden Rd. Plainly marked on the map. (Note: There is another Cashel in county Tipperary.)

ROSLEAGUE MANOR HOTEL
Letterfrack, Connemara, County Galway

The visit to this country house hotel began with a sinking sensation. It all happened this way:

Driving on the Connemara coastal road between Clifden and Leenane, I saw the sign for the Rosleague Manor Hotel, remembered Peter and Moira Haden's recommendation, and turned into a pleasant, woodland road that afforded many glimpses of a splendid bay. Just as I pulled into the car park of a Georgian house, I felt the left front corner of my automobile descending and experienced the said sinking sensation. I had a flat tire.

From that point on, it was all uphill. Anne Foyle, one of the resident owners of the hotel, was good enough to ask a young man to help me change the "tyre," and also conducted me on a tour of the house, which wound up with tea in the library.

"We are essentially a friendly, family-run hotel with much emphasis on what I think is superb home cooking," she said. "My brother, Patrick, is the principal chef."

Her eyes sparkled when I remarked on the unusual number of oil paintings. "Yes, Patrick and I, as well as our mother, are art lovers and we've had a great deal of enjoyment in supplementing the period furniture with bright spots of color."

Characteristic of Georgian houses, the public rooms in the main part of the house have high ceilings and very comfortable, conversation-inviting furniture. A pleasing collection of English bone china was displayed on one wall of the dining room; I believe Anne said it was English Derby, which is basically white with a wide blue border.

The guest rooms in the older portion of the house are large and decorated with harmonious draperies, bedspreads, and wallpaper, as are the bedrooms in the newer part of the house. All have private bathrooms. All of them have a view of Ballinakill Bay.

Back in the main sitting room, Patrick, resplendent in his chef's whites, joined us for just a few moments. He was making his preparations for the evening's repast.

"The one thing that we insist on is fresh food," said Patrick. "Everything comes locally—the vegetables are either from our own garden or are grown nearby, the meat all comes from Galway, and the fish comes from the bay out there. At the beginning of the season we have salmon—that's the main attraction, especially for the tourists. We also serve lamb, veal, and beef. Most of our dishes are served with sauces that give some of them a very nice French touch."

Anne was able to fill me in a little bit more on this beautiful section of Ireland. "Mountains dominate the Connemara landscape," she said. "There are many picturesque, hidden villages, and the coastline, as you've already seen, has dozens of little bays interspersed with very wide beaches. Ireland's language, customs, and crafts are kept alive in Connemara.

"Our guests can fish for salmon or sea trout, enjoy pony trekking, golf, or hill climbing. I think one of our principal virtues is the traffic-free roads."

And so my visit at Rosleague Manor, which began with a sinking sensation, ended with a real lift as I drove out of the driveway, taking one last look at Ballinakill Bay, encircled by the Twelve Bens Mountains. The water looked warm and there were lazy ripples tempting me to stay even longer.

Reader Comment: "This place put us in mind of an American inn—we loved it. Anne Foyle was not there but we had a lovely visit with Patrick, her brother, who was kind enough to show us all around the inn. He well remembered changing your 'tyre.' We were very impressed, as you were, with the beautiful paintings. You didn't mention the very high quality shops that are located in Letterfrack. Charlie had to drag me away by the heels."

ROSLEAGUE MANOR HOTEL, Letterfrack, Connemara, Co. Galway. Tel.: 095-41101. A 16-guestroom country house hotel in the west of Ireland, 100 mi. from Shannon Airport. Open from Easter to the end of Oct. Lunch, tea, and dinner served to non-residents. Salmon and sea trout fishing, pony trekking, golf, and hill climbing nearby. Anne and Patrick Foyle, Resident Proprietors. (See Index for rates.)

Directions: Letterfrack is located on the coastal road in the Connemara section of Co. Galway between Clifden and Leenane.

MOUNT FALCON CASTLE
Ballina, County Mayo

Almost every country house hotelier that I met in Britain and Ireland considered his hotel his home, and his patrons as houseguests, and the Mount Falcon Castle was no exception to this.

Owner Mrs. Constance Aldridge moved here with her husband from England in the 1930s and has maintained it as a country house hotel ever since. "I think I'm probably one of the earliest country house hoteliers in Ireland," she said. "It's become quite fashionable now to run a country house hotel."

The country house feeling is quite pervasive just before dinner, when all of the guests meet in the main drawing room and are introduced by Mrs. Aldridge. She has the knack of making everybody feel most comfortable and very much at home. The room itself contributes to this feeling of well-being with walls that are lined from floor to ceiling with all kinds of books, and with all the family possessions that have been accumulating for more than fifty years. Guests are naturally drawn together, not only by her skillfull conversation, but also by a cheery log fire.

On that particular evening, Constance Aldridge had invited a neighboring friend to join the guests at dinner, and the three of us, plus four other Americans, were a lively group discussing such diverse subjects as salmon and trout fishing and the poetry and drama of William Butler Yeats.

Dinner was announced and we all filed across the imposing entrance hall to an equally imposing and graceful candlelit dining room, where the table was impressively laid with splendid china and silverware.

As it is every evening, dinner was a set meal, and the main dish was a splendid roast beef accompanied by vegetables from the garden, and served on a handsome silver tray. It was presented by two pleasant Irish colleens, who also performed a number of other duties at Mount Falcon.

During the lull in the badinage we all learned that the building, which resembles a small castle and has many acres of grounds and woodlands, was built in 1876. "When we purchased it in 1932, it was known as a fashionable country house," Constance noted. "We brought most of our home furnishings with us from England, but spent many years adding to them. In the early days one could find beautiful things. My husband and I were always collectors, and this has been our home for such a long time."

Because it was originally built as a palatial country home, ten of the eleven bedrooms are double rooms and some are quite large, with views on two sides. Even the smaller guest rooms have their own private bathrooms today.

The "country house" feeling can also be found in strolling about the one hundred acres surrounding the house, where there are many varieties of trees and flowers, including cypress, beech, and chestnut, as well as delphiniums, dahlias, and gladiolas. I saw a flock of goldfinches chattering about in the branches. A clay tennis court is playable during dry weather, and many of the guests enjoy fishing in the River Moy, one of the best salmon rivers in the west of Ireland. Mount Falcon owns seven miles of the river, and fishing for hotel guests is free. Advance notice is needed for boats and gillies.

There's a very pleasant rumpled informality about Mount Falcon Castle, and even if Mrs. Aldridge weren't there, it would be an enjoyable place to visit. However, it is the presence of this gracious lady that makes any stay memorable.

When I asked her about her innkeeping philosophy, she replied, "I don't have any in mind—I just love giving happiness—it's just a part of me." She reached down and patted the two very lovable dogs that all the guests take for walks in the woods. "I know that we're a little different, and sometimes guests who are more used to big formal hotels and obsequious servants find it a bit hard to adjust, but, after all, this is really my home, and I just love having houseguests. I wish that some of your countrymen would arrange for longer stays. I love Americans."

Mrs. Aldridge, I'm sure that Americans would love you.

MOUNT FALCON CASTLE, Ballina, Co. Mayo. Tel.: (096) 21172. An 11-guestroom country house castle hotel, 140 mi. from Dublin. MAP; dinner served to non-resident guests with advance booking. Closed Feb., Mar., and Christmas. Salmon and trout fishing in River Moy; tennis on grounds. Winter shooting for snipe and woodcock can be arranged, but advance planning necessary. Estuary and sea fishing, pony riding, golf nearby. Constance Aldridge, Resident Proprietress. (See Index for rates.)

Directions: Ballina is on the coastal road on Ireland's west side. Mount Falcon Castle is on the Foxford Rd. between Castlebar and Ballina. From Ballina, take the Castlebar Rd. south about 1½ mi. to a Y. Bear left at the Y and drive another 2½ mi. The hotel gate is on the right.

DRUMLEASE GLEBE HOUSE
Dromahair, County Leitrim

Hardly a week goes by that I don't talk to people who would love to own a country inn. A very small number have found "their inn" and have even been subsequently listed in *Country Inns and Back Roads*.

A few years ago, Andrew and Barbara Flanagan Greenstein, in the midst of their travels in Ireland, discovered this handsome Georgian house near Sligo. They decided to leave their home in Rochester, New

York, giving up Andrew's law practice and Barbara's singing and acting career to become innkeepers in Ireland.

Upstate Magazine quoted Barbara to the effect that "it has been a busy, fascinating, funny, occasionally frustrating year. Change is good for people and it has been a great challenge. Hundreds of strangers have become familiar guests in our home and some in our hearts."

This is a delightful country house located in a quiet corner of rural Ireland—unspoiled, peaceful, and far removed from the hustle and bustle of the 20th century. The house is surrounded by a forest, and the River Bonet also provides atmosphere as well as fishing. There are friendly dogs, one of whom originally came from Rochester, as well as three friendly donkeys, O'Casey, Yeats, and Joyce, who make friends with all the guests, especially if there is a handout included.

The dining room, with its gleaming, polished mahogany, Waterford crystal, log fire, and flickering candles, comes alive promptly at eight o'clock every evening. The cuisine might best be described as classic, and the verdant countryside provides excellent vegetables and fruit as well as farm cheese.

Guest rooms are fresh and bright, decorated in Laura Ashley prints.

This is Yeats country, and Dromahair is just a few miles from County Donegal, whose spectacular, brooding scenery and seemingly endless stone fences stir up many an imagination.

Drumlease Glebe House with its two American proprietors would be an excellent place to start or finish a holiday on the Emerald Isle.

DRUMLEASE GLEBE HOUSE, Dromahair, Co. Leitrim. Tel: Sligo 071 64141. A 10-guestroom Irish country house just a few miles from Sligo. Breakfast included in tariff. Dinner served to residents only. Open Easter to early Oct. Swimming pool on grounds. Private beat, along with nearby lakes and rivers for fishing and boating. Two 18-hole golf courses 15 mi. distant, and horse riding nearby. Not suitable for children under 15. Andrew and Barbara Flanagan Greenstein, Proprietors. (See Index for rates.)

Directions: From Sligo take N4 south to R 287 and continue to Dromahair. Turn off the main street onto Manorhamilton Rd. (opp. Breffni Holiday Cottages). Keep left past Nat'l. School, continuing 1½ mi. Well signposted.

For room rates and last time for dinner orders, see Index.

GLENCOLMCILLE

Since I've returned from Glencolmcille I have been amazed at how many people also have either been there or have heard about it. It is located in the southwest corner of county Donegal on a peninsula of land thrust out into the Atlantic about 170 miles northwest of Dublin.

Glencolmcille comprises five parallel glens, each opening out to beautiful expansive beaches and the sea. Within a radius of five miles there are twenty-three lakes, three rivers, and countless streams. The mountains end in precipitous cliffs that hurl defiance at the changing moods of an unpolluted ocean. One of these cliffs is reputed to be the highest in Europe at 1,972 feet.

The lore, legends, antiquities, scenic views, tranquility and peace of Glencolmcille are such that the area is extremely popular among the Irish themselves. I caution against arriving in high season without advance reservations.

Besides all these things I have enumerated, Glencolmcille is very well known in Ireland because of the efforts of Father McDyer, who has become the guiding spirit of a cooperative known as the Glencolmcille Association.

Briefly, and with apologies to Father McDyer, whose small booklet I am paraphrasing, the isolation, poor land resources, and the tyranny of landlordism all conspired in their own way to subject Glencolmcille to massive emigration over the past 150 years.

Father McDyer saw the need for providing a way for the people of the area to help themselves and, among other things, a Holiday Village was built and new industries were fostered. There is an excellent folk museum and a crafts shop.

I have a suggestion: whether you're going to Glencolmcille or not, send $2 in American currency to the manager of the Glenbay Hotel, request an inn brochure and a copy of The Riches of Glencolmcille *by J. McDyer. The booklet contains not only the history of the area, but also several walks in the countryside and some excellent four-color photographs. I promise the reader an unusual literary journey.*

I shall quote briefly from this booklet: "I hope you are not a careless driver, for, although the road to the car park overlooking the cliff (2,000 feet) is quite safe, the driver must proceed very slowly and keep his eye riveted on the road until he parks his car. On the right side of the road driving upwards there can be seen many outcrops of large flagstones, from which the mountain Sliabh a Liag takes its name. I hope, too, that the day is fine and that you brought your luncheon basket and your camera for here you can remain for a long time, absorbed by the riot of colours, the majesty and the peace, and entranced by the distant prospect of the mountains of Connaught far across the bay. It is also an engaging thought as you look westwards that there is no land between you and the American continent. Looking downwards you will see the seagulls gliding lazily on the air currents or occasionally plummeting toward the fish beneath."

The booklet is the next best thing to being there, and being there is to catch a brief glimpse of the magic of Ireland.

GLENCOLMCILLE HOTEL
Malinmore, Glencolmcille, County Donegal

This is the only hotel in the Glencolmcille area. The accommodations are warm and comfortable and the menu is adequate. The hotel also has frequent Irish gatherings and songfests.

Oddly enough, for an accommodation that seems rather remote, there is also a telex service available and arrangements can probably be made by a North American travel agent.

GLENCOLMCILLE HOTEL, Malinmore, Glencolmcille, Co. Donegal. Tel.: 073-30003 Telex: 33517 DWPEI. A 20-guestroom (private baths) conventional hotel on Ireland's west coast, 142 mi. from Dublin. Open all year. Breakfast, lunch, dinner served to non-residents. (This particular section of Donegal is extremely popular and reservations must be made considerably in advance in the high season.) Bicycles, deep-sea fishing, boat trips, archeology, folk museum, evenings of Irish music and dancing, tennis, and sandy beaches all available. (See Index for rates.)

Directions: There are several different choices of roads from Dublin or Shannon to Donegal town. From there follow the road west through Killybegs to the farthest end of the peninsual.

FROM DONEGAL TO DUBLIN VIA NORTHERN IRELAND

The shortest distance between Donegal town and Dublin is to travel across the Black Gap, following the signs to Pettigo, Kesh, Irvinestown, and Enniskillen. This road leads through two border-crossing points which, I must confess, I was through before I had even realized it. It introduced me to the Erne Lakes that afford some of the most beautiful scenes in Ireland.

MANOR HOUSE HOTEL
Killadeas, Enniskillen, Northern Ireland

On the aforementioned journey from Donegal to Dublin across a corner of Northern Ireland, just outside of Enniskillen, I saw the signpost for the Manor House Hotel.

It proved to be an imposing and stately manor house-villa with Mediterranean overtones, filled with "Olde World" atmosphere, on the shores of Lough Erne.

Besides the twenty-four large bedrooms, many with private bathrooms or showers, there is also a group of chalets on the shore of the lake, which offer holidays of a different dimension. A marina supplies boats for hire in which to explore the 300 square miles of waterways.

Almost everything at the Manor House is done in a grand manner. The high ceilings, the dimensions of the dining room, the many large oil paintings, and the length of the hallways and breadth of the terraces all bespeak bygone days of grandeur. It has lovely views of the lakes and countryside and there are a couple of corner guest rooms where I would have loved to settle down for a week's stay.

Among the many scenic forest walks and drives is the Lough Navar Forest Drive that incorporates a wide variety of scenery, picnic areas, and a magnificent panoramic view of Lough Erne. The Manor House Hotel is only twelve miles from Eire and has easy access to Donegal and the Atlantic Coast.

Although this hotel is privately owned, it is a touch on the commercial side. The size of the dining room and bar indicates that it must be very popular with the local people as well as travelers.

MANOR HOUSE HOTEL, Killadeas, Enniskillen. Tel.: (036562) 545/561. Telex: 747912. A manor house hotel on the shore of Lough Erne in the Irish Lake District, 100 mi. from Dublin. Closed on Christmas Day only. Breakfast, lunch, tea, dinner served to non-residents. Cruisers and day boats are available for hire. Many scenic walks and drives nearby. Self-catering chalet cottages also available. (See Index for rates.)

Directions: Enniskillen is 12 mi. from Eire and 86 mi. from Belfast. Make inquiries in village for correct road.

KILLYHEVLIN HOTEL
Enniskillen, Northern Ireland

I stopped at the Killyhevlin Hotel on the recommendation of the manager of the Manor House Hotel, which was just a few miles away. The two places make an interesting contrast, because the Killyhevlin is a bit more "Americanized" and is a conference center as well as a travelers' accommodation.

One of the principal attractions is the fact that it's located right on the Lough Erne shore and is very popular with fishermen.

Bedrooms are available with private bathrooms, television, channel radio, telephones, and a private balcony overlooking the countryside and the lake.

Amenities also include a recreation room and nightly entertainment by a resident pianist.

As in the case of the Manor House Hotel, the Killyhevlin also has some self-catering chalets on the lake shore.

KILLYHEVLIN HOTEL, Enniskillen. Tel.: (0365) 3481. A 25-guestroom hotel with 13 self-contained chalets in the Lake District of Northern Ireland. Open year-round. Breakfast, lunch, dinner served to non-residents. Salmon fishing, golf, boating on grounds. (See Index for rates.)

Directions: Enniskillen is on one of the main roads from Dublin to Donegal. It's tucked into the southwest corner of Northern Ireland. On my visit I found no problems at the border crossing points.

SCOTLAND

11	Borders
7	Central
12	Dumfries & Galloway
8	Fife
5	Grampian
4	Highland
10	Lothian
2	Orkney
1	Shetland
9	Strathclyde
6	Tayside
3	Western Isles

WALES

59	Clwyd
60	Dyfed
58	Gwynedd
64	Gwent
63	Mid Glamorgan
61	Powys
65	South Glamorgan
62	West Glamorgan

NORTHERN IRELAND

70	Armagh
67	Antrim
71	Down
69	Fermanagh
66	Londonderry
68	Tyrone

ENGLAND

45	Avon
42	Bedfordshire
47	Berkshire
41	Buckinghamshire
37	Cambridgeshire
25	Cheshire
17	Cleveland
53	Cornwall
15	Cumbria
26	Derbyshire
54	Devon
55	Dorset
16	Durham
57	East Sussex
44	Essex
39	Gloucestershire
48	Greater London
23	Greater Manchester
50	Hampshire
34	Hereford & Worcester
43	Hertfordshire
21	Humberside
52	Kent
19	Lancashire
32	Leicestershire
28	Lincolnshire
22	Merseyside
33	Norfolk
36	Northamptonshire
13	Northumberland
18	North Yorkshire
27	Nottinghamshire
40	Oxfordshire
30	Salop
49	Somerset
24	South Yorkshire
29	Staffordshire
38	Suffolk
51	Surrey
14	Tyne & Wear
35	Warwickshire
31	West Midlands
56	West Sussex
20	West Yorkshire
46	Wiltshire

Index

The following alphabetical listings under each country provide approximate rates in British pounds sterling (£) for two people for one night, including breakfast. In most cases, these rates include the Value Added Tax (VAT) of 15%. However, it is always wise to check the rates and what they cover when you make your reservation. There are a few places where breakfast is not offered with the room tariff, as well as others where *both breakfast and dinner* ARE included in the room rate. This latter situation is identified in the listing as "MAP" (Modified American Plan). (American Plan includes 3 meals.) These rates are estimated through 1989.

Why "Last Orders"?

It's not that the distances are very long in the British Isles, it's the many diversions along the way that sometimes make it impossible to estimate traveling and arrival times. Last order times for dinner are included in these listings so that you can see what time you must arrive in order not to find the kitchen door locked. If you are going to arrive later, call ahead—there isn't a hotel/inn listed here that will not make some provision to feed you if they know you can't make it before the kitchen closes.

ENGLAND

Rates shown are for lodgings and breakfast for two people for one night, in most cases inclusive of VAT (Value Added Tax, 15%). Prices are in British money: pounds sterling (£). Check exchange rates. Rates estimated through 1989.

	LAST ORDERS	RATES	PAGE
Angel Hotel, The, Bury St. Edmunds, Suffolk	9:45 p.m.	£65–85*	59
Basil Street Hotel, The, Knightsbridge, London	9:45 p.m.	£94*	23
Bell Inn, The, Aston Clinton, Buckinghamshire	9:45 p.m.	£77–115	36
Belstead Brook Hotel, Ipswich, Suffolk	9:30 p.m.	£61–71	52
Bickleigh Cottage Guest House, Bickleigh, Devon	5:00 p.m.	£25	129
Bishopstrow House, Warminster, Wiltshire	9:30 p.m.	£80–230	106
Bryanston Court Hotel, Great Cumberland Place, London	10:30 p.m.	£70	26
Buckland-Tout-Saints, Goveton, Devon	9:00 p.m.	£70–80	116
Calcot Manor (near Tetbury), Gloucestershire	9:30 p.m.	£70–110	149
Castle Hotel, The, Taunton, Somerset	9:00 p.m.	£89–155	131
Cavendish Hotel, Baslow, Derbyshire	10:00 p.m.	£75	167
Chewton Glen Hotel, New Milton, Hampshire	9:30 p.m.	From £140	91
Chicklade Lodge, Chicklade, Wiltshire	7:30 p.m.	£36**	109

*Breakfast additional   **MAP

	LAST ORDERS	RATES	PAGE
Church Farm, Barton Stacey, Winchester, Hampshire	Noon	£40–50	86
Collin House Hotel, Broadway, Worcestershire	9:00 p.m.	£56	156
Combe House Hotel, Gittisham, Devon	9:30 p.m.	£66	113
Congham Hall, King's Lynn, Norfolk	9:30 p.m.	£70	57
Crosby Lodge, Crosby-on-Eden, Cumbria	9:00 p.m.	£58	207
Dedham Hall, Dedham, Essex	4:30 p.m.	£36–46	49
Dedham Vale Hotel, Dedham, Essex	9:30 p.m.	£70–85	48
Dukes Hotel, St. James's Place, London	10:00 p.m.	£165*	24
Dundas Lock Cottage, Monkton Combe, Bath, Avon	—	£25	104
Durrants Hotel, George Street, London	10:00 p.m.	£90*	26
Eastnor House Hotel, Stratford-upon-Avon, Warwickshire	—	£32–44	161
Esseborne Manor, Hurstbourne Tarrant, Andover, Hampshire	9:15 p.m.	£75	84
Farlam Hall Hotel, Brampton, Cumbria	8:00 p.m.	From £100**	208
Feathers, The, Ludlow, Shropshire	8:45 p.m.	£69	149
Felmingham Hall, North Walsham, Norfolk	9:00 p.m.	£52	55
Fifehead Manor, Middle Wallop, Hampshire	9:30 p.m.	£62–72	81
Flitwick Manor, Flitwick, Bedfordshire	9:30 p.m.	£90–150	40
Fox's Earth, Lewtrenchard Manor, Lewdown (near Okehampton), Devon	9:30 p.m.	£70–80	119
George & Pilgrims Hotel, The, Glastonbury, Somerset	9:15 p.m.	£60	135
Gidleigh Park, Chagford, Devon	9:00 p.m.	£150–220**	114
Goring Hotel, The, Beeston Place, London	10:00 p.m.	£150*	27
Grafton Manor, Bromsgrove, Worcestershire	9:00 p.m.	£75–135	162
Gravetye Manor (near East Grinstead), West Sussex	9:30 p.m.	£75–110*	75
Greenway, The, Shurdington, Gloucestershire	9:00 p.m.	From £165**	153
Hark to Bounty Inn, The, Slaidburn, Lancashire	9:00 p.m.	£32	173
Harrop Fold Country Farmhouse Hotel, Bolton-by-Bowland, Lancashire	8:45 p.m.	£45	171
Holbrook House Hotel, Wincanton, Somerset	8:30 p.m.	£50	110
Homewood Park, Hinton, Avon	9:30 p.m.	£95	105

*Breakfast additional   **MAP

**MAP

	LAST ORDERS	RATES	PAGE
Old Vicarage, The, Higham, Suffolk	–	£36	51
Old Vicarage Hotel, The, Worfield Bridgnorth, Shropshire	9:00 p.m.	£53–60	147
Parrock Head Farm, Slaidburn, Lancashire	9:00 p.m.	£39	172
Pheasant Inn, The, Cockermouth, Cumbria	8:30 p.m.	£56	203
Port Gaverne Hotel, Port Gaverne, Port Isaac, Cornwall	9:30 p.m.	£47–55	125
Powdermill House, Battle, East Sussex	6:00 p.m.	£50	66
Priory Hotel, The, Wareham, Dorset	9:45 p.m.	£40–150	95
Rectory Farm, Woolstaston, Shropshire	–	£20	146
Riber Hall, Matlock, Derbyshire	9:30 p.m.	£65–100	165
Rising Sun Hotel, The, Lynmouth, North Devon	9:00 p.m.	From £45	128
Ritz, The, Piccadilly, London	11:00 p.m.	£180–220*	28
River House, The, Skippool Creek, Lancashire	9:30 p.m.	£43–49	177
Rothay Manor, Ambleside, Cumbria	9:00 p.m.	£70–75	194
Rowan House, Great Hucklow, Derbyshire	9:00 p.m.	£18	169
Royal Hotel, The, Deal, Kent	9:15 p.m.	£52	71
Royal Oak Hotel, The, Yattendon, Berkshire	10:00 p.m.	£70	32
Scale Hill Hotel, Loweswater, Cumbria	8:00 p.m.	£52–80**	206
Sharrow Bay Country House Hotel, Lake Ullswater, Cumbria	8:45 p.m.	£190**	200
Somerset House, Bath, Avon	6:30 p.m.	£62**	141
South Sands Hotel, Salcombe, South Devon	9:30 p.m.	£76–100**	118
Stafford, The, St. James's Place, London	10:30 p.m.	£155*	25
Ston Easton Park, Ston Easton, Chewton Mendip, Somerset	9:30 p.m.	£95–225	139
Stone House Hotel, Sedbusk, North Yorkshire	8:00 p.m.	£37	184
Studley Priory Hotel, Horton-cum-Studley, Oxford	9:15 p.m.	£68	33
Summer Lodge, Evershot, Dorset	8:00 p.m.	£110–120**	98
Swalcliffe Manor, Swalcliffe (near Banbury), Oxfordshire	a.m.	£30–60	42
Swan Hotel, The, Bibury, Gloucestershire	8:30 p.m.	£55	151
Thorn Heyes, Buxton, Derbyshire	7:00 p.m.	£35	166
Thornbury Castle, Thornbury, Bristol	9:30 p.m.	£80–180	136
Three Tuns Hotel, Thirsk, North Yorkshire	9:30 p.m.	£46	185

*Breakfast additional   **MAP

LONDON

Rates shown are for lodgings and breakfast for two people for one night, in most cases inclusive of VAT (Value Added Tax, 15%). Prices are in British money: pounds sterling (£). Check exchange rate. Rates estimated through 1989.

WALES

Rates shown are for lodgings and breakfast for two people for one night, in most cases inclusive of VAT (Value Added Tax, 15%). Prices are in British money: pounds sterling (£). Check exchange rate. Rates estimated through 1989.

*Breakfast additional   **MAP

	LAST ORDERS	RATES	PAGE
Rhiwiau Riding Centre, Llanfairfechan, Gwynedd	9:00 p.m.	£20	229
Sygun Fawr Country House Hotel, Beddgelert, Gwynedd	7:30 p.m.	£32	228
Tŷ Mawr Country House Hotel, Brechfa, Dyfed	9:00 p.m.	£45	220
Tyn-y-Cornel Hotel, Talyllyn, Gwynedd	9:30 p.m.	£52–56	224

SCOTLAND

Rates shown are for lodgings and breakfast for two people for one night, in most cases inclusive of VAT (Value Added Tax, 15%). Prices are in British money: pounds sterling (£). Check exchange rate. Rates estimated through 1989.

Albany Hotel, Edinburgh	9:30 p.m.	£55–75	236
Ardanaiseig, Kilchrenan, Argyll	9:00 p.m.	£158**	255
Ardsheal House, Kentallen of Appin, Argyll	8:30 p.m.	£58–78	259
Borthwick Castle, North Middleton by Gorebridge	9:00 p.m.	£60–100	242
Cairn Lodge, Auchterarder, Tayside	9:00 p.m.	£50–60	277
Clifton Hotel, The, Nairn, Nairnshire	9:30 p.m.	£70–75	264
Creggans Inn, The, Strachur, Argyll	8:30 p.m.	£54–68	250
Cringletie House Hotel, Peebles, Borders	8:30 p.m.	£44–60	243
Dalhousie Castle Hotel, Bonnyrigg, Lothian	10:00 p.m.	£60–95	240
George Hotel, Edinburgh	9:45 p.m.	£99–110	234
Greywalls, Gullane, East Lothian	9:30 p.m.	£85–110	239
Hillhead of Dunkeld, Dunkeld, Perthshire	8:30 p.m.	£71–78	274
Howard Hotel, The, Edinburgh	9:30 p.m.	£90	236
Inverlochy Castle, Fort William, Inverness-shire	8:30 p.m.	£35–160	261
Isle of Colonsay Hotel, Colonsay, Argyll	7:30 p.m.	£55	253
Isle of Eriska Hotel, Ledaig, Argyll	8:30 p.m.	£160**	257
Kenmore Hotel, The, Kenmore, Perthshire	9:00 p.m.	£56	271
Knockinaam Lodge Hotel, Portpatrick, Wigtownshire	9:00 p.m.	£100–130**	247
Loch Ness House Hotel, Inverness	9:00 p.m.	£55–76	262
Marine Hotel, Troon, Ayrshire	11:00 p.m.	£86	249
Open Arms Hotel, The, Dirleton, East Lothian	10:00 p.m.	£75	238
Philipburn House Hotel, The, Selkirk	10:00 p.m.	£80–90**	246
Pittodrie House Hotel, Pitcaple, Aberdeenshire	9:00 p.m.	£80	268
Port-an-Eilean Hotel, Strathtummel, Perthshire	8:45 p.m.	£40	273

**MAP

IRELAND

Rates shown are for lodgings and breakfast for two people for one night, in most cases inclusive of VAT (Value Added Tax, 15%). Prices are in Irish pounds, except where indicated in Northern Ireland. Check exchange rate. Rates are estimated through 1989.

**MAP